# Teacher Research
## and
# Special Educational Needs

# List of Editors' Other Relevant Books

Dr Graham Vulliamy is the co-author, with Keith Lewin and David Stephens, of *Doing Educational Research in Developing Countries: Qualitative Strategies* (Falmer, 1990)

Dr Rosemary Webb is the editor of *Practitioner Research in the Primary School* (Falmer, 1990)

# Teacher Research
# and
# Special Educational Needs

Edited by

**Graham Vulliamy and Rosemary Webb**

**David Fulton Publishers**
London

David Fulton Publishers Ltd
2 Barbon Close, London WC1N 3JX

First published in Great Britain by
David Fulton Publishers 1992

*British Library Cataloguing in Publication Data*

A catalogue record for this book is available from the British Library

ISBN 1–85346–187–3

Typeset by Action Typesetting Limited, Gloucester
Printed in Great Britain by BPCC Wheatons Ltd, Exeter

# Contents

vi

# Contributors

**Trefor Davies-Isaac** is the headteacher of a special school in North Yorkshire.

**Thomas Farrell** teaches in a comprehensive school in Cleveland.

**Jean Holgate** is the acting deputy headteacher of a special school in Calderdale.

**Kathleen Murphy** teaches in a large number of ordinary schools as a member of a Special Needs Support Service in Calderdale.

**Joan Normington** is the headteacher of an assessment centre in Kirklees.

**Lynda Peake** teaches in a special school in Cleveland.

**James Powell** is the headteacher of a special school in West Yorkshire.

**Marion Tricker** teaches in a primary school in West Yorkshire.

**Graham Vulliamy** is a Senior Lecturer in the Department of Educational Studies at the University of York.

**Jacqueline Wadlow** is the headteacher of a special school in Bedfordshire.

**Rosemary Webb** is a Senior Research Fellow in the School of Education at the University of Manchester.

# Foreword

Professor Peter Mittler
*Professor of Special Education, Dean and Director, School of Education, Manchester University*

This book celebrates the teacher as researcher. The practitioners whose work is recorded here are teachers who are driven by a wish to explore, by a need to describe what is actually happening, to show what is possible and to try to assess the impact of change and innovation. With support from their tutors, they have shown that the long distance researcher need not be either lonely or lost and certainly not lacking grim determination to reach the finishing post without losing their capacity for insight or humour.

Teacher research of this quality is vital to the health of the profession. It is also desperately needed at a time when very few teachers can expect to attend one year full time taught courses with a research element, and are increasingly expected to pay their own fees even to attend on a part time basis. Hardly any teachers can now expect to be funded to undertake a research degree.

The work reported here is timely because publicly funded research is itself an endangered species. For every pound spent on education, probably more than a tenth of a penny is invested in educational research. Unlike other government departments, the Department of Education has no clear policy for commissioning research. Furthermore, a new sinister trend of direct government interference in research is being noted. A number of projects have been terminated prematurely and others have been prevented from publishing because either the methods or the conclusions of the research were unacceptable to the government.

Work such as that reported in this book which demystifies research and demonstrates its relevance to classroom and professional practice should help other teachers to lose their fear and suspicion of research and encourage them to undertake projects of their own. Furthermore, the results of such research can be put into practice either in the teacher's own classroom or in the school and sometimes in the LEA and further afield.

Professional or full time researchers work hard to get their work published but have no means of ensuring that anyone reads it, far less believes the results to the point where they want to change their work to incorporate the findings. The teacher researcher may have the hardest task – that of convincing colleagues. No audience is more critical of teachers' research than their own immediate colleagues; no one has a greater investment in its success.

A lively profession is one that takes nothing for granted, and has a healthy scepticism about research that appears to be unrelated to their needs or experience. Teachers who undertake research such as that reported in this book demonstrate that research is too important to be left to researchers.

Peter Mittler
August 1992

# *Preface*

The purpose of this book is threefold. Firstly, it argues that teacher research has a vital, but as yet undeveloped, role to play in special educational needs. Secondly, it provides methodological advice on the design and conduct of teacher research. Thirdly, there are accounts by teachers of case-study research and evaluation carried out in ordinary and special schools. It has been written particularly for teachers and tutors involved in research-based courses and for school staff, support staff and LEA advisers participating in enquiry-based institutional development and evaluation. Nevertheless, the book has a wider relevance, given the increasing interest in reflective teaching in initial teacher training and inservice generally.

The book has its origins in the University of York Outstation MA Programme. This two-year part-time course, which began in Cleveland in 1983, is sponsored by a number of local LEAs. Teams of teachers are recruited who work on projects in areas of interest or concern to them and their schools. All the teachers' contributions are derived from research carried out on this programme, with the exception of Chapter 8 by Trefor Davies-Isaac, who was seconded by his LEA to the York full-time MA course.

The teachers come from a wide range of institutions – ordinary primary and secondary schools, special schools, a support service and an assessment centre. Within these they also represent a diversity of roles, experiences and perspectives. In their chapters they both consider key methodological issues related to their projects and discuss the implications of their research findings. Chapters 1, 2 and 12 have a different role. Firstly, they set teacher research in the wider context of the literature on research into special educational needs in general. Here it is perhaps worth stressing that, while in Chapter 1 we are critical of the dominance of traditional positivist research in this area, we recognise that there are many research questions which are best investigated by such methods. However, this dominance has led to some potential research topics, to which teacher research can make a vital contribution, being neglected. Also, in our view, positivist methodologies have in the past often been used to address research questions for which qualitative ones would have been far more appropriate. Secondly, Chapters 2 and 12 provide practical advice on how to conduct teacher-research projects and a guide to the literature on the kinds of qualitative research techniques involved. In doing so, we indicate where information can be found on conventional qualitative data collection techniques, such as interviews and observation, about which much has already been written, and we introduce some less widely used techniques, such as teacher diaries. Paradoxically, much less has been written about two themes which, from our experience supervising teacher-research projects, are found to be the most difficult by teachers conducting research. These are how to focus upon appropriate research questions, which we address in Chapter 2, and how to analyse and validate qualitative data, the subject of Chapter 12.

We owe a debt of gratitude to the contributors to this book who, despite ever-increasing workloads associated with current developments in education, willingly gave much time and effort. We should also like to thank the Department of Educational Studies at the University of York for funding research into the Outstation Programme and the Head of Department, Professor Ian Lister, for his continuing support for practitioner research in the department's higher degrees programme. Finally, our thanks go to Professor Peter Mittler, Head of the School of Education at the University of Manchester, and the staff of the Centre for Educational Guidance and Special Needs for their interest and encouragement.

Graham Vulliamy
University of York
Rosemary Webb
University of Manchester

# CHAPTER 1

# *New Directions in Special Educational Needs Research*

Graham Vulliamy and Rosemary Webb

> My attitude to children with learning difficulties is very different
> now; I'm not prepared to accept that they can't do certain things
> and I'm much better at looking for potential strengths in them.

The above comment was made during an interview with a primary
school teacher researcher whose pedagogy had changed markedly
as a result of her research. It illustrates how teachers enquiring into
their own classroom practice can lead to a greater understanding of
children's needs and capabilities. The aim of this book is to explore
the potential of teacher research to bring about informed changes
in practice and policy in the area of special educational needs.

In this opening chapter, we will examine both why teacher
research has been relatively neglected in special education and
what the essence of its contribution might be. In outline, our
argument, which is developed in more detail in subsequent sections
of the chapter, is that special educational needs research in this
country has tended to be dominated by those trained in the
discipline of psychology. This discipline has characteristically used
positivist research strategies, such as experiments and surveys,
which attempt to produce law-like generalisations based upon
the statistical analysis of large samples. Any shortened statement
on the methodology of positivism is clearly problematic in that
the term is used in very different ways, both in philosophy and
in sociology (Halfpenny's book, 1982), for example, delineates
twelve different usages). Moreover, it cannot do justice to the
varied positions that positivists take on the crucial issues such as
causation and prediction in the social sciences. This said, a positivist
approach is generally taken to imply that 'the methodological

procedures of natural science may be directly adapted' (Giddens, 1974, p.3). More recently, however, two major problems with such approaches have been identified by prominent special educational needs researchers. Firstly, there has been concern that experimental settings and the study of large samples often do little to add to our understanding of the realities of teaching and learning in the natural settings of ordinary or special schools. Secondly, worries have been expressed concerning the lack of impact of research on practice. During the 1980s many special needs researchers have increasingly pointed to the connection between these two perceived limitations of traditional research approaches. This has led to suggested new directions: quantitative studies based upon 'single-subject' and 'small-N' designs; a move from laboratory experiments to studies of the processes of learning in classroom settings; the blending of qualitative and quantitative research; and programmes for teacher-researcher collaboration.

Also, during the 1980s, the established tradition of special needs research increasingly came under attack from sociologists. They argue that much conventional special needs research tends to be atheoretical and, by neglecting the social and political context of disability, tends to focus exclusively on the characteristics of individual pupils at the expense of the institutional context of the school and the labelling processes in the wider society.

Such recent developments in special needs research are still wedded to the traditional educational disciplines of psychology and sociology. In other areas of educational research, however, notably in curriculum evaluation and in the study of classroom practice, it has been argued that a more genuinely 'educational' theory located within a teacher-research tradition has great potential for breaking down the theory—practice split (Elliott, 1978; Bassey, 1983). Such teacher research generally adopts a qualitative research strategy, which tends to be eclectic in its choice of data collection techniques, usually using some combination of interviews, observation and the analysis of documents. We believe that teacher research based, as much of it is, on case studies of the processes of teaching and learning, is particularly suited to the area of special needs, where teachers are often concerned to understand pupils with unique learning difficulties. And yet, with very few exceptions (e.g. Ainscow, 1989), this has not been an approach which has been generally encouraged by the special needs community.

## The broadening of traditional approaches to special needs research

A historical overview of special needs research over the last two decades indicates that many of the marked changes in emphasis during the 1980s were prompted by the implications of the Warnock Report, published in 1978, and the subsequent 1981 Education Act. Wedell (1985a) notes that 'this Act gave "official", recognition to the concept of "special educational need", and to the concern of special education with meeting children's needs rather than with categorizing them' (p.1). Thus the focus of research needed to shift from descriptive studies of children's conditions and disabilities to studies of the ways in which various educational needs might best be met. This, in turn, directed research attention towards ways of improving the learning experiences of children, and evaluating and disseminating improvements, whether in special or in ordinary schools.

Such a change of emphasis is readily apparent in a comparison of reviews of special needs research conducted prior to the 1981 Act (Cave and Madison, 1978; Wedell and Roberts, 1981) – where the more traditional research, including investigations of children grouped by category of diagnostic classification, predominates – with an agenda for future research drawn up by a 1982 special needs research symposium. The latter concluded that priority should be given to six areas:

1. the evaluation of intervention approaches;
2. the methodology for evaluating intervention;
3. within the area of descriptive research, emphasis should be placed on the study of functional impairment, rather than the characteristics of diagnostic categories of children with special needs;
4. the process of innovation;
5. the methods of disseminating research information;
6. the preparation of critical summaries of existing relevant research, particularly in areas which extend across disciplines.

(Wedell, 1985b, p.23)

Such a research agenda inevitably required a shift from the more traditional emphasis of psychology upon studies of specific children, either as individuals or groups, to a broader range of approaches. This range included both new substantive themes, such as implementation and change, and new methodological ones, such as qualitative evaluation styles, which for some time had characterised educational research on curriculum evaluation and innovation in general. This, in turn, brought the special needs research community more directly into contact with alternative research strategies arising from critiques of the methodological positivism underlying more traditional approaches. As early as 1968, the psychologists Bracht and Glass had raised some fundamental problems about such approaches when they developed the concept of 'ecological validity' in their discussion of the external validity of experiments. Ecological validity refers to the extent to which behaviour observed in one context can be generalised to another. Put simply, the problem with more traditional research methods in education, whether experiments or questionnaire surveys, is that they are unlikely to give an accurate portrayal of the realities of teaching and learning in a natural or conventional setting. The strictures of experimental design are such that only rarely does the experimental setting approximate to the normal conditions of schooling to which generalisations need to be made. Questionnaire surveys cannot penetrate the gap between 'words and deeds' (Deutscher, 1966) and, especially in the evaluation of innovations, are prone to the reproduction of the rhetoric contained in the aims and documentation of the innovation. It is considerations such as these which have led to compelling arguments that traditional positivist research strategies in education and the social sciences have been over-preoccupied with reliability (the consistency of a measuring instrument) at the expense of validity (Deutscher, 1973). Somewhat ironically, perhaps, Bracht and Glass's (1968) early discussion of 'ecological validity' was picked up much later by qualitative researchers in education who see the maximisation of ecological validity as one of the main rationales for their approach (see, for example, Atkinson, 1979; Hammersley, 1979; Evans, 1983).

The influence of such critiques of positivism, together with the new research agenda, can be clearly seen in a 1984 special needs research symposium on the methodology of evaluation studies in special education. Thus, for example, Corrie and Zaklukiewicz comment in their paper that much previous work:

has tended to be limited by the somewhat narrow conception of research as being above all, quantitative and statistical in character. Quantitative procedures, particularly survey techniques, have featured prominently throughout the entire history of research in this area ... as have psychometric approaches to individual functioning and development.

(1985, p.123)

Following an overview of the major criticisms being made of previous research in special education (Schindele, 1985), the symposium was devoted to two approaches to evaluation which, in very different ways, marked new departures. The first of these, the use of single-subject and small-N research designs, whilst still operating within a positivist and quantitative research strategy, nevertheless attempts to overcome some of the previous weaknesses of more traditional evaluation strategies by focusing upon an in-depth evaluation of practice. Kiernan (1985) provides an overview of the defining features of single-subject research designs. They involve the investigation of the behaviour of a single individual (or a small group in small-N designs), where the intention is to test specific hypotheses concerning critical variables. However, where in more traditional experiments the use of control groups is intended to enable the replication of effects across individuals, any replication in single-subject designs is across time, context or other variables and the analysis concerns only the behaviour of the single individual.

An example of such a study is Barrera et al.'s (1980) investigation into the effectiveness of three different models of language training – using signs, words and a combination of the two – for a four-and-a-half-year-old 'mute' autistic boy. This involved giving the child 20 minutes of direct language training with each of the three models in a random order each day and using a trained observer, supplemented by video recordings to ensure reliability, to monitor the child's responses. The results showed that the total communication model was substantially superior to both the oral and sign-alone training models.

Evans (1985) suggests that single-subject experimental designs have a particular relevance for special needs research for a number of reasons. Firstly, the nature of some children's special needs may be particularly individualistic in character, with few other children displaying exactly the same range of needs. Secondly, the designs enable teachers to monitor and record the progress of an individual child over time against pre-set objectives. Thirdly, whilst sophisticated statistical techniques have been developed for the interpretation of causal effects in single-subject designs (McReynolds and Kearns, 1982; Halil, 1985), it is still possible for teachers to 'eyeball' the numerical data and reach conclusions which can immediately be put into practice.

The second major evaluation approach considered at the 1984 research symposium was the use of qualitative research. There are several important distinguishing features of such research. It provides descriptions and accounts of the processes of social inter-action in 'natural' settings, usually based upon a combination of observation and interviewing of participants in order to understand their perspectives. Culture, meanings and processes are emphasised, rather than variables, outcomes and products. Instead of testing preconceived hypotheses, qualitative research aims to generate hypotheses and theories from the data that emerge, in an attempt to avoid the imposition of a previous, and possibly inappropriate, frame of reference on the subjects of the research. This implies a far greater degree of flexibility concerning research design, data collection and analysis, with aspects of each of these sometimes occurring simultaneously throughout the duration of a research project, than tends to be the case with quantitative research. (For more detailed summaries of the defining characteristics of qualitative research see, for example, Corrie and Zaklukiewicz, 1984, pp.125−7; Burgess, 1985, pp.7−10; Bryman, 1988, pp.61−9; Vulliamy, 1990a, pp.7−14.)

Hegarty (1985) argues that qualitative research is particularly suited to a number of topics in special education. These include investigations into pupils' and teachers' perspectives and experiences of special education programmes; clarifying the implications of various policy options; evaluating innovations; and providing detailed accounts of various forms of special education provision. However, to date, there have been relatively few published qualitative research studies on the theme of special educational needs, despite the prominent impact of qualitative research on educational research more generally. Moreover, it is noticeable that, of the few such published studies that do exist, a high proportion have been initiated or conducted by researchers from outside the special needs research community, as, for example, with Jamieson et al.'s (1977) study of the integration of visually-impaired children into ordinary schools and Bell and Colbeck's (1989) action inquiry project into the integration of a number of special needs units into a large primary school.

Given the strong legacy of positivist research in the special needs community, but the recent recognition also of the need for alternative approaches, it should not be surprising that calls are made for a judicious blending of quantitative and qualitative approaches (for example, Corrie and Zaklukiewicz, 1985, p.124). As Vulliamy (1990b) notes, in other areas of education and social science research, the integration of quantitative and qualitative research techniques has taken a number of forms, with varying rationales, possibilities and problems. Mittler (1985) suggests that, within special needs research, one of the most fruitful areas for such a combination of approaches is in the evaluation of policy changes and innovations. Thus, for example, Hegarty *et al.*'s (1981) study of the education of pupils with special needs in ordinary schools used a combination of a nationwide questionnaire survey of Local Education Authorities and detailed case studies of schools, including interviews with individual teachers, parents and pupils. Mittler (1985) concludes that 'this approach provides rich possibilities for concentrating on process variables without neglecting product outcomes' and that the detailed case studies of the practice of integration in schools 'are likely to be more influential and useful to policy makers than are any number of multivariate regression analyses' (p.174).

We have suggested that one of the main concerns of special needs researchers during the 1980s has been to broaden their research styles in response to the growing critique of more traditional positivist research. A second central preoccupation has been to address the problem of the perceived gap between theory and practice, which was identified in each of two major reviews of special needs research (Cave and Madison, 1978; Wedell and Roberts, 1981). While the broadening of research approaches discussed above is seen as one potential means of increasing the relevance of research to practice (Corrie and Zaklukiewicz, 1985), other ideas have centred around trying to bring researchers and teachers into a closer partnership with each other. Thus, for example, Wedell (1985b) suggests that more opportunities should be available to practitioners for periods of secondment when they could be engaged on research projects and Kiernan (1982) considers a partnership which 'asks teachers to provide feedback on ongoing research or to act as consumers evaluating the products of research' (p.26). Here there is no attempt to redefine the traditional subordinate roles of teachers in relation to researchers and the approach is similar to the earliest forms of teacher-researcher collaboration advocated by Boone (1904) and by Buckingham (1926), where teachers were used by clinical psychologists as fieldworkers.

However, an alternative strategy intended to break down such hierarchies has been suggested by Mittler (1974), who argues for a communality of approach between teachers and researchers in special needs, whereby 'teaching is better when it is informed by a research attitude' and 'conversely, research can only benefit from retaining the humanity and open-mindedness of the teacher' (p.80). Wood (1981) also discusses the benefits of the close collaboration between researcher and teacher in an investigation into teaching strategies with hearing-impaired children. He argues that unless researchers and teachers work together in classrooms 'it seems inevitable that we shall continue to spawn unworkable, unrealistic or invalid theories and that the teachers' intuitions about what works and what does not will go unheard and untested' (p.432). A recent example of the increased collaboration between teachers and researchers in special needs research can be found in the work of the National Curriculum Development Team (Severe Learning Difficulties) based at the Cambridge Institute of Education. The team sought to provide INSET on key issues associated with the implementation of the National Curriculum in Special Schools and were commissioned by the National Curriculum Council to produce a publication in the curriculum guidance series (NCC, 1992a) together with an INSET pack to support the implementation of the advice in the guidance (NCC, 1992b). Seconded teachers from seven LEAs in the Eastern region collected evidence through spending a series of two-week periods in schools working with staff on National Curriculum related development. The resulting materials, which the team produced to address the issues identified, were revised and extended as a result of widespread piloting in schools and the collection of staff feedback (see, for example, Rose, 1991, on strategies for promoting groupwork in schools for pupils with severe learning difficulties).

This review of new directions in special needs research has so far restricted itself to developments from within, what might be termed, the mainstream special needs research community. However, the 1980s also witnessed a dramatic increase in research and theorising on special education from writers who do not share many of the basic assumptions of the traditional psychological and medical models of special needs. Such critiques came from sociologists, and also from those with disabilities themselves who sought to provide a more radical perspective on the provision of education for those with special educational needs.

## The sociological contribution

Whilst the publication of the Warnock Report helped generate a new research agenda for the special needs community, it also contributed to sociologists taking a more direct interest in special education than had previously tended to be the case in Britain. Thus, in an early critique of the Warnock Report, Lewis and Vulliamy (1979; 1980) argue that for both methodological and theoretical reasons the Report's definition of 'special educational needs' is misguided and that the Report compounds its definitional problem by an implicit theory which neglects the importance of social factors in the creation of learning difficulties. Rather than accepting psychological categories as given, sociologists consider the social processes leading to the construction of such categories and the social and political implications of their use, both at the micro and the macro level. This has involved examining the ways in which legislation and the vested interests of various professional groups may contribute to the legitimation of inequalities in the education of specific groups of pupils. A detailed example is Tomlinson's (1981) study of the decision-making processes involved in the categorisation of 'educational sub-normality'. She draws an important distinction between normative categories, such as 'blind' or 'deaf' where there is widespread agreement as to the nature of the label used, and non-normative ones, such as 'educationally subnormal' or 'disruptive'. For the latter, she argues that:

> There are no adequate measuring instruments or agreed criteria in the social world to decide upon these particular categories whether descriptive or statutory. There can be, and is, legitimate argument between professionals, parents, other interested groups and the general public, over what constitutes these categories. The answer to the question 'what is' an ESN-M child or a maladjusted child will depend more upon the values, beliefs and interests of those making the judgments than on any qualities intrinsic to the child.
> (1982, pp.65−6)

Using a combination of historical research and a case study of the provision for 40 ESN-M children in one Local Education Authority in the mid-1970s, she found that those given such provision were mainly the unwanted and troublesome pupils. These were largely from lower socio-economic backgrounds, with a severe over-representation of black children. As she herself points out, such research is conducted from an entirely different value position from mainstream psychological research on this theme:

> It turned back-to-front the literature on ESN-M children which attempts to trace causal explanations for educational subnormality in low social class or cultural disadvantage. It pointed out that . . . categorising children as ESN-M may be more of a solution to a problem of social order than an aid to education.

> (1982, p.10)

The writings of disabled sociologists go further in advancing a radical political and social theory of disability. Barton and Oliver provide a useful summary of this work and its underlying theoretical orientation:

> They are critical of 'personal-tragedy' models of disability. For them, the difficulties of participating in society are not due to personal limitations, but arise from the prejudices, discriminatory policies and practices and social restrictions of an unadaptive society. Disability is a fundamentally political, social issue, which is a form of oppression.

> (1992, p.70)

The successful establishment of a new academic journal, *Disability, Handicap and Society*, in 1986 is testimony to the influence of these newer sociological approaches. The latter are critical of the privileged status previously given to psychological explanations in discussions of special educational needs and disability in general. By individualising problems, attention is wrongly diverted from the inherently political nature of the social and educational processes which help produce such 'problems'.

## Approaches to teacher research

The above review of new directions in special needs research throughout the 1980s indicates that a variety of fresh theoretical and methodological orientations have been pursued. What is striking, however, is that such new directions are still firmly placed within the traditional educational disciplines of psychology and sociology. The development of various styles of teacher research, which have come to the fore in mainstream educational research (see, for example, Elliott, 1991; Webb, 1990b; Lomax, 1989; Hustler *et al.*, 1986), are conspicuous by their absence, with the exception of Ainscow's (1989) book and a few other isolated examples, such as Burton's (1989) project on combating sexism in a special school and Stephenson's (1990) research on the integration of four young children with special educational needs in a nursery department.

While the origins of various brands of teacher research go back to the turn of the century, where as suggested earlier teachers remained in a totally subordinate role to researchers, contemporary approaches in Britain are best viewed as being derived from the pioneering work of Lawrence Stenhouse in the 1960s and 1970s (for a review of teacher research from its origins to the present day, see Webb, 1990a). He argued that both curriculum development and teachers' professional development would be enhanced by teachers systematically studying the processes of teaching and learning (Stenhouse, 1975). He questioned the traditional model of the relationship between educational research and educational change, whereby teachers were expected to adopt those curricula and pedagogic styles that had been 'proved' by academic researchers to be successful. Instead, he argued that teachers should take the fruits of researchers and curriculum developers as working hypotheses to be systematically tested in order that they might be evaluated, rejected or refined. An early example of this was the use of teacher researchers in the development of the Schools Council Humanities Curriculum Project between 1967 and 1972 (see Elliott, 1991, Ch.2). Since that period, and especially within the last decade, the influence of teacher research has grown considerably, giving rise to some distinct 'schools', each with its own set of intellectual and theoretical influences − for example, the case-study tradition developed at the Centre for Applied Research in Education at the University of East Anglia (Walker, 1985) and the 'living educational theory' approach associated with Whitehead's group at the University of Bath (Whitehead, 1989).

It might be helpful here to differentiate three very broad approaches to teacher research which, between them, account for the vast majority of current teacher research enquiries. The first broad approach is case study. As a research strategy, case study has a long history in both anthropology and sociology where it is associated with ethnography and the intensive study, using participant observation, of a particular group or institution. Where schools have been the objects of study, this has led to the development of theories of schooling located either within an anthropological framework (for example, Spindler, 1982) or a sociological one (for example, Hammersley and Woods, 1976). However, Stenhouse specifically distinguished the use of case study in teacher research from its anthropological and sociological counterparts. He argued that, since ethnographers are strangers to the situations they study, this was an inappropriate strategy for teachers and educational researchers who tend to be very familiar with classrooms. Instead of using participant observation, he envisaged that the analysis of schools and classrooms would be based upon an accumulation of documents ('the case record') which would include those created through interviews and direct observation (Stenhouse, 1978). Compared to the more traditional ethnographic participant observation studies, this involves much shorter periods of fieldwork with a greater reliance on data derived from the transcripts of tape-recorded interviews. While interviews usually play a central part in teacher-research case studies, a variety of other research techniques may also be adopted, including observation, teacher and pupil diaries, questionnaires and the analysis of teachers' and pupils' written materials (see Chapter 2).

A second broad approach to teacher research is represented by evaluation studies. Stenhouse (1975) argued that it should be teachers themselves who should play the major role in evaluating the potential of new innovations in their own classrooms or schools. However, he was very critical of the traditional 'evaluation by objectives' model, arguing that undue attention to learner outcomes and objectives restricted the scope of evaluation. Thus traditional approaches tend to neglect key aspects, such as the actual processes of innovation and a sensitivity to the context in which innovation is attempted. In this, he shared with a growing body of evaluators, both in the United States and in Britain, a desire to promote alternative qualitative approaches to educational evaluation based upon the disciplined use of case study (for a review of such approaches, see Norris, 1990).

Many of the key characteristics of case-study evaluations are exemplified in Parlett and Hamilton's (1977) depiction of 'illuminative evaluation'. This has a special relevance here for two reasons. Firstly, it has become a popular approach for teacher researchers. It forms the basis, for example, of Holgate's evaluation of the leavers' curriculum in her special school (see Chapter 3) and of Davies-Isaac's evaluation of the use of conductive education (see Chapter 8). Secondly, Parlett and Hamilton set their alternative approach to evaluation, which is strongly influenced by sociological and anthropological traditions, in the context of a critique of the traditional experimental design which has been dominant in psychology and special needs research. They characterise the traditional pre-test/treatment/post-test design for curriculum evaluation as operating within an agricultural-botany paradigm. They argue that this has five major weaknesses:

1. It is impossible to control all relevant parameters in an educational context.
2. It assumes that innovations do not change over time, and can even prevent policy-makers adapting to changed circumstances for fear of contaminating the research design of the evaluation.
3. It concentrates only on that which can be measured and only on the intended consequences of an innovation.
4. The use of large samples for adequate statistical control leads to the neglect of atypical cases, which may be of great interest.
5. Such evaluations often fail to address the concerns both of the participants in the innovation and its sponsors.

(1977)

In a striking analogy, they liken the traditional evaluator 'to a critic who reviews a production on the basis of the script and applause-meter readings, having missed the performance' (1977, p.22).

Parlett and Hamilton describe their alternative approach as follows:

> Illuminative evaluation takes account of the wider contexts in which educational programmes function. Its primary concern is with description and interpretation rather than measurement and prediction ... The aims of illuminative evaluation are to study the innovatory programme: how it operates; how it is influenced by the various school situations in which it is applied; what those directly concerned regard as its advantages and disadvantages; and how students' intellectual tasks and academic experiences are most

affected. It aims to discover and document what it is like to be participating in the scheme, whether as teacher or pupil; and, in addition, to discern and discuss the innovations' most significant features, recurring concomitants and critical processes. In short, it seeks to address and to illuminate a complex array of questions.

(1977, p.10)

The third broad approach to teacher research is action research. While this term can be used in a variety of different ways, within the context of teacher research it has come to be identified specifically with teachers' enquiries which consist of a cycle or spiral involving identifying a problem, devising and implementing a proposed solution and researching the effects of this (see, for example, McTaggart and Kemmis, 1981; McNiff, 1988). Elliott connects this process specifically with the heightened teacher awareness required for improvement to practice: 'this total process − review, diagnosis, planning, implementation, monitoring effects − is called *action research*, and it provides the necessary link between *self-evaluation* and professional development' (1981, p.ii).

Action research is always a form of self-reflective enquiry. It is an approach which requires teacher-researchers to use evidence to identify issues and gain understanding of problems with which they are directly concerned. As with case study, a wide variety of data-collection techniques tends to be used. While action research can be undertaken by individuals, it is frequently a collaborative enterprise (Westgate *et al.*, 1990). This emphasis on collaborative enquiry can make it particularly appealing to groups of teachers, who share common pedagogic, curricular or policy concerns. This is because it facilitates the investigation of a problem from a variety of perspectives and across different subject areas and hierarchical levels. Also, if a number of teachers are involved it strengthens the likely impact and take-up of change.

While in some action-research traditions the emphasis is upon improving practice through insights derived from critical reflection following the systematic collection of evidence, in others it is upon improving practice through changing the values and perspectives of teachers. Thus, for example, Whitehead (1989) advocates the use of video to highlight for teachers the 'living contradictions' of their values in action; Griffiths and Tann (1991) consider a range of techniques, such as the use of images and metaphor, to help uncover teachers' 'personal theories'; and Lomax (1991b) discusses the importance of communities of 'critical friends' in providing

validation of explorations of the relationships between teachers'
values and educational change.

What distinguishes all three broad approaches to teacher research
from more conventional educational research, whether positivist or
qualitative, is that research questions are derived directly from the
practical experience and concerns of the teacher, rather than being
derived from traditional educational disciplines or areas, such as
sociology, psychology or curriculum studies. Bassey (1981; 1983),
in drawing a distinction between 'disciplinary' and 'pedagogic'
research, argues that much traditional educational research,
carried out by specialists and couched in their language, has
been rejected by practising teachers as of little use in assisting
them to analyse classroom situations and in devising solutions to
practical problems. By contrast, 'pedagogic' research has as its main
aim the improvement of practice (rather than the contribution to
theoretical knowledge within a discipline) and employs research
techniques, ways of presenting findings and publication outlets
that are eclectic, pragmatic and readily accessible to teachers. Such
an orientation characterises the research reported throughout this
book, as it does the work of other edited collections of teacher
research (for example, Hustler *et al.*, 1986; Ainscow, 1989; Lomax,
1989, 1990, 1991a; Webb, 1990b).

## The implications of teacher research

Some of the advantages and disadvantages of teacher research,
together with the purposes to which such research can be put,
are illustrated by our recent research (using questionnaires and
in-depth interviews with seven cohorts of students) into the impact
of the York Outstation MA Programme on teachers and on schools
(Vulliamy and Webb, 1991; 1992). Of the three broad approaches to
teacher research, we found that far the most popular was case study,
despite the fact that most teachers hoped to bring about changes in
their research and might therefore have been expected to adopt an
action-research strategy. The reason appeared to be that teachers
did not have enough time during the two-year course to work
through a complete action-research cycle. Thus some teachers,
who were very clear about their research focus from the outset,
used an early pilot study required of them during the first year
of the course to complete the initial stage of an action-research
cycle (see, for example, Gregson, 1990; Winter, 1990). However,

many projects, which were conceived as action-research ones at the outset, became instead a more detailed case study analysing the problem, culminating perhaps in a suggested solution to be implemented once the MA course and thesis had been completed. A case in point is Peake's project which was intended to try out and evaluate a new motor programme for a pupil with physical disabilities (see Chapter 5).

Our research suggested that teacher research could potentially make important contributions in three areas: personal and professional development, changing classroom practice and influencing school policy. An increase in confidence was identified as the major personal contribution of participation in the research process — confidence 'in my own abilities', 'as a teacher', 'to say and act on what I believe to be right', 'in group activity', 'in educational debate'. Other frequently mentioned areas of personal gain were heightened awareness of alternative perspectives on issues, a willingness to question existing assumptions and predilections, a more analytical approach to problems and open-mindedness to new ideas.

Interview data suggested a range of ways in which teachers' research affected classroom practice. A common theme throughout these was teachers' changed attitudes towards their pupils and the value that they came to ascribe to their views, following the collection of data from pupils in their projects. Pupil data also led in some cases to reassessments of their perceived abilities. For example, in an action-research project, one primary class teacher recorded the children's discussion in science as they worked in collaborative groups. She had her expectations of pupils' achievements challenged by the data:

> One thing that I was quite stunned by was the ability of some children, who you would class as having learning difficulties, and the contribution that they made in the working groups ... One of the boys, who went for special remedial lessons, quite clearly in his group was organising the work and coming up with some very good ideas and questioning a lot of what was happening ... I thought well this isn't right, if a child has this ability and I haven't recognised it.
>
> (Quoted in Vulliamy and Webb, 1991, p.228)

She described how she learned about teaching through groupwork from the process of collecting and reflecting on the data, which involved visiting a science co-ordinator in another school, keeping a diary, the observations of her classroom by her tutor and a colleague, taping groupwork and interviewing pupils. The data continuously generated ideas to be tested out and refined in her classroom. As the project progressed, her changed approach to science teaching began to affect her classroom organisation and teaching style in other curriculum areas. As with many of the other teacher researchers we interviewed, there was a strongly held view that systematically collecting and analysing data concerning their own practice was a much more powerful stimulus to change than the more traditional forms of INSET where new ideas were presented to them by others.

While some teacher researchers prefer to conduct projects within their own classrooms, others operate at a wider level in an attempt to inform school policy. Examples in this book include policies for parental involvement (Chapter 4), for record keeping and assessment (Chapter 11), for curricula design (Chapter 3), and for the use of support staff (Chapter 9). In some action-research traditions, such as Lomax's (1989; 1990; 1991a) work at Kingston Polytechnic, action research is viewed as an important component of a school's overall management and staff development strategy. Similarly, Somekh (1989) considers the ways in which INSET co-ordinators in schools might use action research to facilitate whole school development. Such examples raise interesting questions concerning possible tensions between the democratic and collaborative ideals associated with action research and the top – down hierarchical nature of most school management structures. Thus Griffiths (1990) sees a danger in the grass-roots investigation of a teacher's *own* practice giving way to senior management's use of action research as a tool to direct and evaluate the practice of subordinates.

Our research also indicated some of the main limitations of teacher research. On a personal level teachers found that it tended to be very time-consuming which could prove stressful, especially given the other rapidly increasing demands being made upon teachers resulting from the implementation of the 1988 Education Reform Act. Pressure from other school initiatives and innovations was also cited as a major factor in constraining the implementation of changes arising from a teacher-research project. We also found that the attitudes of senior management, especially the head, and the general ethos of the school — whether, for example, it had a participative decision-making structure — were key aspects influencing the extent to which teacher-research enquiries could bring about change. Contrary to the rhetoric of collaborative teacher research, we found that for many teachers their research remained a very private enterprise, not to be shared with other staff, reflecting, we argue, deep-seated individualist aspects of the culture of teaching (Vulliamy and Webb, 1992, pp.46−9).

A final perceived limitation of teacher research, and one frequently argued by other educational researchers, is that, whilst such research might lead to improved practice for isolated teachers, the findings are not generalisable to other contexts and cannot be used to advance theoretical understanding. Here we believe that Bassey's (1981; 1990) distinction between 'generalisability' and 'relatability' is an important one. He argues that the products of much traditional educational research, whilst supposedly generalisable because they have been derived from large samples, are perceived by most teachers as unrelatable to the realities of their specific classrooms. By contrast, given the in-depth portrayal of a particular case, be it the use of a specific curriculum package or a certain classroom management style, then teachers can readily relate aspects of such a portrayal to their own experiences. For example, teachers are likely to recognise the kinds of disruptive behaviours by pupils and their effects on comprehensive school classrooms portrayed by Farrell in Chapter 7. Through his analysis as to why pupils felt the need to resort to such behaviours as a means of coping with the demands of school, teachers can deepen their understanding of the underlying reasons for any similar behaviours occurring in their own classrooms. They may also find it helpful to adopt some of the approaches Farrell's colleagues used to try to remove the need for such coping strategies. Thus one intention of edited collections of teacher research such as this is to help publicise and generate pedagogic theories which are of direct relevance to other teachers, by offering them alternative ways of understanding and acting in their own situations.

## References

Ainscow, M. (ed) (1989) *Special Education in Change*. London: David Fulton.

Atkinson, P. (1979) *Research Design in Ethnography*. Course DE304, Block 3B, Part 5. Milton Keynes: Open University Press.

Barrera, R.D., Lobato-Barrera, D. and Sulzer-Azaroff, B. (1980) 'A simultaneous treatment comparison of three expressive language training programs with a mute autistic child'. *Journal of Autism and Developmental Disorders* 10, 21−37.

Barton, L. and Oliver, M. (1992) 'Special needs: personal trouble or public issue?', in Arnot, M. and Barton, L. (eds) *Voicing Concerns: Sociological Perspectives on Contemporary Education Reforms*. Wallingford: Triangle Books.

Bassey, M. (1981) 'Pedagogic research: on the relative merits of search for generalisation and study of single events'. *Oxford Review of Education* 7, 73–94.

Bassey, M. (1983) 'Pedagogic research into singularities: case studies, probes and curriculum innovations'. *Oxford Review of Education* 9, 109–21.

Bassey, M. (1990) 'On the nature of research in education (Part 2)'. *Research Intelligence* 37, 39–44.

Bell, G. and Colbeck, B. (eds) (1989) *Experiencing Integration*. London: Falmer Press.

Boone, N. (1904) *Science of Education*. New York: Scribner.

Bracht, G.H. and Glass, G.V. (1968) 'The external validity of experiments'. *American Educational Research Journal* 5, 437–74.

Bryman, A. (1988) *Quantity and Quality in Social Research*. London: Unwin Hyman.

Buckingham, B.R. (1926) *Research for Teachers*. New York: Silver, Burdett and Co.

Burgess, R.G. (ed) (1985) *Strategies of Educational Research: Qualitative Methods*. Lewes: Falmer Press.

Burton, K. (1989) 'Bringing about gender equality of opportunity in a special school', in Lomax, P. (ed) *The Management of Change*. Clevedon: Multilingual Matters.

Cave, C. and Maddison, P. (1978) *A Survey of Recent Research in Special Education*. Windsor: NFER.

Corrie, M. and Zaklukiewicz, S. (1984) 'Leaving special education: issues for research'. *Scottish Educational Review* 16, 10–18.

Corrie, M. and Zaklukiewicz, S. (1985) 'Qualitative research and case-study approaches: an introduction', in Hegarty, S. and Evans, P. (eds) *Research and Evaluation Methods in Special Education*. Windsor: NFER-Nelson.

Deutscher, I. (1966) 'Words and deeds: social science and social policy'. *Social Problems* 13, 233–54.

Deutscher, I. (1973) *What We Say/What We Do: Sentiments and Acts*. Glenview: Scott, Foresman and Co.

Elliott, J. (1978) 'Classroom research: science or commonsense?', in McAleese, R. and Hamilton, D. (eds) *Understanding Classroom Life*. Windsor: NFER.

Elliott, J. (1981) *Action-research: A Framework for Self-evaluation in Schools*. Cambridge: Schools Council 'Teacher – Pupil Interaction and the Quality of Learning' Project, Working Paper No.1.

Elliott, J. (1991) *Action Research for Educational Change*. Milton Keynes: Open University Press.

Evans, J. (1983) 'Criteria of validity in social research: exploring the relationship between ethnographic and quantitative approaches', in Hammersley, M. (ed) *The Ethnography of Schooling*. Driffield: Nafferton Books.

Evans, P. (1985) 'Single case and small-N research designs: introduction', in Hegarty, S. and Evans, P. (eds) *Research and Evaluation Methods in Special Education*. Windsor: NFER-Nelson.

Giddens, A. (ed) (1974) *Positivism and Sociology*. London: Heinemann.

Gregson, D. (1990) 'Why do pirates have peg legs? A study of reading for information', in Webb, R. (ed) *Practitioner Research in the Primary School*. London: Falmer Press.

Griffiths, M. (1990) 'Action research: grassroots practice or management tool?', in Lomax, P. (ed) *Managing Staff Development in Schools: An Action Research Approach*. Clevedon: Multilingual Matters.

Griffiths, M. and Tann, S. (1991) 'Ripples in the reflection', in Lomax, P. (ed) *Managing Better Schools and Colleges: An Action Research Way*. Clevedon: Multilingual Matters.

Halfpenny, P. (1982) *Positivism and Sociology: Explaining Social Life*. London: George Allen and Unwin.

Halil, A. (1985) 'Statistical methods in single-case studies', in Hegarty, S. and Evans, P. (eds) *Research and Evaluation Methods in Special Education*. Windsor: NFER-Nelson.

Hammersley, M. (1979) *Analysing Ethnographic Data*. Course DE304, Block 6, Part 1. Milton Keynes: Open University Press.

Hammersley, M. and Woods, P. (eds) (1976) *The Process of Schooling*. London: Routledge and Kegan Paul.

Hegarty, S. (1985) 'Qualitative research: introduction', in Hegarty, S. and Evans, P. (eds) *Research and Evaluation Methods in Special Education*. Windsor: NFER-Nelson.

Hegarty, S., Pocklington, K. and Lucas, D. (1981) *Educating Pupils with Special Needs in the Ordinary School*. Windsor: NFER-Nelson.

Hustler, D., Cassidy, T. and Cuff, T. (eds) (1986) *Action Research in Classrooms and Schools*. London: George Allen and Unwin.

Jamieson, M., Parlett, M. and Pocklington, K. (1977) *Towards Integration: A Study of Blind and Partially-sighted Children in Ordinary Schools*. Windsor: NFER.

Kiernan, C. (1982) 'Teachers and researchers in special education'. *Special Education: Forward Trends* 9, 25–6.

Kiernan, C. (1985) 'Single-subject designs', in Hegarty, S. and Evans, P. (eds) *Research and Evaluation Methods in Special Education*. Windsor: NFER-Nelson.

Lewis, I. and Vulliamy, G. (1979) 'Where Warnock went wrong'. *Times Educational Supplement*, 30 Nov.

Lewis, I. and Vulliamy, G. (1980) 'Warnock or Warlock? The sorcery of definitions: the limitations of the report on special education'. *Educational Review* 32, 3–10.

Lomax, P. (1989) (ed) *The Management of Change*: Clevedon: Multilingual Matters.

Lomax, P. (ed) (1990) *Managing Staff Development in Schools: An Action Research Approach*. Clevedon: Multilingual Matters.

Lomax, P. (ed) (1991a) *Managing Better Schools and Colleges: An Action Research Way*. Clevedon: Multilingual Matters.

Lomax, P. (1991b) 'Peer review and action research', in Lomax, P. (ed) *Managing Better Schools and Colleges: An Action Research Way*. Clevedon: Multilingual Matters.

McNiff, J. (1988) *Action Research: Principles and Practice*. London: Macmillan Education.

McReynolds, L. and Kearns, K.P. (1982) *Single Subject Designs for Intervention Research in Communicative Disorders*. Lancaster: MTP Press.

McTaggart, R. and Kemmis, S. (1981) *The Action Research Planner*. Geelong: Deakin University.

Mittler, P. (1974) 'Research and the teacher'. *Special Education: Forward Trends. Proceedings of the Annual Conference, National Council for Special Education, Birmingham*. London: NCSE.

Mittler, P. (1985) 'Approaches to evaluation in special education: concluding reflections', in Hegarty, S. and Evans, P. (eds) *Research and Evaluation Methods in Special Education*. Windsor: NFER-Nelson.

National Curriculum Council (1992a) *The National Curriculum and Pupils with Severe Learning Difficulties*. York: National Curriculum Council.

National Curriculum Council (1992b) *The National Curriculum and Pupils with Severe Learning Difficulties: INSET Resources*. York: National Curriculum Council.

Norris, N. (1990) *Understanding Educational Evaluation*. London: Kogan Page.

Parlett, M. and Hamilton, D. (1977) 'Evaluation as illumination', in Hamilton, D. *et al.* (eds) *Beyond the Numbers Game*. London: Macmillan Education.

Rose, R. (1991) 'A jigsaw approach to group work'. *British Journal of Special Education* 18, 54–8.

Schindele, R.A. (1985) 'Research methodology in special education: a framework approach to special problems and solutions', in Hegarty, S. and Evans, P. (eds) *Research and Evaluation Methods in Special Education*. Windsor: NFER-Nelson.

Somekh, B. (1989) 'Action research and collaborative school development', in McBride, R. (ed) *The In-Service Training of Teachers*. London: Falmer Press.

Spindler, G. (ed) (1982) *Doing the Ethnography of Schooling*. New York: Holt, Rinehart and Winston.

Stenhouse, L. (1975) *An Introduction to Curriculum Research and Development*. London: Heinemann.

Stenhouse, L. (1978) 'Case study and case records: towards a contemporary history of education'. *British Educational Research Journal* 4, 21–39.

Stephenson, S. (1990) 'Promoting interaction among children with special educational needs in an integrated nursery'. *British Journal of Special Education* 17, 61–5.

Tomlinson, S. (1981) *Educational Subnormality*. London: Routledge and Kegan Paul.

Tomlinson, S. (1982) *A Sociology of Special Education*. London: Routledge and Kegan Paul.

Vulliamy, G. (1990a) 'The potential of qualitative educational research strategies in developing countries', in Vulliamy, G., Lewin, K. and Stephens, D. *Doing Educational Research in Developing Countries*. London: Falmer Press.

Vulliamy, G. (1990b) 'Research processes: postscript', in Vulliamy, G., Lewin, K. and Stephens, D. *Doing Educational Research in Developing Countries*. London: Falmer Press.

Vulliamy, G. and Webb, R. (1991) 'Teacher research and educational change: an empirical study'. *British Educational Research Journal* 17, 219–36.

Vulliamy, G. and Webb, R. (1992) 'The influence of teacher research: process or product?' *Educational Review* 44, 41–58.

Walker, R. (1985) *Doing Research: A Handbook for Teachers*. London: Methuen.

Webb, R. (1990a) 'The origins and aspirations of practitioner research', in Webb, R. (ed) *Practitioner Research in the Primary School*. London: Falmer Press.

Webb, R. (ed) (1990b) *Practitioner Research in the Primary School*. London: Falmer Press.

Wedell, K. (1985a) 'Foreword', in Hegarty, S. and Evans, P. (eds) *Research and Evaluation Methods in Special Education*. Windsor: NFER-Nelson.

Wedell, K. (1985b) 'Future directions for research on children's special educational needs'. *British Journal of Special Education* 12, 22–6.

Wedell, K. and Roberts, J. (1981) Survey of Current Research in the UK on Children with Special Educational Needs. SSRC Unpublished report.

Wedell, K. and Roberts, J. (1982) 'Special education and research: a recent survey'. *Special Education: Forward Trends* 9, 19–25.

Westgate, D., Batey, J. and Brownlee, J. (1990) 'Collaborative action research: professional development in a cold climate'. *British Journal of In-Service Education* 16, 167–72.

Whitehead, J. (1989) 'Creating a living educational theory from questions of the kind "How do I improve my practice?"'. *Cambridge Journal of Education* 19, 41–52.

Winter, V. (1990) 'A process approach to science', in Webb, R. (ed) *Practitioner Research in the Primary School*. London: Falmer Press.

Wood, D. (1981) 'Theory and research in classrooms: lessons from deaf education', in Swann, W. (ed) *The Practice of Special Education*. Oxford: Basil Blackwell.

# CHAPTER 2

# *Designing a Teacher-research Project*
Graham Vulliamy and Rosemary Webb

This chapter begins by considering how the current educational context and its implications for the education of pupils with special educational needs creates an important agenda for teacher researchers.

Having suggested some of the key aspects of this agenda which could form the focus of research projects, the chapter goes on to explain how research questions can be formulated and a research project designed. To illustrate this process in more detail five vignettes describe research proposals for case-study research, evaluation and action research. Through discussion of the proposals a range of appropriate data collection techniques open to teacher researchers are reviewed and suggestions made for further reading.

## Choosing a focus for teacher research

The Education Reform Act (ERA) of 1988 legislating for the National Curriculum, its associated assessment, Local Management of Schools (LMS) and opting out has brought about sweeping changes in the educational system. There has been much speculation as to the likely positive and negative effects of the reforms for pupils and teachers, especially those pupils with special educational needs. However, as argued by Ball and Bowe (1992) in a report of their research in four secondary schools, the question of the actual rather than the anticipated effects of the ERA must remain an empirical one. Teacher research has a major role to play in providing evidence to inform debate on the resultant educational issues and controversies at school, local and national level. While such a time of multiple change causes much stress and anxiety, it also legitimates undertaking a reappraisal of existing school structures and teaching methods and the development of creative additional or alternative policies and practices. In relation to special educational needs, teacher research has a powerful part to play in evaluating the impact of the new legislation on pupils, their parents and teachers, devising, implementing and monitoring strategies to finance and administer schools in ways that meet the requirements of pupils with special educational needs and designing teaching approaches and materials to give all pupils the fullest possible access to the National Curriculum.

Implicit in the ERA is the right of all pupils to a broad and balanced curriculum including the National Curriculum. However, a consideration of pupils with special educational needs was over-looked by the working parties for the core subjects which meant that teachers in special schools were initially concerned that their pupils would be marginalised from the education system, or in the case of pupils with profound and multiple learning difficulties, even placed outside it. Teachers' commitment to their pupils with special educational needs has resulted in numerous working parties producing suggestions as to how the National Curriculum can be made accessible to pupils with a range of needs, especially those with severe and profound and multiple learning difficulties (see, for example, Fagg *et al.*, 1990). Teacher research can be used both to devise new curricula based on the orders and to evaluate the pupils' experience of these once they are in place.

The work of special educational needs co-ordinators and the drawing up of whole school policies on special educational needs are vital for supplying advice to teachers in ordinary schools and in meeting the individual needs of pupils. Consequently, they provide an important focus for teacher research. Support teachers also play a key role in promoting integration of pupils moving from special to ordinary schools. However, as pointed out by Murphy in Chapter 6 and Normington in Chapter 10, LMS is viewed as a major threat to the continued existence of the support services. If LEAs cease to be able to fund these services centrally, schools may find themselves unable to pay for the services or unwilling to do so if there are few pupils in their schools who are perceived as likely to benefit. Also, as schools opt out and become grant maintained, support services are unlikely to be available to their pupils as the schools are no longer accountable to the LEAs. Teacher research needs to monitor the effect of these changes on the ability of LEAs and schools to meet their responsibilities to pupils with statements under the 1981

Act and to improve schools' awareness of special educational needs issues through INSET and guidance.

Despite the widely publicised fears of the adverse effects of national assessment procedures on the teaching-learning process and relationships with parents and pupils, Broadfoot *et al.* (1991) also found evidence to suggest 'that we might be at the beginning of a very creative phase of development in the use of assessment' (p.163). Teacher research can evaluate the effects of the content and implementation of SATs and the publication of SAT results and other decisions relating to assessment − such as the restrictions on GCSE coursework − upon the access of pupils with special educational needs to the National Curriculum and other courses. It can also provide a valuable contribution to the 'creative phase' of using teacher assessment to diagnose pupils' individual learning needs and to devise approaches to differentiation in the classroom to meet those needs.

The current situation regarding progress on integration is very variable. Progress has been much greater in some parts of the country than others. For example, 'the percentage of pupils in special schools varies between 0.6 per cent in places as different as Cornwall and Barnsley to just under 4 per cent in some of the new London boroughs' (Mittler, 1991, p.13). Also, pupils with some types of special need appear to be more readily integrated than others. In relation to the implementation of the National Curriculum, research undertaken by the National Curriculum Council found that:

> although 20% of heads thought that ordinary schools would become less willing to link up with special schools to support pupils with learning difficulties, the majority anticipated a growth in integration projects for special school pupils helped by the common language of the National Curriculum, shared attainment targets and greater curriculum breadth.
>
> (NCC, 1991, p.121)

As discussed by Holgate in Chapter 3 and Powell in Chapter 11, parents and teachers are pessimistic about the prospects of pupils with special educational needs finding employment or continuing in full-time education when they leave school. HMI (1991) have recently criticised the poor transition arrangements between schools and colleges and the lack of support for these students in further education. Teacher research provides the possibility of gaining greater understanding of the factors constraining and promoting integration in all phases of education and of action research to develop new initiatives.

Wadlow's research in Chapter 4 demonstrates the importance of teachers building relationships with parents which promote the exchange of information and create a basis for co-operation over the education of their children. Both Wadlow's and Murphy's research demonstrate that there is still much to be done to improve communication with parents by the professionals involved in the support of pupils with statements and to co-ordinate the assistance that they provide. The implementation of the 1989 Children Act has the potential to effect considerable improvement in this area, providing the professionals in the LEA departments of Education, Social Services and Health capitalise on the opportunity for co-operation. Action research across departments offers exciting possibilities to establish co-operation in order to meet children's needs and fulfil parents' rights.

## Research questions and project design

Once a research focus is identified the next stage in getting started is to formulate some research questions to clarify the nature of the investigation and to guide initial data collection. Likely sources of research questions are:

1. The purpose of the research — for example, whether it is to gain a deeper understanding of an issue, evaluate an existing policy or to design, implement and monitor a new initiative.
2. A teacher researcher's role and status in the school and the particular demands and possibilities associated with these.
3. A particular problem experienced by the teacher researcher or of concern throughout the school.
4. The attitudes, values and views of colleagues.
5. A surprising set of facts, such as unanticipated examination successes or failures.
6. A major event, such as the amalgamation of two schools or the opening of a nursery or special unit.
7. Published research, guidance or pupil materials.
8. Media coverage of current controversies or legislation.

Frequently, once research questions begin to be formulated the initial research focus appears too vast for the time available and the depth of information required and so a specific aspect of this must be selected. As described by Wadlow in Chapter 4, on the Outstation course the course requirements of a research assignment and a pilot study often provide valuable information assisting teachers to identify for their research important and manageable aspects of their areas of interest. Once data collection begins some questions are likely to be discarded and others added. Sometimes the nub of the problem being investigated emerges from the data as something quite different from what was originally anticipated requiring a considerably modified or even new set of research questions. Throughout the research, referring back to the research questions can serve as a reminder of the overall purpose of the research and data required and prevent the researcher from getting diverted or carried away into interesting areas that are not really relevant.

A major problem for teacher researchers when they begin collecting data is finding ways of getting beyond the 'everydayness' and the taken for granted routines and expectations of classroom life. Becker acknowledges the difficulty of observing in classrooms experienced by all researchers and attributes this to it:

> all being so familiar that it becomes impossible to single out events that occur in the classroom as things that have occurred, even when they happen right in front of you ... it takes a tremendous effort of will and imagination to stop seeing the things that are conventionally 'there' to be seen.
>
> (1971, p.10)

This is even more the case for teachers researching in schools and classrooms which they have worked to shape, possibly over a number of years. Delamont considers that the problem is not so much one of not noting events, but rather of how they are interpreted:

> The teacher observer may not be bored, or see 'nothing', but will see the interaction through the eyes of a teacher or an educationalist rather than those of a social scientist. Here the familiarity brings into play common-sense interpretations of events rather than formal sociological ones.
>
> (1981, p.71)

While few teacher researchers on the Outstation course draw on sociological theories to inform their research questions and give meaning to their data, it is vital that their investigations involve ways of challenging existing assumptions and seeking alternative explanations of events. Delamont (1992) returns to the theme of 'fighting familiarity' when offering advice on carrying out fieldwork in educational settings. She suggests four strategies for making the familiar strange:

1. Study unusual, bizarre or different classrooms, such as those for adults.
2. Study schools and classrooms in other cultures, such as Judaism and Islamic instruction.
3. Study non-educational settings chosen for their parallel features, such as aspects of hospitals, prisons, factories and shops.
4. Adopt gender as the focus of the study. In relation to gender she argues that 'the attempt to focus on a neglected, taken-for-granted feature of school life can highlight other aspects of it' (1992, p.45).

Four years ago an opportunity to research in schools in Poland demonstrated for us how the familiar can be thrown into sharp relief by the unfamiliar. Interestingly, gender became a major focus of our study as we increasingly came to realise the mistaken nature of our assumptions about why female teachers predominated in key positions and in science teaching and why girls outnumbered boys in science classes in grammar schools (Webb and Vulliamy, 1989). While acknowledging that few teachers will have the opportunity to research abroad, or indeed in alternative classes and institutions, we recommend deliberately seeking out and taking advantage of TV documentaries, fiction and autobiographies which can provide challenging contrasts or novel perspectives on the area being studied.

Teachers have a wide range of demands made upon them and, as is recognised in Chapter 1, research – even when closely related to their role – increases their workload. There is, therefore, a very understandable tendency to only read or watch that which is obviously specifically and immediately relevant, so reducing possible sources of ideas at a time when they are most needed.

Simultaneously with drawing up research questions thought needs to be given to the techniques of data collection to be used, the criteria determining the selection of the research sample and the timescale within which the data must be collected, analysed and written up.

It is important to plan how to set up and carry out the research. This involves considering who needs to be consulted, which information should be gathered first and from whom (pupils, colleagues, parents and governors) and what ideally their level of participation in the research should be. Resources to aid data gathering, such as tape or video recorders and cameras or particular teaching materials or equipment, may be required. Decisions will need to be made about who should be kept informed or ought to know about the progress of the research and whether adequate mechanisms exist to enable this to happen. It may be necessary to create additional means for providing feedback. Although those not directly involved in the research may or may not be interested in it, unexplained information gathering activities can at best be irritating to colleagues and at worst appear subversive or threatening.

As part of ensuring colleagues understand the purposes and processes of the research and its possible implications, some teacher researchers choose to make explicit the ethical code guiding the collection, control and release of data. Information should be confidential to the person concerned until its release has been negotiated with that person. This may involve sharing notes of observations of colleagues' lessons, giving back transcripts or notes of interviews for comment or asking for feedback on early attempts at writing up. As discussed in Chapter 12, such procedures can generate further useful data and assist in validating the research. Research participants should always be anonymised. However, when considering whether and how information should be used, the researcher must take into account the fact that within their own institution or LEA research participants may be recognisable by their role, actions or views.

It is important to draw up a timescale for the research and set deadlines within it. However, they must be realistic enough to take account of minor but common setbacks, such as colleagues finding they are needed elsewhere at the time arranged for an interview and to allow for additional unforeseen school or personal commitments. Also, until personally experienced it is likely that the time required for certain aspects of the research may be underestimated, such as transcribing audio or video tapes, struggling to derive meaning from some of the data, tracking down elusive references in the library or clarifying complex ideas in writing.

Teacher research will always involve a process of sampling, since one cannot possibly study everything. It is therefore important to be clear as to the purposes of such sampling. If the aim is to generalise the findings from one's sample to a wider group, then the sample needs to be representative and should be chosen according to statistical principles (see, for example, the discussion of random and stratified sampling in Munn and Drever, 1990). This may sometimes be the intention in teacher research where, for example, a 50 per cent random sample of a school staff might be selected for interviews. However, in much qualitative research a process of theoretical sampling is used, by which is meant choosing people or situations to study which seem to give the greatest possibilities for generating new ideas (Glaser and Strauss, 1967). Thus a decision might be made to interview a particular teacher, not because it is thought that this teacher's responses will be typical of others, but because they are likely to cast the most light on an emerging hypothesis. The important point is to be as explicit and systematic as possible as to how and why a particular sample was chosen, bearing in mind that sampling involves not just people, but also different contexts and different time periods.

Guides to the process of educational research usually emphasise that it is the nature of the research questions that should dictate the methodological approach and data collection techniques adopted (Bell, 1987). However, as suggested by Walker, this choice is often influenced by researchers' personal preferences:

> Just as an instrumentalist will not change from playing the clarinet to playing the trumpet because a particular piece demands it, but will instead usually turn to another piece of music, so researchers generally give a lot of time and thought to the formulation of possible and potential research problems, looking for those that appear to fit their interests and preferred methods.

> (1985, p.47)

Teacher researchers also have to take account of pragmatic concerns, such as the lack or amount of non-contact time available for carrying out research, as this is likely to dictate whether data may be collected in colleagues' classrooms or in other schools. Other influential factors are which members of staff are likely to be willing to participate in the research, in what ways and to what degree and what kinds of data collection can best take place alongside, or most readily fit in with, other school commitments.

There is a wealth of advice on a wide range of techniques for data gathering as the growth of teacher research over the last decade has given rise to a steadily expanding literature (see, for example, Bell, 1987; Hopkins, 1985; McKernan, 1991; Patton, 1980; Pollard and Tann, 1987; Walker, 1985; Woods, 1986). First-hand experience of some of these techniques is provided by the contributors in the following chapters, who have each chosen to write about one or two methodological issues of particular importance to their study. Additional advice and suggestions for further reading are given in the remaining part of this chapter, which gives vignettes of five proposals by teachers for research into an aspect of special educational needs. These are:

1.  Action research into integrating hearing-impaired pupils into a comprehensive school classroom.
2.  Case study of the role of a SEN co-ordinator in a comprehensive school.
3.  Action research into differentiation in a primary school.
4.  Case study of a middle school's policy and practice for managing behaviour.
5.  Evaluation of the science curriculum in a school for pupils with severe learning difficulties.

## Examples of project proposals

The vignettes describing these proposals are based on genuine interests and problems experienced by teachers in real settings. However, the proposals have been constructed to illustrate different kinds of teacher-research projects involving the combination of a range of data collection techniques either used solely by the researcher or in co-operation with colleagues.

*1. Action research into integrating hearing-impaired pupils into a comprehensive school classroom*

David Bean recently took up a new post in the humanities department of a comprehensive school. Attached to the school is a unit for pupils who are partially hearing and they are integrated into ordinary classes for as much time as is considered beneficial for them. Currently there are four staff based in the unit supporting 32 pupils. David, who has no experience of working with pupils with hearing impairments, decided that for his research project he would carry out action research to improve his knowledge and practice in this area. Talking to colleagues in the department it appeared that there was considerable variation in the amount of extra time and attention and modifications to teaching style that they were prepared to make for these pupils. However, he was committed to putting himself in a position where he could adequately meet the needs of hearing-impaired pupils integrated into his lessons.

He began by reading around the subject of hearing impairment and discussing the types of hearing loss and the implications of these for teaching and learning with teachers from the unit. The unit staff helped him to become *au fait* with the working and checking of hearing aids. They made suggestions as to the changes he would need to make in his classroom organisation and teaching style to provide for hearing-impaired pupils. They also advised on how class materials might need to be modified to take account of the fact that many hearing-impaired pupils do not read as well as their peers.

In answer to his initial research question 'How can I make my history lessons accessible to pupils with hearing impairments?' David identified classroom environment and aiding communication as the two major inter-related areas requiring attention:

a. Classroom environment
- seating arrangements (e.g. curved rows) needed to allow hearing-impaired pupils to easily pick up visual cues from teacher and peers;
- bright evenly distributed lighting without glare and with the source situated behind the pupil;
- use of additional visual aids and visual cues − especially the overhead projector which allows the teacher to face the class while discussing transparencies;
- ensuring classmates are aware of consequences of hearing impairment and techniques to improve communication;
- use of a friend of a pupil, whose hearing is impaired, to act as an assistant when books and maps are being used while explanations offered;
- ensuring children with hearing impairments are independent.

Important ways in which the teacher can help the hearing-impaired child are suggested in the information pack on meeting special educational needs in the ordinary classroom 'Signposts to Special Needs' (1992) produced by the National Children's Bureau. Dave tried to take account of the following to aid communication:

b. Aiding communication
- keep the face unobstructed and avoid putting the hands in front of the mouth;
- stand in one place while talking rather than moving around;
- stop talking when you turn away;
- avoid changing the subject abruptly;
- look directly at the child; talking from the side will reduce his or her understanding;
- be ready to repeat or change vocabulary if it is not understood;
- writing down information and instructions may help;
- maintain the normal rhythm and intonation of speech;
- be conscious that group work may present problems if several people are talking or interrupting;
- check if the child could benefit from a radio aid.

(Pupils with Hearing Impairment 10.2)

Over the duration of the following term he intended to try to incorporate these suggestions into his practice in order to achieve good communications with the two boys (one in year 7 and one in year 8) who were to be integrated into his history classes. He decided to collect data on his progress and the effect it was having on the boys' motivation and learning through:

- interviews with the boys' parents enabling discussion of their sons' integration in the school generally and how they were coping with Humanities classwork and homework.
- interviews with three members of staff considered by the staff in the special unit as knowledgeable and experienced in the integration of the hearing impaired.
- fieldnotes containing:
  a. notes on modifications to lesson plans and material prepared to increase access;
  b. reflections on the lesson written at lunchtime or after school;
  c. feedback from the two boys on how they found the lessons;

d. analysis of the boys' work;
e. perceptions of classmates on the effects of hearing impairment and the effects on their learning of the changes he has made to his practice;
f. observations of the two boys at breaks and lunchtimes to ascertain their status and relationships within their peergroups.

- oral and written feedback from the teacher from the special unit who would be supporting the two boys during some of David's lessons.
- audio tapes of a sample of lessons to check pace, rhythm, intonation and vocabulary.

Many teacher research studies, like David's, involve gathering interview data because of the potential of interviews to give speedy access to much needed information and to supply considerable detail in a short space of time. All books on qualitative research methods have sections on interviewing which categorise the various approaches as 'structured' and 'unstructured', 'focused' and 'unfocused', 'informant' and 'respondent', and so on. Patton (1980) identifies and elaborates on three basic approaches to qualitative interviewing which serve somewhat different purposes and involve different types of preparation, conceptualisation and implementation:

1. The informal conversational interview 'which relies entirely on the spontaneous generation of questions in the natural flow of an interaction, typically an interview that occurs as part of ongoing participant observation fieldwork' (p.198).
2. The general interview guide approach involves drawing up a checklist of issues to be covered prior to the interview. The issues 'need not be taken in any particular order and the actual wording of questions to elicit responses about those issues is not determined in advance' (p.198). The checklist provides a framework within which the interviewer can decide where to probe and which information to pursue in greater depth.
3. The standardised open-ended interview 'consists of a set of questions carefully worded and arranged with the intention of taking each respondent through the same sequence and asking each respondent the same questions with essentially the same words' (p.198).

David intends to use the first approach to gain data from the pupils during opportunities for conversation arising within lessons and at break and lunchtimes. Informal conversational interviews with small groups of pupils allow them to take the interview in directions which are meaningful to them and to clarify recollections with, and to bounce ideas off, friends (for example, see Webb, 1990). David will use the second approach when he interviews teachers and parents as a result of making formal arrangements to do so. The general interview guide tends to be the most common approach to interviews in teacher research. Hammersley and Atkinson (1983), Patton (1980) and Woods (1986) provide helpful discussions of the role of different kinds of interview questions, pitfalls to be avoided and the advantages and disadvantages of notemaking and tape recording. For those who require more detail and examples there is a fund of information in two books specifically on the subject by Powney and Watts (1987) and Spradley (1979). Powney and Watts (1987) give particular consideration to children as interviewees and include accounts of interviews with groups of secondary and junior school pupils (pp.48–9 and pp.100–16). Readers, who may be interested in the steadily growing use of interviewing to compile life histories and to document oral folklore and popular culture in education, will find Delamont (1992) provides useful references to different kinds of published studies (pp.110–11).

David also intends to keep fieldnotes about the integration of the two boys in the school and in his lessons and on the steps he is taking to assist in this. Fieldnotes contain detailed descriptions of events, settings and interactions, quotations from what people have said, the teacher researcher's own reactions to experiences and insights, interpretations and emerging theories and hypotheses. As stressed by Hammersley and Atkinson meticulous note making is vital:

> The memory should never be relied on, and a good maxim is 'If in doubt, write it down'. It is absolutely essential that one keeps up to date in processing notes. Without the discipline of daily writing, the observations will fade from memory ...
>
> (1983, p.150)

Hammersley and Atkinson (1983), Patton (1980) and Woods (1986) discuss the form and content of fieldnotes and provide an analysis of some examples of entries. However, these examples are taken from 'outsider' research. Teacher researchers making notes of events in their own classroom in which, like David, they may be fully participating face additional constraints on time and memory as is evidenced by Peake in Chapter 5.

*2. Case study of the role of a co-ordinator for special educational needs (SEN) in a comprehensive school*

Richard Stones is the SEN co-ordinator at Heathend Comprehensive which has 500 pupils on roll. His role, which has evolved and changed during the ten years that he has worked there, has four main dimensions:

1. Teaching of individuals and small groups withdrawn for intensive help with the basic skills of reading, writing and computation. When he was first appointed three-quarters of his time was spent in this way.

2. Supporting pupils with special educational needs within the classroom by enabling individuals to understand the content of the lesson, tasks set and the teachers' expectations. In classes where there were statemented pupils they were given particular attention. As time spent on withdrawal diminished, time involved in in-class support had grown.

3. Fulfilling a pastoral role for pupils with emotional and behavioural problems by offering them counselling, withdrawing them on specific occasions where they were likely to be disruptive, alerting pastoral staff to any adverse personal circumstances experienced by pupils and providing advice to subject teachers on coping strategies for behaviour problems.

4. A more recent dimension of his role, which evolved from requests to build in provision for pupils with special educational needs into National Curriculum schemes of work, was to provide consultancy to subject departments. Working with one department each term he advised on individual pupils' needs and how to make subject lessons more accessible through the use of alternative curriculum materials and teaching approaches. When invited, he observed lessons and provided feedback on the involvement of pupils with special educational needs.

Richard viewed his research as an opportunity to establish exactly how much time was spent where and with whom and to critically reflect on the four dimensions of his role in order to improve his effectiveness and decide on future priorities. He was particularly interested in gaining information on his in-class support work and discussing this with staff in order to move to more of a team teaching approach.

Richard decided to collect data through:
- a daily diary;
- interviews with a sample of subject teachers and the heads of departments to identify their needs and views on how these might best be met;
- interviewing pupils with special needs whom he regularly helped to gain their perceptions of support teaching and withdrawal groups;
- interviewing a sample of other pupils who were prepared to give their understandings of his role.

The daily diary was to be his main data source and the vehicle for gaining a deeper understanding of his work.

Hook states that:

> Diaries contain observations, feelings, attitudes, perceptions, reflections, hypotheses, lengthy analyses, and cryptic comments. The entries are highly personal 'conversations with one's self', recording events significant to the writer; they are not meant to be regarded as literary works, as normally the accounts or remarks are read only by the writer and no one else.
>
> (1981, p. 128)

While diaries have much in common with fieldnotes as described in the previous vignette — and in fact the terms are sometimes used interchangeably — diaries generally contain a chronological description of facts, events and anecdotes as they unfold with the personal beliefs and feelings associated with these recorded as they occur or soon after (see, for example, in Holgate, Chapter 3). Holly (1984) provides advice on keeping a diary/journal for research and professional development purposes. She argues (Holly, 1989) that keeping such a journal 'enables the author to develop an educational archive which serves as an evolving database for gaining understandings and insights which inform and enrich professional judgement' (p.71). As expressed by Ferrucci the act of writing itself is a powerful tool for coming to know one's self through making unconscious values and views explicit and therefore open to analysis:

> If we start by freely writing about the issue that concerns us, we will find ourselves expressing things not previously thought of. We have to formulate explicitly that which we feel implicitly, thereby clarifying to ourselves what may have been a confused morass. In this process we may also come to new conclusions and ideas about courses of action to take. We should not be surprised that unconscious material surfaces so readily in our writing ... Writing stimulates this interchange and allows us to observe, direct, and understand it.
>
> (1982, p.41)

It is perhaps not surprising that few Outstation teachers engage in deep reflection in their diary writing, or where they do, are willing to share it with others. As Gregson (1990), whose personal writing has this quality, found, such revelations about one's teaching can be very upsetting and depressing. Also, moving from the destruction of one's confidence and beliefs to an imaginative reconstruction of ideas and practices can be extremely difficult and require peer and tutor support. Apart from keeping diaries themselves teacher researchers sometimes ask research participants to keep diaries or notes. Both Peake in Chapter 5 and Wadlow in Chapter 4 asked parents to keep diaries of their children's behaviours and interactions at home in order to supply additional data to which the researchers would not otherwise have had access. However, while such data can prove extremely useful, it is important to remember that these diaries/notes are documents prepared specifically for the researcher and as such may deliberately seek to get certain points across or to supply what it is perceived the researcher wants. This can be a particular drawback in relation to pupil diaries written for the teacher researcher which are likely to be viewed as additional work to be marked.

## 3. Action research into differentiation in a primary school

There have been increasing criticisms of primary class teaching for its lack of differentiation from both research and HMI inspections. These criticisms together with the requirements of the National Curriculum that children should work on the programmes of study and attainment targets at an appropriate level caused Janet

Bennett, who is a deputy headteacher at Hillside Primary, to make differentiation the subject of her research. Hillside has 185 children on roll and serves a collection of small villages and hamlets. There are nine teaching staff including the headteacher.

Janet planned to undertake action research as she wanted not only to develop additional strategies to achieve differentiation in her own classroom but also to heighten staff awareness of its importance in order to influence practice throughout the school. The initial research questions that she drew up were:

1.  What do staff understand by differentiation?
2.  How are pupil tasks differentiated?
3.  What additional strategies might be used to differentiate tasks?

The resources which supplied ideas to help Janet to get started on her project are listed in Figure 2.1:

Figure 2.1 Resources on differentiation

---

Barthorpe, T. and Visser, J. (1991) Differentiation: Your Responsibility, an in-service training pack for staff development, NARE Publications.
British Journal of Special Education (1992) vol.19, no.1, March, Theme for this issue: Differentiation.
Lewis, A. (1991) Primary Special Needs and the National Curriculum, London, Routledge.

---

She began by gaining the support of the headteacher and the agreement of colleagues for two introductory 'twilight' staff meetings to be held in consecutive weeks. At the first she explained the purpose of her research and asked for assistance with it. Staff also began to share current understandings of the meaning of differentiation by reviewing the curricular materials that they had each used that day and in so doing examining the types of differentiation of access that existed. As the focus of the second meeting, Janet provided the staff with a profile of two children in her year 4/5 class − one whose vision was impaired and one who experienced considerable difficulty with reading and was poorly motivated. Using Janet's outline plans for the next week's work on a flight topic, staff brainstormed to produce a range of ways in which differentiation might be achieved to meet the needs of these two children. The list included:

a. Content − depending on child's prior knowledge and interests;
b. Pace − similar activities undertaken at varying speeds;
c. Level − same curricular content but different level of manual, intellectual or affective demand;
d. Access − task presented in alternative forms;
e. Outcome − learning presented in different forms;
f. Structure − breaking down learning goals into broad stages or small steps;
g. Teaching methods − varying the approach according to the aims and objectives for learning and the child's preferred mode of learning;
h. Grouping − individual, paired, whole class, across classes.

Staff considered that they most frequently differentiated by pace and sometimes by access, level and teaching method. However, they thought that they seldom used differentiation by content, outcome or structure and hoped that Janet's project would particularly concentrate on these. Also, although they used a range of pupil groupings they were uncertain of the implications of this for differentiation. Janet agreed that she would make the areas that they had identified a major part of her research. Two teachers volunteered to work with her on devising, implementing and monitoring strategies, the one concentrating on differentiation by outcome and the other on differentiation by structure. They were also willing for her to observe in their classrooms and the head agreed to provide cover to allow this to happen. The rest of the staff agreed to be interviewed about their classroom practice, to make notes on the forms of differentiation they were using in topic work and to participate in further meetings throughout the phases of the research to discuss findings in order to develop a whole-school approach.

After these two meetings Janet added three more research questions to the original three. These were:

4. How far are staff views on the use of alternative ways of differentiating tasks borne out in their classroom practice?
5. What are the implications for pupil motivation and learning of differentiation by content, outcome and structure?
6. How can approaches to differentiation be built into curriculum planning at both whole-school and classroom level?

Janet intends to collect data on practice throughout the school by:

- interviewing staff;
- notes on differentiation strategies kept by colleagues;
- observations in colleagues' classrooms;
- taping future staff meetings.

In relation to trialling differentiation strategies in her own classroom she intends:

- to keep detailed lesson plans with descriptive and evaluative notes on differentiation in practice;
- to audiotape samples of paired work and groupwork in order to be able to study and reflect on the children's approach to the tasks and their interactions with each other;
- to discuss tasks set and the work resulting from the tasks with children in much more detail than she would otherwise do;
- to plan and monitor differentiated work based on staff suggestions for the two pupils for whom profiles were drawn up for the second staff meeting.

Hopkins (1985) provides a simple introduction to the range of ways of collecting and analysing classroom observation data. Bailey (1991) has researched the available checklists in this area and produced his own 'nudge sheet' detailing the kinds of information that he considers need to be collected in relation to: the classroom as a working environment; physical setting; task-related factors; what the teacher did and communication issues. Janet could adapt this as an *aide-mémoire* for her observations of differentiation in colleagues' classrooms. More detailed advice on how to develop observation skills and examples of structured and unstructured classroom observation are given in Hook (1981) and Walker and Adelman (1975). Rowland's (1984) detailed and sensitive account of children learning in his classroom demonstrates the depth of understanding that can result from observations and reflections as a teacher researcher.

### 4. Case study of a middle school's policy and practice on managing behaviour

Elm Tree middle school is a three stream entry middle school catering for 7–12 year olds in an urban area just outside a city centre. The school mainly serves the community living on an extremely large council housing estate. The headteacher, who is deeply committed to the school, has been there for fifteen years during which time he has forged strong links with parents. Since being designated an Educational Priority Area during the Plowden era the school has been regarded 'as one of the roughest in the city'. Anxiety over maintaining classroom control and the management of disruptive behaviour of certain pupils with emotional and behavioural difficulties is ongoing and a constant topic of conversation. The school has a discipline policy setting out ways in which behaviour should be censured — for example, through detentions and criticisms in 'the Friday book' the contents of which are read out during assembly. Praise and the enhancement of self-image are regarded as most important and achieved through mechanisms such as displays of pupil work throughout the school, mentions of good work in assembly, the award of merit points, and small prizes awarded in each class at the end of each half term for effort. The school also has an exclusions policy which involves consultations with parents and governors and, after a clearly set out sequence of procedures if the disruptive behaviour does not improve, leads to a child being excluded from school for a week or longer.

An increase in theft within the school, outbreaks of aggressive behaviour especially towards the dinner ladies and several exclusions made Vicky Blake, the year 6 teacher with responsibility for pupils' pastoral and social education, decide to research into the school's policy and practice for managing behaviour. Drawing on colleagues' worries expressed in the staffroom and the findings of the Elton Report (DES, 1989), Vicky drew up the following research questions:

1.  What kinds of disruptive behaviours occur most frequently, when and by whom?
2.  What explanations do teachers give for this behaviour?
3.  How far do teachers recognise the kinds of needs this behaviour may express?
4.  What classroom management strategies do they use to maintain order?
5.  What are the most useful/least helpful aspects of the school's discipline policy for avoiding/managing disruption?

6. What are pupils' perceptions of discipline problems and how they should be managed?
7. How do teachers perceive the school's exclusion policy and its effect on keeping discipline within the classroom?
8. What formal or informal support systems help teachers to find their own solutions to the problems they face in the classroom?

Vicky decided to use the following techniques to collect data to answer these questions:

- analysis of documents, such as the school brochure, entries in the 'Friday book', letters to parents relating to discipline, minutes of governors' meetings concerned with exclusions, pupils' records;
- interview with a sample of teachers, parents and governors;
- a survey of disruptions over a two week period compiled by asking staff to complete a simple daily checklist;
- notes on disruptions occurring in her own classroom;
- simulations with her own class of cases of theft, aggressive behaviour and exclusions to explore their feelings about these and views of what should be done;
- pupil group interviews covering topics such as school rules and how teachers attributed praise and blame;
- fieldnotes on pupil behaviour during breaks and lunchtimes;
- photographs of incidences of disruptive behaviour and/or its consequences taken by herself and a non-teaching assistant.

Vicky considered that the tone and language used and the explicit and implicit messages contained in documents appertaining to school rules, discipline and exclusion would provide a useful starting point for her research. Documents often provide information relevant to problems under investigation. Reflections on the intentions and aspirations contained in the rhetoric of documents and the reality of what actually happens in schools and classrooms can generate additional research questions or provide a focus for interviews or observations. Documents for study might include: syllabuses and schemes of work; working party reports and curriculum guidelines; school development plans; policy statements; minutes of meetings; tests; workcards, worksheets and textbooks; pupils' work; pupils' records; LEA policy documents and guidance; National

Curriculum Orders and Non-Statutory Guidance. Discussion of the contributions to research that the study of documents can make and the factors to consider when evaluating their reliability and validity as data sources are provided by Hammersley and Atkinson (1983), Hitchcock and Hughes (1989) and Plummer (1983).

In the past photography has been little used in educational research, but it can be a very useful tool for the teacher researcher. At the most basic level it serves as an adjunct to fieldnotes supplying information about the physical lay-out of the classroom, displays, the organisation of pupils, pupils working on tasks, the roles of adults either in one's own classroom during the research period or in other schools and classrooms visited. This photographic evidence should be cross-referenced to related sections of fieldnotes or diaries. Vicky's photograph collection was both to serve as evidence of disruptive behaviour and the contexts in which it occurred and to be used to generate discussion about such behaviour with staff and pupils. Prosser, who provides a fascinating illustrated account of how he used photography extensively in his case study of a comprehensive school, employed photographs in different ways to elicit interview data. In one approach he presented a photograph with recognisable content, such as one of 'smokers' corner', and:

> with little, other than an encouraging 'tell me about them', participants made comments about the images which usually led to a 'what do you mean by that?' sort of question. Using this approach it was possible to illicit a variety of interpretations, affiliations, beliefs, attitudes and perspectives from participants and make comparisons.
>
> (in press)

He also occasionally used more provocative photographs, such as one showing pupil grafitti, 'to identify the range of attitudes from progressive/liberal teachers to the more traditional "elderly statesman type"'. Finally he used ambiguous and enigmatic photographs to trigger 'a gamut of insightful but unexpected comments from interviewees'.

## 5. Evaluation of the science curriculum in a school for pupils with severe learning difficulties

Moortop is a seventy-place day school for pupils with severe learning difficulties. Prior to the publication of the first set of National Curriculum Science Orders Jane Baker had been given responsibility for co-ordinating science across the school. Although a non-specialist she was enthusiastic about the subject, as she believes that science activities can be fun and stimulating for pupils with severe learning difficulties and provide a range of experiences which help them to explore the world and to develop skills of observation and investigation. As a first step to extending the school's science curriculum, she and her colleagues carried out an analysis of their regular class activities and matched the scientific skills, content and concepts that they identified to the science programmes of study and attainment targets. Then they brainstormed to devise ways of extending existing routine activities, personal and social education, subject focused tasks, topic work, outings and day trips to draw out the science content. During the first year of National Curriculum implementation in ordinary schools they devised and trialled science-based schemes of work and compiled a 'bank' of science activities together with lists of resources required and record sheets to be completed by the teacher and/or pupils. After two years of implementing these activities and with the issue of the new Science Orders, Jane decided to undertake an evaluation of the school's science curriculum for her research and the other teachers agreed to give her their full co-operation.

Jane intended to collect evaluation data through:

- teacher interviews;
- teachers' notes recording descriptions of, and reflections on, science activities over a two week period;
- the use of video as an aid to classroom observation in a sample of science-based activities taught by her;
- discussions of notes and video extracts in staff meetings.

A member of the LEA science advisory team also agreed to help by assuming the role of 'critical friend' (Lomax, 1991) and offering her additional interpretations of the video data. In order to assist teachers to compile notes which supplied similar kinds of information to aid later staff discussion, Jane supplied a checklist of questions to be considered after each session:

- What lesson preparations were carried out?
- How adequate were these preparations?
- Which children took part?

- What resources did they use?
- What did they actually do?
- How did they react to the activities?
- What learning took place?
- Were there any unexpected outcomes?
- What was the most successful aspect of this lesson?
- How could the lesson have been improved?

The main purpose of the video was to enable Jane to review critically what had taken place and to enable her to share aspects of her practice with colleagues to get their interpretations and reactions to what was happening. However, she also thought that she might use extracts to inform parents and governors about the role of National Curriculum science in the school. This opened up the possibility of adding parents' views to the other sources of data.

Video cameras are slowly but steadily contributing to data collection in teacher research especially on teacher-research courses, such as that offered by the University of Bath. There they are frequently used to identify how far teachers' educational values are realised in their classroom practice and to share their claims about their practice with fellow course members and tutors (see McNiff, 1988). Using video recorders has a number of advantages. Videotape can quickly give teachers information on the overall teaching situation in their classroom and on many facets of their teaching — some of which they may examine further through the use of other techniques. It enables teachers to observe and analyse privately, or with colleagues, their interaction with pupils. Pupil behaviours and peer interactions can be recorded in situations where teachers either cannot be present or are unable to observe in detail at the time (see, for example, the use of video to record the experiences of Mirpuri Pakistani infant pupils in McCann, 1990). Videos of classroom situations can be studied intensively to allow teaching and learning problems to be diagnosed, the reactions of individual pupils to be charted or alternative interpretations to be developed. Patterns of progress for pupils over a long period of time can be clearly documented, which is particularly useful in special schools where aspects of the learning of pupils with severe learning difficulties occurs slowly and in small steps.

The main disadvantages are that video cameras are not readily available to many teachers, especially in primary schools, are costly, and require some specialist knowledge to operate them.

They are initially distracting to pupils and so if the data are not to be distorted pupils will need to grow accustomed to the equipment in the classroom and to being filmed prior to data collection. Where the camera is being directed by the researcher or a colleague, rather than set up and left to record an overview of the classroom, that person will edit the data by only filming occurences and behaviours which seem of interest at the time. If a specific focus − for example, on a particular child or group, or on certain kinds of interactions − is the intention and colleagues are filming then they need to be well briefed beforehand. Finally, transcribing video tape is immensely time-consuming.

## Conclusion

The five vignettes include reviews of the data collection techniques available and offer particular comment on those which, while very appropriate to teacher research, are probably less widely used, such as personal journals, photographs and video recordings. Teacher research provides the opportunity to develop diverse and creative approaches to data collection − especially from pupils − derived directly from teachers' skills and experience in the classroom, such as the use of discussion groups, simulations, poems and artwork. However, it is likely to be the more confident and experienced teacher researchers who experiment and seek to push back the boundaries of research methods − for example, the use by Winter (1991) of fictional-critical writing as a method of organising, collecting additional interpretations of, and theorising about data. It is not easy to be immediately confident and innovative in an area of experience that is completely new. However, one of the aspirations of this book is that it will provide a clear and thorough introduction to teacher research in order to provide a basic platform from which teachers working with pupils with special educational needs can launch into research with enthusiasm and imagination.

This chapter provides advice on how to translate an area of interest or concern into a research project. Chapters 3 to 11 build on this chapter by providing teachers' descriptions and reflections on the process of carrying out such research projects, their findings and the uses to which these were put.

# References

Bailey, T. (1991) 'Classroom observation: a powerful tool for teachers?'. *Support For Learning* 6, 32–6.

Ball, S.J. and Bowe, R. (1992) 'Subject departments and the "implementation" of National Curriculum policy: an overview of the issues'. *Journal of Curriculum Studies* 24, 97–115.

Becker, H. (1971) Footnote to Wax, M. and Wax, R. 'Great tradition, little tradition, and formal education', in Wax, M. and Wax, R. (eds) *Anthropological Perspectives on Education*. New York: Basic Books.

Bell, J. (1987) *Doing Your Research Project*. Milton Keynes: Open University Press.

Broadfoot, P., Abbott, D., Croll, P., Osborn, M., Pollard, A. and Towler, L. (1991) 'Implementing national assessment: issues for primary teachers'. *Cambridge Journal of Education* 21, 153–68.

Delamont, S. (1981) 'All too familiar? A decade of classroom research'. *Educational Analysis* 3, 69–83.

Delamont, S. (1992) *Fieldwork in Educational Settings: Methods, Pitfalls and Perspectives*. London: Falmer Press.

Department of Education and Science (1989) *Discipline in Schools* (Elton Report). London: HMSO.

Fagg, S., Skelton, S., Aherne, P. and Thornber, A. (1990) *Science For All*. London: David Fulton Publishers.

Ferrucci, P. (1982) *What We May Be*. New York: St Martins Press.

Glaser, B. and Strauss, A. (1967) *The Discovery of Grounded Theory*. Chicago: Aldine.

Gregson, D. (1990) 'Why do pirates have peg legs? A study of reading for information', in Webb, R. (ed) *Practitioner Research in the Primary School*. London: Falmer Press.

Hammersley, M. and Atkinson, P. (1983) *Ethnography: Principles in Practice*. London: Tavistock.

Her Majesty's Inspectorate (1991) *Transition From School to Further Education for Children with Learning Difficulties*. London: Department of Education and Science.

Hitchcock, G. and Hughes, D. (1989) *Research and the Teacher*. London: Routledge.

Holly, M.L. (1984) *Keeping a Personal-Professional Journal*. Geelong, Victoria: Deakin University Press.

Holly, M.L. (1989) 'Reflective writing and the spirit of enquiry'. *Cambridge Journal of Education* 19, 71–80.

Hook, C. (1981) *Studying Classrooms*. Geelong, Victoria: Deakin University Press.

Hopkins, D. (1985) *A Teacher's Guide to Classroom Research*. Milton Keynes: Open University Press.

Lomax, P. (1991) 'Peer review and action research' in Lomax, P. (ed) *Managing Better Schools and Colleges: An Action Research Way*. Clevedon: Multilingual Matters.

McCann, A. (1990) 'Culture and behaviour: a study of Mirpuri Pakistani infant pupils', in Webb, R. (ed) *Practitioner Research in the Primary School*. London: Falmer Press.

McKernan, J. (1991) *Curriculum Action Research: A Handbook of Methods and Resources for the Reflective Practitioner*. London: Kogan Page.

McNiff, J. (1988) *Action Research: Principles and Practice*. London: Macmillan Education.

Mittler, P. (1991) Meeting Special Educational Needs: Towards the 21st Century and Beyond, 6th lecture in series Continuing the Great Debate, commemorating the 15th anniversary of Lord Callaghan's Ruskin speech.

Munn, P. and Drever, E. (1990) *Using Questionnaires in Small-scale Research: A Teachers' Guide*. Edinburgh: Scottish Council for Research in Education.

48

National Curriculum Council (1991) *Report on Monitoring the Implementation of the National Curriculum Core Subjects 1989–1990*. York: NCC.

Patton, M. Q. (1980) *Qualitative Evaluation Methods*. London: Sage.

Plummer, K. (1983) *Documents of Life*. London: George Allen and Unwin.

Pollard, A. and Tann, S. (1987) *Reflective Teaching in the Primary School: A Handbook for the Classroom*. London: Cassell Education.

Powney, J. and Watts, M. (1987) *Interviewing in Educational Research*. London: Routledge and Kegan Paul.

Prosser, J. (in press) 'Personal reflections on the use of photography in an ethnographic case study'. *British Educational Research Journal*.

Rowland, S. (1984) *The Enquiring Classroom: An Introduction to Children's Learning*. London: Falmer Press.

Spradley, J.P. (1979) *The Ethnographic Interview*. New York: Holt, Rhinehart and Winston.

Walker, R. (1985) *Doing Research: A Handbook for Teachers*. London: Methuen.

Walker, R. and Adelman, C. (1975) *A Guide to Classroom Observation*. London: Methuen.

Webb, R. (1990) 'Information gathering in topic work: the pupil experience', in Webb, R. (ed) *Practitioner Research in the Primary School*. London: Falmer Press.

Webb, R. and Vulliamy, G. (1989) 'Education and economic crisis in Poland'. *Educational Review* 41, 55–71.

Winter, R. (1991) 'Interviewers, interviewees and the exercise of power (fictional-critical writing as a method for educational research)'. *British Educational Research Journal* 17, 251–62.

Woods, P. (1986) *Inside Schools: Ethnography in Educational Research*. London: Routledge and Kegan Paul.

# CHAPTER 3

# An Evaluation of a Leavers' Curriculum in a Special School

Jean Holgate

In special schools a dilemma exists. The very nature of such schools inhibits the attainment of goals which might, ideally, be set for their pupils. Progress is prejudiced by an artificial social situation as there are restricted opportunities for pupils to experience living and learning amongst others in the community. Thomas (1978) argues that the problem is compounded by the failure of many special schools to identify themselves as educational establishments as distinct from para-medical aid centres or a branch of the social services.

In 1984, in the special school where I worked, a new curriculum was designed for disabled school leavers, aged 14 to 19. It was felt that the school functioned as an almost closed community. Disabled pupils were transported there, taught there and para-medical services were available on site. The system almost precluded normal experiences. The new curriculum was an attempt to address the problem. It had to be purposeful and relevant, yet sufficiently flexible to accommodate the needs of a wide ability range and degree of physical disability and it had to achieve this against a background of changing attitudes to special education.

A curriculum can only achieve credibility when it serves the needs of the pupils but the small numbers in special schools can be restrictive, especially in relation to the number of staff available for deployment. There was an inherent risk of producing a curriculum which accommodated the idiosyncracies of staff rather than one which made appropriate provision for the pupils, for it was essential to enlist the support of staff. Additional to the seven special school staff it was also important to win the confidence of teachers in link schools and colleges, to whom physically disabled pupils were an unknown quantity. Similarly, the co-operation of the parents and of the governing body was required. This was less of a problem than anticipated in that most were willing to offer support whilst leaving curriculum issues to the professional judgement of teachers.

The school buildings – modern, spacious and well appointed – offered more possibilities than they imposed restrictions, but access to the outside world still depended upon one critical resource, the school minibus. The catchment area of the school was a complex mixture of urban and rural environments, with an equally intricate pattern of social groupings and this provided scope for a range of out of school activities. Secondary schools and the College of Further Education were also within a radius of 1.5 miles, offering the possibility of some measure of integration.

The concept of a new curriculum was also in accord with the then current trends in education. Central to the Warnock Report of 1978 was the insistence that attention should be focused upon the educational needs of a child rather than upon the nature and degree of disability. This report was the lever by which thinking in the school could be directed away from the medical model. Warnock's emphasis upon external links with ordinary education also gave weight to the case for more purposeful co-operation in the case of this one school. The reaction of the LEA was to express public support for such initiatives but, like so many author- ities, it was equally anxious to justify the fixed capital invested in special schools by retaining them as distinct units.

In essence this new curriculum contained the following elements:

(1) life and social skills:
    (a) practical component,
    (b) language and numeracy,
    (c) Preparation for leaving school;
(2) examination courses;
(3) creative and leisure activities.

I decided to evaluate the curriculum once it had completed its first two year cycle. The aim was to ask six questions of each of the curriculum areas:

(1)  Are the assumptions fundamental to the planning and implementation of the curriculum valid?
(2)  To what extent do resources influence the direction of the curriculum?
(3)  Is the content relevant and realistic for the full ability range and degree of physical disability?
(4)  Are the teaching methods appropriate for the resources available and do they achieve the purpose intended?
(5)  To what extent do the perceptions of staff, pupils and other individuals and their attitudes toward the curriculum influence it?
(6)  To what extent do research findings validate present thinking, which recommends that, where practicable, pupils with special educational needs be taught in integrated settings?

Given the limitations of traditional evaluation approaches, as discussed by the editors in Chapter 1, it was decided to adopt Parlett and Hamilton's (1977) 'illuminative evaluation' strategy (see pp.12–14).

This approach is not without its critics. Parsons (1976) argues, for example, that it concentrates on method and data collection to the detriment of a consideration of formal theory, which is needed to make sense of the data. He also argues that participant evaluators tend to accept the status quo and not challenge it. The great merit of illuminative evaluation in assessing a curriculum is, however, that it reflects the teaching and learning processes and not just the outcomes. It allows for examination of the attitudes, values and assumptions underlying information. It was, therefore, considered right for the task of evaluating the curriculum for 14-to-19-year-old pupils in a special school.

## Data collecting techniques

Data were gathered by using four main techniques: semi-structured interviews, research diary recordings, structured observation and documentary evidence.

### Semi-structured interviews

The key to success, or otherwise, in this technique lay in the format and nature of the interview itself. It was decided that

52

the six research questions should be the basis of the interview
schedule and that they would be applied to the curriculum areas
'life and social skills', 'examination courses' and 'creative and
leisure activities'. Interview schedules were deliberately flexible.
In the case of pupils, for example, questions had to be adjusted
to their level of understanding. This was in accordance with
guidance given by McCormick and James (1983) who stress
that vocabulary should be at the correct level to ensure clarity.
They also advise that for the same reason, each question should
contain only one idea and should not be 'leading'. The phrasing
of a question was considered significant. Some were worded so
as to produce predictable results, perhaps the response 'yes' or
'no', with some opportunity to elaborate. Others were more
open ended, virtually inviting respondents to formulate less
predictable replies. Less planned were the probes intended to
follow up the initial questions and elicit further information.
An occasional 'really' or 'yes' or a nod of encouragement was
sometimes found to be effective and did not disrupt the flow of
conversation whilst contrived naivety could induce interviewees
to elaborate upon issues about which they might otherwise have
been dismissive. This probing could not be planned in that the
tactic most likely to be advantageous varied with the individual.
It became apparent, however, that supplementary probing was an
important aspect of interview technique in that issues uppermost
in the interviewee's mind began to emerge and these could, in turn,
change the emphasis in the individual interview and perhaps even
lead to adjustments in future interviews. The schedules remained
the same but the balance changed.

The manner of an interview was also considered important.
Stenhouse admitted that 'As an interviewer I try to be polite,
attentive, sensitive, thoughtful, considerate but not familiar, ...
rather respectful' (1984, p.222). It was not always possible to
achieve all these objectives. Many of those interviewed were, for
example, colleagues and friends and were familiar. Given this
situation familiarity was turned to advantage, with encouragement
offered to some whilst others were steered, quite firmly, along a
desired course.

An attempt was always made to conduct the interviews in a
favourable environment. Pupils were found to be more relaxed in
the familiar setting of their own classroom and this applied equally
to the headteachers of the special school and the secondary link

school. They were interviewed in their own rooms. In practice, however, many interviews had to be conducted in less than ideal circumstances. As part of the new curriculum some special school pupils attended courses at the local college of further education. Some interviews here were conducted in workshops, with more than half an eye turned to ensure that irreparable damage was not done to either work or the student. Even when a suitable room could be secured this did not guarantee an ideal atmosphere. Telephones proved to be a major source of disturbance with caretakers, anxious to clear the premises of teachers, a close second. Pupils in discussion groups came and went to physiotherapy, hydrotherapy and to see the appliances man. Exhausted by their efforts some children went to sleep, others woke them up and visitors arrived and departed unaware that research was in progress. The only uninterrupted interview was that with an HMI, suggesting that one law of research is that the level of interruption is inversely proportional to the hierarchical status of the interviewee.

A decision had to be reached about who was to be interviewed. Sampling was considered but was dismissed in favour of an attempt to interview all who were direct participants in the Leavers' Curriculum — teachers, pupils and those who had a professional or personal interest such as careers officers and parents. Within the special school this posed no problems but some pupils also attended college and some a secondary school. Here, practical problems dictated who could be interviewed and in what circumstances whilst in the case of parents it had to be accepted that specific meetings, designed solely for purposes of research, were not possible and instead views expressed during routine careers interviews were noted. In total, 38 interviews of differing length were conducted.

In order to maintain a rapport with interviewees note making was kept to a minimum. Corrie and Zaklukiewicz (1985) write of the superiority of tape recording over note taking and despite the inhibiting effect of the recorder upon some individuals audio recordings were used in most interviews, including discussion groups with pupils. There were exceptions. It was not convenient, or appropriate, to use a recorder in the college. The interviews here were short and conducted during either breaks or lecture times, in rooms which were scattered. Additionally, I had the dual role of interviewer and support teacher. Neither did it seem appropriate to use a recorder in meetings with parents, when the prime object of the exercise was a careers interview. The remaining interview to go unrecorded was that with an HMI where there were restrictions imposed by his code of practice. Even notes made during and after the interview could only be used in a general way to validate opinions held by others and in no instance could he be quoted.

When possible, tape recordings were transcribed immediately following an interview. The process was quicker because it was possible to remember and anticipate remarks whilst interruptions, facial expressions, causes of silences or of laughter, could be recalled. The recordings were carefully transcribed but only in part, adopting a method recommended by Stenhouse (1984). Two adjacent columns allowed for a record of the interview to be made in catchword and brief note form whilst, alongside, the second column was reserved for literal quotation (see Figure 3.1).

*Diary recordings*

Through direct involvement in the organisation and teaching of the Leavers' Curriculum I was in a position to observe events and developments and record them as they happened (see Figure 3.2 for an extract from my research diary). Informal and spontaneous remarks, sparked off by circumstance, were frequently more revealing and pointed than measured responses given in reply to questions posed in an interview. A stair-climbing machine for pupils in wheelchairs was described in an interview as being a 'splendid means of overcoming access problems within the secondary school building'. Teachers using the machine in practice were, on occasions, heard to swear at it.

The question of bias in selecting what to observe and record could not be ignored. It was my job to ensure that the Leavers' Curriculum provided, successfully, for the needs of pupils of a wide ability range and degree of physical disability. It was, therefore, in my own interests that pupils and teachers should adopt positive attitudes towards the curriculum. This, at times, made it difficult and occasionally impossible to maintain the neutrality and detachment required of a researcher. The diary recording for Tuesday 18th November (see Figure 3.2) noted teacher J's thoughts about the reception afforded special school pupils attending a local secondary school. The sentiment 'the influx wasn't received with quite so much enthusiasm in two departments', was not in accord with my own ambitions, which were to see this

Figure 3.1 Method of transcribing interview tapes

<u>Interview with Headteacher + Deputy Headteacher (Secondary School)</u>

| NOTES | QUOTATIONS |
|---|---|
| Integration of pupils from Special into Secondary School: are there any benefits for pupils from Secondary School? | (H.T.) 'Absolutely – this is a very major point isn't it – that children in a normal school don't understand the existence of children with difficulties + disabilities.' |
| –both say they haven't seen any unpleasantness or teasing between pupils of the 2 schools | (H.T.) 'When children from our school meet these kind of situations outside school they're very much better prepared – they're not going to be part of that big awful public who are going to be embarrassed + doesn't know how to cope.' |
| D.H.T. feels that children are better at coping than adults | (D.H.T.) '--- there are lots of lessons in caring for others, teamwork + doing your bit when something needs doing --- I think it's enriched us.' |
| Any difficulties in the sharing of teaching a group? | (D.H.T.) 'I think there is always the possibility of problems – we do need the will to get over them. One can imagine a variety of personalities in the classroom when it may not work!' |
| ROLE of support teachers from Special School. Is 'M' who shares teaching of group with D.H.T. seen as 'support' teacher? | (D.H.T.) 'Oh NO NO NO – I didn't say that at all! I think that would demean 'M'. I think 'M' and 'J' when they are here, are members of our staff.' |
| D.H.T. doesn't just see 'M' as being there to help Special School pupils. He admits that on occasions he is called out and she has to take the class. | (H.T.) 'But I think there's a co-ordination aspect isn't there. For example, who was it 'J' has been 'fixing' up for?' |
| H.T and D.H.T. discuss pupil and timetable | (D.H.T.) ''J''s fixed it has he!' (LAUGHTER) |

Figure 3.2 Section of notes taken from research diary

MONDAY, Nov. 17th

Leavers' group and teachers watched a Y.T.S. video in the morning session. Feeling of teachers afterwards was that it wasn't very informative and went 'over the heads' of some of the children but 'C' thought it served to reinforce what we discussed the previous week.

TUESDAY, Nov. 18th

I take 'Y' shopping in the afternoon to buy some warm clothes for Winter. She uses S.D.A. money (parents are unaware that she gets this allowance) – Would this happen in a 'normal' school?

'J' seems to be under pressure with pantomime imminent. He refers to the group of pupils who attended the Secondary School that morning – he felt the 'influx' wasn't received with quite so much enthusiasm in two departments (could just be the way he is feeling.')

WEDNESDAY, Nov. 19th
College

Discuss P.E. Group with teacher concerned. We decide to separate pupils from the two Special Schools and design a course more suitable for the needs of the physically disabled.
Meeting: Secondary School 4·00 p.m.

Purpose: – To discuss use of 16 N.T.A. hours offered by L.E.A. to support pupils from Special School in Secondary School.
Possible full-time integration of 4 pupils discussed.
N.T.A. assistance will make it possible for 'N' in a wheelchair to stay for a full day. (She needs help going to the toilet)
Access for wheelchairs is difficult in the Secondary School building. Discuss need for a 'Gimson' (a stair climbing machine) Headteacher of Secondary School is willing to find ½ of the cost if the L.E.A. will fund the rest.
On the return journey to the Special School after the meeting the Headteacher expresses concern over the 'creaming off' of brighter pupils – this could affect the curriculum and the ethos of the School. It also reduces pupil numbers and we could be 'doing ourselves out of job.'

N.B. Later extracts from the Diary record: –
TUESDAY Jan 6th

L.E.A. agrees to purchase 3 'Gimsons' (stair climbing machines) – 1 for the Secondary School.
WEDNESDAY April 1st

N.T.A. appointed for 16 hours to work with Special School pupils in the Secondary School.

exercise in integration succeed and hence the personal bracketed note 'could just be the way he was feeling' had been added. This was not objective neutrality. Recognising that this conflict of roles existed did not eliminate the bias but helped to control it, through increased self-awareness.

The diary entries could be categorised in five main ways:

(a) Formal meetings: all planned meetings such as staff meetings, governors' meetings and consultations with parents were included.
(b) Record of events: the direct noting of miscellaneous events, such as the appointment of a non-teaching assistant and taking a child shopping.
(c) Observations: random and unplanned observations in both formal and informal situations relating to staff, pupils and other individuals. These embraced a whole range of environments as diverse as dining rooms, shops, lifts and staffrooms.
(d) Record of impromptu remarks: casual remarks relevant to the issues under examination.
(e) Personal reflections: subjective assessment of circumstances and of individuals and their reactions.

Categorising the contents of the diary in the above manner, however, could detract from one of its major virtues. By their nature, the diary entries were chronological and this could highlight a sequence of events. It did, for example, reveal the strengthening links between the special school and a secondary school and also mark the stages by which pressure from parents, consultation with administrators and discussions with the careers officer began to determine a child's future beyond school.

*Structured observation*

Detailed observations of selected lessons were made over a seven month period. These were chosen to embrace all curriculum areas and as interviews and pupil discussions examined a particular curriculum component, observation of lessons concerned with the same topic took place. It was thus possible to judge the data collected against evidence from other sources. During the selected lessons notes were made about seating positions, pupil and teacher movement, verbal and non-verbal communication, tasks attempted and completed, concentration and disturbances and their causes. In the special school pupils and teachers were conditioned to the presence of support teachers, non-teaching assistants and students. My presence as an observer was, therefore, accepted as normal. Equally, in the college and secondary school I had become accepted in my role as support teacher. When there was a specific teaching commitment a cassette recorder was placed in the classroom and the subsequent transcript was used to supplement any notes which it had been possible to make.

## Documentary evidence

Documentary evidence was gathered from a variety of sources including minutes of past and current meetings and relevant reports. Material was also taken from transcripts of personal research assignments carried out in the past. This evidence was useful in two ways. Firstly, it provided a background of information against which the current research could be set and secondly it added credence to data collected by interview, observation and diary recording.

## Data analysis

> This task essentially involves a sifting process in which distinct points are first located and separated and in which related points are assembled for discussion under a particular heading ... Analysis consists of discovering groupings and relationships among the body of the data as a whole.
>
> (Corrie and Zaklukiewicz, 1985, p.133)

This sifting process had to be attempted in logical stages. An indiscriminate pick and mix approach would not serve. The technique chosen was very similar to that advocated in a later publication by Hopkins (1989). This envisaged an analytic process as having four distinct phases.

## (1) Immersion in the data and the initial generation of categories

In the collection of data the researcher becomes more familiar with the content of the research topic and also begins to develop an awareness of the trends emerging. Discrimination and sorting began in step with data collection and ideas about future tactics began to form. It was decided to make an initial distinction based on the curriculum areas. It was assumed that, for the practical component in the curriculum, data from an earlier attempt at evaluation could be transferred, unaltered. This judgement proved unsound in that additional information had accumulated, almost incidentally, and therefore had to be part of the sifting process. Issues also began to emerge which ran across the curriculum divisions and twenty-one such cross-curricular issues were eventually identified:

1. Learning environment
2. Group composition
3. Organisation
4. Definition of teacher roles
5. Future developments
6. Teaching methods
7. Attitudes
8. Ethos of school
9. Time
10. Resources
11. Teacher records
12. Pupil records
13. Parental involvement
14. Socialisation
15. Disability
16. Integration
17. Curriculum content
18. Communication
19. Vested interests of individuals
20. Inter-relationships of curriculum components
21. Relationship of learning experiences to social background

Thus, in the fabric of information the curriculum topics were the warp, running throughout, whilst the cross-curricular issues were the weft.

## (2) Validation of categories

by employing analytic techniques such as saturation and triangulation, evaluators can produce hypotheses and concepts from qualitative data that are valid, methodologically sound and to an extent generalizable.

(Hopkins, 1989, p.69)

Two techniques were used to help validate the emerging categories. The first was saturation where data were collected until they became repetitive, adding nothing new to the fund of information. On the basis of the information the categories were then judged, with one of three outcomes:

(a)   one or more of the categories adopted was inappropriate in that it did not match the data collected. That category was discarded;

(b)   a category was inappropriate but the data revealed that it needed to be retained and modified;

(c)   data collection confirmed the validity of the categories adopted in that repeated observation neither contradicted nor amplified the categories.

One of the cross-curricular issues, for example, was that of communication. As data were collected there was a repetitive reference to the difficulties arising from problems of communication, especially when pupils were being taught in different schools and had, simultaneously, to keep contact with para-medical staff, careers officers and others. Communication was, therefore, confirmed as a valid category.

The second validation technique was triangulation. This involved gathering accounts of teaching situations from at least three sources and then confirming or rejecting a category on the basis of cross-reference. In the role of observer and researcher a decision was made to include, as a cross-curricular issue, the constraints upon the curriculum imposed by disability. The data collected demonstrated that both teachers and pupils considered it a critical issue, thus confirming the validity of its inclusion as a category.

### (3) Organisation and interpretation of categories

Having categorised the data analysis began, seeking patterns, linkages and explanations in an attempt to give the data meaning in the context of the initial questions set. The need for validation remained but now it was a matter of validating the analysis. The principle of triangulation was again relevant. For example, analysis of data from various sources and collected using different techniques led to the conclusion that the special school pupils integrated into Maths and English GCSE lessons in an ordinary school coped well. Personal observation suggested that they did not appear to be under pressure. The pupils themselves spoke of their excitement at being 'in proper lessons' whilst staff commented on the stimulus of pupils working in groups of twenty rather than two or three.

A second technique was to study the data seeking support for alternative interpretations. Failure to find strong support for any alternative increased confidence in the original, preferred, explanation. Closely linked with this was a technique where negative cases were sought. This involved a conscious attempt to find cases which did not fit with the pattern emerging from analysis. Negative cases, if few, did not invalidate the principal explanation but could, in fact, assist in the refining or confirming of ideas. In the context of teaching material for Maths and English the over-riding consensus was that internally prepared material was preferable. There was one dissenting voice. A teacher regretted 'the inadequate use of standard published material'. This contrary response served simply to highlight the unanimity of support, elsewhere, for the use of non-published teacher-prepared material.

Validation, first of the categories used in collating data and then of analysis, based on the data, was vital for as Hopkins insists 'internal validity is the basic minimum without which any evaluation is uninterpretable' and 'if the various threats to validity are not taken into account then one cannot claim that one's interpretation is correct' (1989, p.79).

## (4) The presentation of theory and conclusions

The organisation and analysis of the collected data had helped to give meaning to hitherto discrete observations and enhanced the understanding of the issues involved in the overall enquiry. It was now possible to engage upon the final stage, that of drawing conclusions about the performance of the Leavers' Curriculum after its first two year cycle and contemplating future action on the basis of this information.

## Research findings

The headteacher of the special school had expressed the view that such schools 'sap the morale of children because they provide an environment where they are fed, watered, taught, brought, sent, bent and fitted into our way of life'. The prime aim of the new curriculum was to release pupils, progressively, from the shelter of the special school and place them in the real world. A range of activities under the blanket heading 'life and social skills' was central to this curriculum. Practical experience was a major element on the assumption that the children, deprived of normal experiences through disability, would learn more readily if they experienced an event or circumstance.

Within the curriculum plan each module of work hinged upon a practical component. Flexibility, continuity and repetition were the guiding principles in the choice of this practical work. Activities out of school figured prominently as they were thought likely to bring understanding and realism into the classroom.

The recording of work demanded skills in language and numeracy but beyond this they were linked, whenever possible, to the practical work. In the context of language the opinion of one teacher was that 'whatever I do it's down to reducing oddness, removing stigma'. This epitomised the thinking of all staff who felt 'a child can be labelled as odd for not being able to ask for help in an acceptable way, sign their name, read and fill in a form, or express their feelings adequately'. In terms of numeracy staff agreed that 'money is the most important because money has consequences in terms of everyday practical use'. These views supported the personally held belief that language and numeracy were best approached via practical work.

Finally, there was provision in the planning for assessment of pupil progress, recorded on a 5-point scale. It was envisaged from the outset that pupils would contribute to this final assessment.

The research study suggested that the general philosophy of the curriculum was appropriate. The headteacher, frank in his earlier criticism of the ethos of special schools, observed 'this curriculum is training them in a routine. They're learning the consequences of their actions ... management strategies; how to manage their lives'. The emphasis upon practical work as a vehicle for learning also appeared to have gained acceptance amongst staff. The remark 'there's no point doing things with pencil and paper if they can't do it practically because they don't have the concept to understand', was typical. Many parents, however, saw it differently. Some had become conditioned to accept Maths as pages of sums and English as reading practice and written exercises. One was only reassured when her child was given sums and exercises as homework and was then content that the child was spending her time 'in a useful way'. Other weaknesses were more concerned with practicalities than principles. A recurrent complaint was that of limitations imposed by time; standard published material was deemed inappropriate and there was criticism of inadequate use of some resources. These criticisms were accepted and the outcome of the evaluation of this part of the curriculum has been to ally language and numeracy work even more closely with practical experience.

An integral part of the new curriculum was a one year course designed to prepare pupils for leaving school. The evaluation of this part of the curriculum led to the conclusion that some of the conventional content of a leavers' course was irrelevant to many pupils in the special school. What emphasis should be placed on 'finding a job' or 'the world of work' when, as one teacher expressed it, 'You can't not relate it to the economic situation and for 75 per cent of them they are just not a proposition'. This view was echoed by the careers officer and by the pupils themselves, where only two out of nine spoke, with any conviction, about job prospects. The issue of future employment often had to be forced as with 'When we throw you out what are you going to do?'. This provoked some response but even then there were individuals who simply imitated others. One seemed prepared, at different times, to suggest 'I'll go to college', 'I wouldn't like it', 'I'll go on the dole', and eventually 'I want to be a motor mechanic'. The two main questions raised were 'Are we being too up-market in intellectual terms?', from one teacher and 'Is it unfair to sow the seeds of job expectations in the minds of disabled pupils?' from another.

More positively, the research confirmed that immediate and practical issues like finance did have a place. They reinforced other parts of the curriculum and 'after all they need to know what their dues and rights are, even if they're unemployed'.

The most unexpected development, however, was the way in which the 90 minutes per week allocated to the course had developed into a type of open forum, probably because all relevant staff and pupils were gathered together. Mundane issues, such as finding the culprit responsible for leaving ten tea bags festering in a cup, were tackled and proved to be useful exercises in themselves. The pupils realised how group pressure could be applied, although the remedies suggested were occasionally drastic. 'Stop tea and coffee and such', 'stop it for the bad ones', 'play heck', and the ultimate sanction, 'kill 'em', were offered as appropriate courses of action. The same group pressures were applied in less trivial cases, as when dealing with an assault in which punches had been thrown. There had been a move away from the original curriculum and towards a programme for 'helping them to cope with meeting people, mixing with people, building up self confidence and taking pride in their own appearance and their own work'. The research had, therefore, revealed a case for re-writing this part of the curriculum document.

Given the reality that a high percentage of pupils were likely to remain unemployed, the new curriculum included a component devoted to creative and leisure activities. The general reaction was favourable on condition that these did not become 'just time fillers'. Craft activities could, for example, 'allow the pupils to think creatively ... practice problem solving ... and increase self confidence'. Leisure activities also involved pupils in 'something which is normal' and as one lecturer remarked, in the context of those courses conducted at college, 'they gain socially just by being on the corridors with other students'.

Some pupils latched upon activities initiated by the curriculum and extended them out of personal interest. Swimming, fitness training, computer skills and sewing were amongst these and appeared likely to develop as long-term interests. Horse-riding, metalworking and others seemed less likely to generate long-term commitment because of expense and lack of facilities. The crucial issue raised, however, was whether 'the school provides activities which the staff consider worthwhile but which do not reflect the natural interests of the pupils'. The ultimate conclusion was that 'if there is a mismatch between what the school offers and the natural interests of the pupils then it has to be accepted that, in a number of cases, the interests promoted by the school will be short lived. The most the school can do is to familiarise pupils with some of the alternative uses of leisure'.

The part of the new curriculum which caused most concern involved the smallest number of pupils. There were physically disabled children who had the intellectual ability to attempt GCSE work in some subjects. There was a strong inclination to satisfy this need within the school. It could be perceived as enhancing the reputation of the school and staff involved could derive professional satisfaction from the academic work. Against this it was hard to justify the administrative cost of presenting the school as an examination centre. Also, the interests of the pupils had to be the priority issue. It was decided that these would be best served by partial integration with a neighbouring secondary school and the college. The issues of examination provision and integration became inextricably linked.

Research revealed that all concerned with this development acknowledged undoubted benefits for the able pupils. Academically, they were stimulated by working alongside others and they gained socially. There were, however, drawbacks. Commuting between schools was time consuming and intruded upon other curriculum components. It was also physically taxing. Integration, though, seemed to cause more disquiet amongst staff than amongst pupils. The head of the secondary school was supportive, feeling that her own students gained in understanding so that 'when our children meet disability now they're not going to be part of that big awful public who are going to be embarrassed and don't know how to cope'. The head of the special school, whilst equally approving, did harbour misgivings. His own position he saw as ambiguous, asking 'where does responsibility lie once pupils leave my school for another?'. He also expressed regrets about the periodic loss of able staff, as they accompanied pupils to ordinary schools or the college for a variety of courses. This, he considered to be to the detriment of the majority of pupils who remained. These were doubly disadvantaged because 'creaming off the more able students is in some ways sad for those left because you've no models to aim for, no leaders'. The teaching staff quite independently also voiced concern about the increasing ambiguity in their professional lives. They felt responsible to two headteachers and even began to question their own status suspecting in one case that 'I'm regarded as a wheelchair pusher and linkman and not seen as a proper teacher'. There was little doubt from the research that although ideologically sound the practical path towards integration was going to be far from smooth.

## Conclusion

Since the evaluation of the senior curriculum adjustment has continued partly in response to the review and partly in response to other factors. Within the authority the number of pupils in special schools has decreased and this has provided an opportunity for rationalisation. It is proposed that the school for physically disabled pupils should become a comprehensive secondary special school. The moves toward integration already started have continued but at a progressively earlier age and the proposed reorganisation could well increase the trend. The school will continue to change in character as able pupils are integrated into ordinary schools and those with multiple learning and physical difficulties remain. As the very nature of the school changes there will be a constant need to review and revise the curriculum.

Pupil assessment routines have already changed. The setting out of objectives in coded form has been replaced by simple statements to which children can relate during the self-assessment process. This contributes to the pupil's Record of Achievement. Each will leave with a formal document identical in style to that possessed by all secondary school pupils. The Record of Achievement will acknowledge amongst other things the extension of residential courses which has been made possible by TVEI funding.

There are some who might like to pretend that the introduction of a National Curriculum has little relevance to special education. Special schools however are required to respond. It will be necessary to work at the appropriate Key Stage in the Programme of Study adjusting to a level of attainment which is appropriate. The National Curriculum could become a charter for mediocre teaching. Boxes ticked, as topics are 'done', could create a false illusion of progress. It could also lead to the belief that the responsibility for evaluation and revision of a school's curriculum lies elsewhere. A curriculum however is more than content; it is concerned with how that content is organised and delivered to a changing school population. This is still very much the domain of the teacher and the Leavers' Curriculum in this special school whilst trying to accommodate the demands of the National Curriculum will do so via the established pattern of a modular approach linked with a strong practical element.

Special education is not immune from all those changes at both local and national level which are currently re-defining the shape of education. Like others, it will have to respond to these changes and an on-going flexibility of curriculum will be central to this. Critical evaluation of current practice by teachers is the catalyst which can initiate change.

## References

Corrie, M. and Zaklukiewicz, S. (1985) 'Qualitative research and case study approaches: an introduction', in Hegarty, S. and Evans, P. (eds) *Research and Evaluation Methods in Special Education*. Windsor: NFER-Nelson.

Department of Education and Science (1978) *Special Educational Needs (The Warnock Report)*. London: HMSO.

Hopkins, J. (1989) *Evaluation for School Development*. Milton Keynes: Open University Press.

McCormick, J. and James, M. (1983) *Curriculum Evaluation in Schools*. London: Croom Helm.

Parsons, C. (1976) 'The new evaluation: a cautionary note'. *Journal of Curriculum Studies* 8, 125–38.

Stenhouse, L. (1984) 'Library access, library use and user education in academic sixth forms: an autobiographical account', in Burgess, R. (ed) *The Research Process in Educational Settings: Ten Case Studies*. Lewes: Falmer Press.

Thomas, D. (1978) *The Social Psychology of Childhood Disability*. London: Methuen.

# CHAPTER 4

# *Creating a Basis for a Partnership with Parents of Pupils with Profound and Multiple Learning Difficulties*

Jacqueline Wadlow

> for only by listening to what parents say can professional service providers and administrators give help which is both appropriate and appreciated.
>
> (Glendening, 1983, p.8)

The school in which I worked during the period of the research catered for children with severe learning difficulties. One third of these children, who experienced profound and multiple learning difficulties, were taught in a special unit for which as Head of Department I was responsible. The individual curriculum for each child in the unit was very intensive and often needed considerable follow up at home in order to maximise the efforts of the staff and consolidate the children's progress. The children's behaviours frequently created barriers to learning which meant it was important that ways of handling these should be consistent at home and at school. Consequently, it was of vital importance that parents should have access to the information and skills that they needed to work in partnership with the school and that school staff should be able to draw on the knowledge and experience of parents.

I became increasingly aware of the need for more discussion and negotiation with parents about the learning opportunities made available to their children and the skills we sought to help them to develop. I realised the importance of recognising the individuality of families and the uniqueness of each child's needs. Skills developed at school can pose difficulties in the home setting – for example, the use of scissors and the turning on of taps. Children in the home setting often reveal the need for particular skills which have not been recognised as necessary at school – for example, stair walking. Mittler and Mittler suggest that flexibility of approach is vital to partnership; professionals must seek to understand and meet the needs of individuals to avoid at all costs the dangers of generalisations about disabled children and their families:

> Obvious examples include the concept of guilt and over-protection on the one hand and rejection on the other that a handicapped child means a handicapped family and that all parents must be helped to accept that their child is handicapped.
>
> (1982, p.49)

As I became increasingly involved with parents and other family members their concerns affected my view of what I should teach in the classroom. In order to plan a curriculum that was more responsive to children's needs and to promote working with parents on an open and equal basis throughout the school I considered that I needed to have deeper knowledge of these concerns and the contexts that gave rise to them. The research that I undertook on the Outstation MA course provided an opportunity to gain that deeper knowledge. It also helped me to identify ways of assisting in the solving of problems experienced by parents when they tried to further their children's learning in the home. Not all the children in the unit lived in their parental home. Some lived in a foster home or a community home and so my study needed to include data from a range of settings.

## Research methodology

For the first research assignment of the Outstation course a questionnaire was sent to the parents of children in the unit. This requested information on parents' perceptions of the most urgent needs of their children and on their own requirements for information or skills to meet those needs. The question-naire responses described home difficulties, many of which were extremely stressful to all members of the family and affected their health, resources and social lives. In some instances – for example, the practical difficulties experienced in lifting heavy children and bathing and caring for doubly incontinent children – the school was subsequently able to respond by offering some support in the form of demonstrations by the physiotherapist and workshops on 'handling hygiene' by the school nurse. Two major interrelated needs were cited in the questionnaires. One was for greater communication between them and their children's teachers. The other was for help in understanding and influencing their children's behaviours, in particular those that were undesirable or aggressive. In response to these, staff developed a short course which brought together teachers and parents to work towards handling difficult behaviours. As a pilot study for the main research the course was monitored to gain feedback as to its usefulness and to trial participant observation and interviewing as techniques for data collection for the main part of the study.

These techniques were chosen because they seemed to lend themselves particularly to obtaining substantive descriptions of the realities of being a prime carer for a child with profound and multiple learning difficulties. I also thought that the research would have credibility with both school staff and parents who would be able to recognise and relate to the issues portrayed.

As the school catered for children from all walks of life and home situations I identified three types of home settings which best represented those experienced by the group of children with whom I worked. I selected the parental home of parents that I shall refer to as Derek and Kath Davis. They were chosen because I had begun to build a trusting relationship with them when, in order to help their son Daniel, they attended the course which was the subject of my pilot study. The other two homes that I selected, both of which are referred to by pseudonyms, were Heathfields the well-established community home in the catchment area and Newstead the recently established home to cater for children who had come from long stay placements in psychiatric hospitals. I hoped to identify the diverse needs of parents and substitute parents in the three homes and to understand the reasons for similarities and differences. I intended to have regular weekly contact with the three homes and to conduct interviews with staff and the natural parents. I hoped that the parents of the children in care would be willing to provide information on their short-term needs when they took the children home. Four families subsequently contributed data for my research.

Interviews conducted in the parental home setting enabled me to have greater access to the views of parents because it was easier for them to describe situations when I knew the nature and layout of their houses. My interview data were complemented by data from participant observation. As noted in Cohen and Manion:

> Because case study observations take place over an extended period
> of time the researcher can develop a more intimate and informed
> relationship with those he is observing, generally in more natural
> environments than those in which experiments and surveys are
> conducted.
>
> (1980, p.103)

I thought perhaps it might be difficult for parents to make
explicit the nature of their roles and the stresses and problems
they encountered. In some cases they have lived and coped with
these for so long that it seemed likely that aspects of their situation
might be taken for granted and therefore not come to light in an
interview. Observing children's behaviour in the company of their
parents prompted questions and discussion.

Mr and Mrs Davis felt after a few weeks of my research that
during my visits and in their interviews they were concentrating on
Daniel's behaviour on specific occasions only. They were concerned
to provide me with an ongoing overview of how it was to live and
care for a disabled child. They suggested that they keep a 24
hour — midday Saturday to midday Sunday — weekend diary. It
was therefore agreed that they should do this for the remaining
period of data collection. Mrs Davis admitted at the end of the
research that she had found the information provided by the diary
extremely depressing as she had previously not realised just how
many incidents that there were in the course of 24 hours: 'It's not
what Daniel does that makes our lives seem hopeless sometimes, it
is the fact that what he does, he does ceaselessly, day after day, year
after year'. Some idea of the stress created by caring for Daniel can
be seen from the following short extract from this diary:

> 4.00 p.m. Tea time begins with the usual unbearable noise from
> Daniel.
> 4.03 p.m. He's thrown his tea all down his front, on the chair etc.
> 4.05 p.m. Daniel's pulling at my arm, more mess.
> 4.07 p.m. He's tried to grab my tea, he wasn't fast enough!
> 4.08 p.m. His spoon and contents are on the floor.
> 4.10 p.m. Daniel's rocking back and forth on his chair, he's
> knocked everything over on the table.
> 4.12 p.m. Daniel has finished his tea complete with all the mess
> that we accept as normal.
> 4.20 p.m. Daniel's screaming again. He's got the photographs.
> 4.23 p.m. He's climbing up me again. I should have known

better than to sit down! I'll give him a biscuit, should give me five minutes.

During the pilot study I felt torn between fulfilling the aims of the study and trying to respond to the immediate needs of the parents. For example, I felt selfish about wanting my research questions answered and in order to achieve that end and owing to the pressures of time I addressed the research participants to my agenda again and again. To have allowed the interview conversation to digress might have resulted in conversation of more value to them. These difficulties were partly resolved at the conclusion of the pilot study with the realisation that the study itself had contributed to meeting some parents' needs by providing an opportunity simply to share problems.

One of the most difficult areas of the research was deciding on the use of time. Frequently, I felt I had insufficient time for the interviews, although the time that I allocated was generous and they generated more than sufficient data for the research. It probably takes a skilled researcher to be able to estimate the time required to meet with people and genuinely listen and explore their views. What I found most distressing was that when the interview had reached its anticipated length, or I had other commitments to go to, it was extremely difficult, when being trusted with details of parents' lives and problems, to terminate the discussion. The personal issues revealed in the interviews were extremely important to the parents and could not be rushed over or treated with anything less than respect.

Another difficulty to be overcome was that of readjustment to work in school after spending the lunchtime interviewing parents or substitute parents. I found it emotionally very draining to discuss with parents issues, such as the nursing of a child involved in a tragic accident and worries about their survival, or to discuss with community home staff the admission of a new child who was covered from the shoulders to the knees in cigarette burns. It became increasingly hard to push this knowledge into the background of my consciousness in order to return to school and continue as normal. As the weeks progressed the content of the interviews became even more personal and intense. Inevitably the period of the research became a time when I questioned past assumptions and thought a great deal about the stresses experienced daily in the homes. It demonstrated how greater involvement with parents would put increased pressure on teachers and that this would have to be acknowledged and catered for by senior staff. Also, if parents were to respond to the additional demands expected of them, then they must have more support from school.

During the interviews the natural parents without exception all raised very emotionally disturbing topics. If they had not chosen to do so, I suspect that I would have avoided raising them as I had no intention of adding unnecessarily to the stress that they were under. I discovered, for example, that for parents, who had decided to place their child in residential care, this decision still deeply troubled them and was raised time and time again in the interviews. On several occasions parents became so deeply involved in such discussions between themselves that they forgot that they were in an interview situation. It is doubtful whether any techniques of data collection could capture such moments adequately.

I found myself constantly questioning why this choice had to be so final and why part-time care arrangements were not available. Parents could then be reassured that time in care was all part of their children's education and managed by teaching staff with whom partnerships could be forged. The heartbreaking choices which face such parents and their subsequent feelings of loss of rights appeared harsh and archaic. Since the research I have encountered residential facilities attached to special schools which allow children with profound and multiple learning difficulties to stay in their own community and retain considerable contact with their families. Such arrangements benefit families who are better able to cope with the reduced and therefore more manageable demands.

As the home settings were so different, so were the ways in which I built up relationships with those involved in the research. The natural parents welcomed my interest in their situation. The sharing of concern for the children acted as a genuine bond. The interviews were regarded as an opportunity to tell someone 'what it is really like'. Relationships with parents appeared relaxed, friendly and increasingly characterised by trust and respect.

Relationships were fairly easy to build at the larger of the two community homes. As Heathfields was an established home, most of the staff had been there a long time and were very committed to it. Trust soon developed as we shared our knowledge and understanding of the children and their difficulties. Information was soon readily exchanged. By the last few weeks of the interviews, regular future meetings between the school and the home were planned. A problem arising from this situation was that because I felt very aware of the work done by staff and sympathetic to their problems my data are not as detailed in key areas as they might have been. Assuming I understood the situation, I think that I may have failed to probe responses with vital questions that would have furnished clearer explanations. Although substantial information was also gained from Newstead, the smaller community home, the formation of working relationships was adversely affected by the lack of continuity of staff. Each time I visited I seemed to meet and interview different members of staff.

The weaker the relationship formed with research participants the easier it was to withdraw from the situation at the end of data collection. The more trusting and supportive the relationship the more concerned I felt about ceasing my regular visits at the end of the research. Through my years of experience of teaching in special education in order to carry out my work I have had to develop a degree of detachment (not to be confused with insensitivity) to situations and families. This is forced on teachers who witness a terminal illness, and who have to come to terms with the occasional death of a child and the distress of parents. Inevitably, working closely with families over the period of my research that detachment gradually lessened. I found it was impossible not to become aware of and respond to the warmth and care displayed in all the parental homes which inevitably led to an emotional involvement with the children and their parents or substitute parents. This was especially the case in relation to the Davis family whose strength, support for each other and care of Daniel I came to admire. Such 'going native' (Ball, 1983, p.88) is obviously an important issue in research involving participant observation and one I had to come to terms with when considering how it might have influenced my data analysis (for a more general discussion of ethical problems involved in educational research, see Burgess, 1989).

## Research findings

The analysis of the data revealed that four main themes predominated in the interviews – isolation, fear and suspicion, community facilities and school contact. In this section I shall discuss each theme in turn.

*Isolation*

Perhaps the most obvious difference between the situation of the natural parents and the substitute parents is the fact that caring for a disabled child does not isolate the substitute parents in any way from their friends, family or interests outside of their jobs. The stresses of 'being alone' simply do not apply. At the end of each shift, the substitute parents return to an 'outside life'. Future commitments are in their own hands:

> Some days you go home and your head is throbbing from the noise. It's nice just to sit in the quiet and think things out. My family soon get me going again though – wanting a meal.
>
> (Substitute parent)

In contrast to the natural parents, there was the knowledge that if the physical or mental strain of the work became too great, or ambitions changed, they could leave.

Isolation appeared to be woven through every aspect of the life of the Davis family. The ways in which Daniel caused his family to be isolated were many. The time he took up was enormous and the mental energy even greater. Both parents agreed that there was little else in their lives. When he was at school they spent their time caring for the house and tackling the vast amount of laundry, mainly generated by their son continuously soiling his clothing and bedding. There was also the baking for his special diet which they did to try to offset some of the cost of caring for him.

Both Mr and Mrs Davis thought that while most children took up a tremendous amount of time initially this decreased as they grew up. Ultimately parents were able to resume a separate life again and take up old friendships, hobbies and careers. This would not be possible in their case and the isolation appeared to be deepening:

> Rebecca [their daughter] grew away from us; she went through the stages and sort of separated herself from us. With Daniel it's just got worse. If you've a mentally handicapped child you've got no space in your life.
>
> (Kath)

Apart from the physical workload of looking after Daniel when one parent coped alone in order that the other could go out 'it was difficult to switch off from the anxiety'. Taking Daniel out anywhere beyond walking distance was difficult as they did not have their own transport and if they tried to take him on a bus he screamed and they received complaints from other passengers.

To them it seemed that few people had any real knowledge of how caring for Daniel had changed their lives. Some friends did still call on them but rarely offered any practical support or real understanding. The needs of a child with profound and multiple learning difficulties and complex behaviours are outside the experience of most people. However, such visits from friends were welcomed if not relied upon. The acceptance of their situation was also an isolating factor. Their awareness of the present and likely future quality of their lives left them stripped of any pretence that they were an average family. Relating to other families was harder because of this realisation.

They were worried about their daughter, who had very few friends in the neighbourhood. No one ever called for her at home despite the fact that she was a popular girl at school. The pain they felt on their daughter's behalf appeared much harder to cope with than their own. Derek felt that 'Rebecca's got to find a way around it. We don't know how to help her, but we'll try ... Rebecca knows we'll support her. She knows we love her'. Derek said 'We don't think we've done too badly with Rebecca'. He considered that despite their problems and bleak outlook on life 'she still has lots of fun and laughter at home'.

The other three sets of natural parents interviewed had taken the decision to accommodate their profoundly disabled children in a community home because of the intolerable stress they caused. They felt that the situation created for their other children meant that the decision had to be made and faced up to. They all agreed that the activities in which they now participated from hobbies to holidays had previously been severely restricted. Their other children had received insufficient time and interest and had few friends. Each family felt that while they were able to cope with short-term commitment to their disabled child during regular home visits, the physical and mental stresses and strains of full-time care were beyond their capabilities.

The community homes were both situated in expensive residential housing areas. They were separated from their nearest neighbours by extensive grounds. There was little, if any, interaction between the staff and children in the homes and the local residents which apparently suited both parties. As stressed previously, the substitute parents had lives beyond the community homes in which they worked. The children in the homes were also much less isolated than Daniel. There was a range of activities in which they could participate and few difficulties over raising the necessary funding. Swimming, horseriding and trips to the beach or countryside were readily undertaken. Transport was not a problem as each establishment had its own vehicle. Often extra helpers were taken on to assist with special trips or for the school holidays.

All the natural parents described the difficulties, which echoed those of the Davis family, that they had experienced prior to their children being admitted into residential care. They also expressed concern about the way the behaviours of the disabled child had isolated their other children from neighbours, friends and boyfriends. Two parents were also aware that their anxieties over their child had caused them to cut themselves off from others. However, the parents of the children in both comunity homes were no longer isolated in the way Mr and Mrs Davis were. Two of the mothers had returned to their careers and the third, who had worked occasionally, was now enjoying contact with her grandchild. All of the fathers worked and all of the couples enjoyed a social life, although this ceased during the occasional visits home of their disabled child.

## Fear and suspicion

Children with profound and multiple learning difficulties appear to generate fear and prejudice among the general public, particularly when their behaviour is unusual or bizarre. Kath and Derek Davis described how, when they were out in the local community, people stared and were rude to them when Daniel did odd things. Shopping at the local supermarket was often a nightmare because Daniel was extremely noisy or ill tempered and would hit the side of his head. If he managed to reach stacked shelves he would knock items to the floor or eat his way through the packaging to get to the food. People were either insulting about their handling of Daniel or offered inappropriate advice.

Mr and Mrs Davis repeated many times that attempts over the years at forming good relationships with neighbours were hardly worth the effort. Kath pointed out that she had given up trying 'to explain to neighbours and relatives that mental handicap was not infectious'. Daniel's most difficult behaviour to control was his continuous screaming which, whilst reducing, could go on for hours at any time of day or night. This particularly caused tensions with neighbours:

> the man across the back, his wife is a friend – ha! He had to go into another bedroom one night, in the front of the house because he had to go to work in the morning. It's hard for us to keep on apologising, when that's what our life is like every night. No one cares a jot unless it puts them out. How could they know how bad things are ... or would they even care.
>
> (Derek)

The Davis family felt that they were unwelcome and an inconvenience to others.

The community homes, due to their physical position and the reduced need for local contact – for example, food was delivered in bulk – rarely encountered the rudeness meeted out to the Davis family. Crying and temper outbursts were seldom heard by neighbours because the gardens separated the homes from their houses. The transport owned by the homes meant that the children were rarely seen entering or leaving the building and in any case spent less time there than Daniel did in his house. There were no daily encounters on route to the shops and no need to explain the children's behaviours and apologise for intrusions on the lives of others.

When they took the children out into the community the competence of the substitute parents was not challenged. There had apparently never been any criticism of the way they coped with the children when they behaved in bizarre ways in public – for example, at the local park; one substitute parent said 'People know that we are employed to do this job and that we know how to handle them'. They did, however, occasionally feel embarrassed when the children behaved badly but thought that passers by were generally kind and just ignored the behaviour if asked to do so.

The natural parents of the children in the community homes had also experienced problems arising from neighbours' suspicions. Simon's mother found that babysitters were not prepared to babysit for a profoundly disabled child. Even longstanding friends, who regularly sat for her other children before her disabled son was born, were frightened in case he woke up. Another mother, whose daughter experienced epileptic fits, stated how these could arouse terror in some people who made no attempt to hide their feelings, 'People would just stare at you or protect their children or pets. You can't take too much of that, it just makes you so upset'. Simon's mother felt similarly, 'I simply didn't take him out if I didn't feel up to all that'.

The data reflected how little the general public know about caring for children with profound and multiple learning difficulties. It raised haunting questions regarding how communities could become more understanding and what role special schools might play. The data also suggested that people are supportive of those caring for the disabled when they have chosen to do it as a vocation but not when they have to do so through family commitment.

## Community facilities

In the community where the Davis family lived the services provided were not geared to help them to meet Daniel's needs. They related the problems that they had experienced getting medical attention for Daniel. If he needed the doctor, they had to wait with him in the waiting room at the surgery, which caused problems with other patients. The local dentist refused to treat him. Kath explained that even when Daniel was hospitalised the nursing staff complained that they were unable to cope with him. They insisted that Kath stay with him at all times in order to contain him. She felt that that was particularly unacceptable because of Rebecca. Eventually Mr and Mrs Davis discharged Daniel themselves and cared for him at home.

The situation seemed little improved regarding the relationship with the support services. Kath and Derek felt that, if anything, their dealings with the support services had increased rather than alleviated the stress of their situation. They spoke of how initially they were not informed of allowances available to them and how often after finding their way through the maze of forms they always seemed to be the exception to the rules. They had particularly wished for a mobility allowance, but because Daniel could walk they were ineligible despite the fact that travelling on public transport inevitably brought on a bout of screaming. Rather bitterly they claimed:

> We see the support service as us supporting them. We give them the information they need — we hope it will help someone else; if they get the right form that is. We hope that we are hardened to it now.
>
> (Derek)

They described how they were assigned a community nurse whom they rarely saw, concluding:

> They do no good anyway. They have a good gossip and go. We had a visit from a speech therapist once. She spent an hour talking about nuclear disarmament and then left. We just laughed. That's all you can do. We think they come because they need someone to talk to.
>
> (Derek)

In contrast, the local community services offered more to the community homes than to the Davis family. The local swimming pool made lifting apparatus and an attendant available when the staff took their children swimming. The local doctor paid a weekly visit to the homes to check on the health of the children. This removed the stress experienced by Mr and Mrs Davis of trying to keep a distraught child amused in a waiting room for up to an hour. Perhaps the most obvious difference in terms of community facilities was in relation to social services provision. The necessary facilities were provided at both the community homes. There were modern lifting aids, laundery facilities and access to the medical and psychological services. Staff considered that there were no unneccesary delays experienced when claiming benefits on the children's behalf.

Community facilities were little used by the natural parents when their children made short visits from their residential care. Simon's mother described the difficulties of taking him out with her because the local shopping centre had so many levels and steps. This made pushing a wheelchair and carrying shopping extremely difficult. Even the seafront was hard to visit because it involved going up a steep hill. Catherine's parents withdrew from the community when she was at home because of her difficult behaviours. On the rare occasions when they took her out the whole family went along so that she was well-accompanied. Sophie's behaviour did not present drastic problems. However, her health could deteriorate rapidly on occasions, which her parents found a constant worry, and therefore they preferred to stay at home for the duration of their child's visit.

## The school

Mr and Mrs Davis both felt that the school was one of the few places where staff listened to them and tried to understand their circumstances. Derek commented 'We trust the staff. They know Daniel and what he's like. They have him all day. They know we're telling the truth'. They were positive about the notion of partnership with the school and saw it as helping Daniel and themselves:

> We need help too; it's a new ball game to us. You might be able to help your normal kid with their sums but where do you start with mental handicap? We need to be taught too. No one is going to do it for us, but if they'd just listen to us and not be afraid to approach us.

They considered that they had benefited already from a jointly planned feeding programme for Daniel that was carried out both at home and at school. They now felt that they needed some help in planning short- and long-term goals, possibly through regular meetings at the school. Regular visits were viewed as likely to help establish staff confidence in parents and trust between parents and the school. Mr and Mrs Davis thought that seeing regularly what Daniel could do at school would encourage them to try things out at home:

> Sometimes, when I've been into school, I've seen staff handling Daniel and getting him to do things that I know we couldn't do. But they wouldn't think to tell you these sort of things because they don't know we can't do it.
>
> (Derek)

They felt that they were often excluded from his life at school, not deliberately, but because there was no definite policy to include them which was agreed and known about by staff and parents. They were concerned that without such a policy for partnership parents seeking greater involvement and understanding of staff teaching strategies could be misconstrued as parental criticism of school practices.

Without exception, all of the natural parents wanted greater contact with the school. They were worried that because their children were living in a community home, they were excluded from school events and educational planning. This was not the intention of course and that point was emphasised to them. Despite the restricted opportunity for carrying out educational programmes at home, they thought that if a particular approach was being taken at school and in the residential home, then they should know about it and maintain that approach during visits. Most parents also had specific questions about how to deal with difficult behaviours which they thought could be addressed through regular meetings at school.

As suggested by Mittler and Mittler (1982), 'parents need to be aware of the precise teaching methods and strategies being used by teachers and other professionals to achieve any particular goal' (p.9). Most parents were unaware of the teaching techniques being used with their children. They stated that they were often at a loss to deal with some problems. They realised that their own, often desperate, measures occasionally resulted in conditions worsening. They wanted help from the school. They sometimes asked for it, but usually only when the situation had become unbearable.

The substitute parents varied in their range of qualifications and depth of experience. They included psychiatric nurses, general care assistants of many years experience and those who had attended short courses on working with children with profound and multiple learning difficulties. Staff from both community homes welcomed greater communication with the school and wished to work in partnership on educational programmes. They stated that they would like staff to visit the homes on a regular basis but accepted that it was easier for them to visit the school. They were aware of the dangers of putting the children under too much pressure if they were expected to work all day at school and then repeat the work sessions at home. They wanted to ensure a balance of expectations. They were particularly concerned to set up a communication system between the home and the school to report any problems experienced, changes in behaviours, factors likely to affect the children in order to improve continuity and avoid confusion.

## Conclusion

Clearly there are restrictions on how far schools can develop the notion of partnership. The time a teacher has available for parents is already much in demand and in most special schools there is no non-contact time. There must, therefore, be a commitment from senior management to enable teachers to participate in sessions with parents. As suggested previously, deeper involvement with parents could prove stressful for staff and would certainly demand additional counselling skills for which training would be required. Teachers would also need to be more aware of the inter-related roles of the support services. This would assist in parents receiving timely and appropriate information on, for example, the allowances to which they are entitled.

The experience gained through carrying out the research and reflecting on the data was put into immediate use and has subsequently been added to. I have moved schools twice and been able to apply my findings to new settings. This has helped me to appreciate that the different communities, parents and children which each school serves require alternative approaches to building partnerships with parents. In schools where such ideas are alien it may initially prove difficult and may take considerable time to develop the necessary staff commitment. I feel very fortunate that the school of which I am now head has staff who recognise the value of, and are enthusiastic about, working with parents.

We have established close home – school links to ensure that support is provided for parents as soon as their children enter the school. Support is provided not only from staff but from other parents. We also offer specific sessions to parents to address areas of need – for example, opportunities for parents and their children to use the hydrotherapy pool and to access the sensory curriculum through the light/darkroom facilities and sound equipment. Since the Education Reform Act of 1988 the implementation of the National Curriculum has generated a need to explain its implications and to remove fears that children in special schools might become marginalised from their peers in ordinary schools. Practical sessions on mathematics, science and English have demonstrated to parents the kinds of activities provided within the National Curriculum, how these meet their children's needs and the possibilities these provide for integration projects with ordinary schools.

Over the last twenty years research into home – school communication and relationships has steadily accumulated and given rise to an increasing number of articles and books providing advice on how to set up partnership schemes. Wells (1989) provides a useful overview of a review of the research findings on all aspects of parental involvement of parents in the education of pupils with severe learning difficulties which was commissioned by the Department of Education for Northern Ireland. This could provide a useful starting point for teacher researchers looking for a way into surveying the literature in this area which at first can seem a daunting prospect. On a more practical note, the components of a theoretical model of parental involvement provided by Hornby could be used as a set of research questions to guide an evaluation of existing practice and to indicate the data that needs to be gathered to translate staff commitment to the principle of partnership into further action:

> Information: how can maximum use be made of the information which parents can contribute?
> Support: what efforts can be made to encourage parents to reinforce school programmes at home?
> Leadership: which parents would be willing and able to provide training for professionals or help in running parent support groups?
> Communication: what can be done to promote effective communication with all the children's parents?
> Regular contacts: what are the best ways of maintaining regular contact with parents?
> Education: which type of parent education programmes should be organised?
> Counselling: how can opportunities for counselling be made available to parents?
>
> (1989, p.162)

## References

Ball, S.J. (1983) 'Case study research in education: some notes and problems' in Hammersley, M. (ed) *The Ethnography of Schooling*. Driffield: Nafferton Books.

Burgess, R.G. (ed) (1989) *The Ethics of Educational Research*. London: Falmer Press.

Cohen, L. and Manion, L. (1980) *Research Methods in Education*. London: Croom Helm.

Glendenning, C. (1983) *Unshared Care*. London: Routledge and Kegan Paul.

Hornby, G. (1989) 'A model for parent participation'. *British Journal of Special Education* 16, 161–2.

Mittler, P. and Mittler, H. (1982) *Partnership with Parents*. Stratford-on-Avon: National Council for Special Education.

Wells, I. (1989) 'Parents and education for severe learning difficulties'. *British Journal of Special Education: Research Supplement* 16, 153–60.

# CHAPTER 5

# *Devising Motor Programmes for Children with Physical Disabilities*

Lynda Peake

> Is there anything special you would like to be able to do when
> you are with your friends?
> I want to be able to turn my bike around.

I taught in ordinary schools for many years prior to working in
a school for physically disabled children. At this special school
I became increasingly aware of the importance of movement
education for those who are unable to move around freely
and are therefore often denied the satisfaction of developing
physical skills and using them as a means of further exploring
the world. Working extensively with small groups of disabled
children necessitated an in-depth knowledge of the range of ways
in which children learn. I soon came to realise how little I knew
about the learning difficulties they experienced.

Hillside special school was purpose built, staffed and equipped
to meet the needs of up to 120 pupils in the age range from 2 to 19
years. The main school was organised in two departments, primary
and secondary, and age, ability and attainment were the criteria
which determined when children progressed from one group to
another and from the primary to secondary department. I was
employed in the primary department which comprised three class
groups with four teachers. My own class group of 14 pupils, aged
between 4 and 7, was shared between myself and a colleague and
we taught as a team for most afternoons. The pupils for whom
I was directly responsible entered my classroom on leaving the
school's nursery, and, at any one time their numbers ranged from
5 to 7.

There were several children within my class group who were

diagnosed as having cerebral palsy, a non-progressive (but not unchanging) disorder of movement or posture, beginning in childhood and due to a malfunction or damage of the brain (Bleck, 1975). These children were experiencing difficulties with classwork and also in physical activity. Although their difficulties were not the same, there were some similarities. In addition to the individual motor disorders experienced by the pupils with cerebral palsy they often also had to contend with speech defects, sensory impairments, convulsions and learning difficulties.

In order to make my teaching of these pupils more appropriate and effective the aims of my research were:

1.   to increase my own understanding of the motor difficulties experienced by young children with cerebral palsy;
2.   to discover what was involved in devising individual motor programmes;
3.   to assess the feasibility of a non-specialist engaging in the construction of individual motor programmes;
4.   to identify and suggest ways of alleviating some of the difficulties teachers and parents experience when engaging in activities to meet the needs of children with cerebral palsy.

## Data collection

My original intention was that my research project, which was conducted during the two years of the Outstation course, should be action research whereby having devised a motor programme for at least one of the children in my class, I would implement it and record the outcomes. In common with others new to research the timescale I initially envisaged turned out to be unrealistic. I underestimated the length of my investigation into the condition of cerebral palsy which was infinitely more complex than I had anticipated and posed many questions that could only be answered by seeking out the expertise of individual specialists. The research therefore became a case study of the physical difficulties experienced by children with cerebral palsy and the process of devising individual motor programmes to assist with these.

I began my research by consulting the literature on cerebral palsy (for example, Bobath, 1985; Hardy, 1983; Levitt, 1985). Then I tapped the expertise of human sources of information who were readily accessible because they were often on site — such as medical staff, the physiotherapist and parents. Further information was obtained from the pupils' files which contained medical and school reports and their statements of special educational needs. My examination of the school files on individual pupils also took longer than anticipated and as a result I felt that there was much work to be done to make the files of more practical use. This documentary evidence enabled me to view the pupils and their difficulties from a variety of perspectives in addition to my own, before drawing on all the information available to compile individual profiles which I hoped would be representative of a majority opinion.

I believe children's parents are the most important teachers as they spend more time with their children than anyone else and therefore have a more intimate knowledge of them and a greater opportunity to help them. Therefore, as a pilot study for my research I carried out interviews with parents to discover their perceptions of their children's physical needs and abilities.

Before any motor programme could be devised I needed through observations to establish the functional level of the four pupils who were to be the subjects of my research. I chose four of the children whose parents I had previously interviewed. I used open-ended observation rather than any of the published observation schedules as they were too rigid in their categorising of the information required. Also, I did not want to produce a fixed schedule of my own as I was not sure at that stage of the details of my focus. Initially my observations were conducted during PE lessons in the hall and soft play therapy sessions. These lessons were not contrived for the purpose of the research. I observed one child (occasionally two) for the duration of the lesson which was never more than 50 minutes. Physical activity in the hall usually included the whole group of 14 pupils and I was therefore in a team teaching situation. On those occasions the taking of notes was made easier because I could take a break from my involvement in the activity to make notes without fear of any pupils being unattended. In soft play therapy I taught a group of 5 to 6 pupils myself, and even observing and taking notes on one child was extremely difficult. I sometimes found myself resorting to communicating instructions to a nursery nurse in order to concentrate on note-making. I attempted to record the performance of each child under observation for the whole session as I did not want to miss anything of importance. I found that during the analysis of notes taken in this way, events which seemed unimportant at the time, took on greater significance. I was also surprised by the number of pages of notes generated.

I was concerned that the other pupils may have suffered as a result of this mode of classroom observation. As my research progressed, I found that I became increasingly involved with the activities of the individuals I was observing. Unfortunately, those pupils on the periphery of my research seemed 'less important' for a time. I had not anticipated the depth of my own involvement with the subjects of my research. The realisation that I was in fact almost 'ignoring' others left me with a considerable feeling of guilt long after the research was completed. When teacher researchers are planning how they are going to collect data in their own classrooms, they need to be aware of the extent to which preoccupation with their research can unconsciously and adversely affect the quality of their teaching.

Bell (1987) points out that one of the difficulties for the participant observer researching a familiar environment is that this familiarity may affect objectivity. It was impossible for me, even in my attempts at non-participatory observation, to distance myself from the group of pupils I was studying. Familiarity with the characteristics of those being observed can cause the observer to overlook aspects of behaviour that would be apparent to a non-participant observer seeing the situation for the first time. To try to overcome these problems I endeavoured to compare and contrast findings from the observation data with data from a variety of other sources, to look for alternative interpretations for myself and the reader.

My observations in soft play therapy and physical activity took place over a period of five months for the majority of the weekly sessions. Lessons were still conducted very much on the basis of a 'what shall we do to-day' approach, and I became concerned about the range of pupil activities I was observing. Because our lessons were not properly planned we were perhaps limiting the pupils' experiences of movement. I decided to use a recommended motor development assessment chart on the four children who were the subjects of my research. This chart included a wide range of age related movement activity and I hoped that by its use I might discover activities we may have omitted. However, nothing new was revealed by the test which suggested that we had in fact covered most of the motor activities of which our pupils with cerebral palsy were capable. Also my own observations had already revealed most of the problems illustrated during the test.

As my observations progressed, I decided that if I was to complete my research in the anticipated timescale I could study only one child in the depth that I considered necessary for devising a motor programme and I chose a child whom I shall call Robert. I realised that in order to understand the full range of Robert's movement problems I would need to observe him doing everything, that is, working, playing, dressing and eating – activities I should have included in addition to observation of physical activity periods. I was able to acquire non-contact time for two non-participant observation sessions. I observed Robert during number and writing sessions, and it was these single-minded observations that produced some of the most important material for analysis.

My examination of the literature, together with discussion with his parents and interviews with the school physiotherapist, provided me with an added awareness of the type of difficulties that Robert would be expected to experience, and served as excellent background knowledge as I conducted my observation of him. I did not observe Robert at home and on reflection that was an important omission. Children often behave differently in their home situation and it would have been interesting to make comparisons. I did, however, produce a simple diary chart for Robert's mother who agreed to note particular activities he performed for a period of one week. Her complete chart (see Figure 5.1) was thorough and contained the type of information I had hoped to obtain. I felt that my belated observation of Robert in the classroom, and in social situations, gave me a more complete picture of his movement problems without which information vital to the nature of the motor programme would not have been included.

Figure 5.1  Chart completed by Robert's mother

The observation schedule below is a copy produced, with the permission of Robert's mother. Prior to observations conducted at home a meeting was arranged between us. I supplied her with a written list of points we had discussed for her to consider during her observation — for example, social skills, balance, concentration, body awareness and self-help skills.

| Monday | Tuesday | Wednesday | Thursday | Friday |
|---|---|---|---|---|
| Built different things with legs (used both hands most of the time) concentrated well. Refused to use right hand when eating. Has to open and climb through middle of safety gate at top of stairs — did very well (used both hands). Balance good, getting through and going up or down the stairs. | Played out alone did not want to mix, used left and right hands when using tool set. Watched TV but lost interest after half an hour. Played 'chasing' with brother but got annoyed and upset because he could not keep up or catch him, and kept falling over. | Played with musical organ using both hands, also pots and pans (drums) again both hands in use. Likes musical things. Really concentrates. | Got annoyed with brother for interfering with a game, quite angry, showed great strength in left hand. I moved safety gate to bottom of stairs, harder to get through but managed it himself. Would not allow us to help (stubborn and independent, will of his own). | All week he has dressed/undressed himself (except buttons), no help at all. Socks most difficult for him. Never used his right hand once at any meal. Running around outside — goes too fast, does not realise he will hurt himself if he falls. Sometimes does not put his hands out to save himself. |

# Case study of Robert

*Medical history*

Robert was born in September 1982. His mother stated that he was not diagnosed as having cerebral palsy until he was nine months old when a weakness of the right arm and hand indicated the presence of some spasticity. Because of this weakness Robert's gross motor functions were limited and he was slow to walk. His fine motor co-ordination was also affected by the limitations of his right hand. Robert showed delays in feeding himself and in the manipulation of toys. Even at the age of six his mother stated that he refused to use his right hand at any meal.

Prior to entering Hillside, Robert's vision and hearing were satisfactory, although his speech remained at a single word level for some time. At the age of two Robert was admitted to Hillside Nursery and received a Statement of Special Educational Needs which classified him as 'multi-handicapped (a spastic quadriplegic suffering from epilepsy and asthma)'. He was to be provided with a full nursery curriculum which allowed for medical supervision, nursing care, physiotherapy and speech therapy. However in another section of the same statement, Robert was classified as a cerebral palsy − a right hemiplegia with indications of weakness in his right leg, and suffering from disturbed behaviour. This discrepancy illustrates the confusion when classifying a condition. By the age of two and a half years Robert's understanding of language was good, but his limited expressive language frustrated him as others failed to understand. Robert was also disadvantaged at this stage by the weakness of his right hand. At the age of four he was still not able to catch a large ball with both hands over a short distance. At three years old Robert was still using a walking frame for short periods and wearing calipers, and later soft splints. He was falling a lot and displayed a stubborn streak which occasionally resulted in a temper tantrum.

During the final stages of my research Robert became six years old and was in his second year of the infant class at Hillside. He had been walking with the aid of splints for over three years but did not require a walking aid when he came into my class. The most recent information concerning his condition was supplied by the school physiotherapist and the school's Senior Medical Officer. It was now evident that Robert had difficulties with all four limbs, although his legs were more affected. His left hand was the least affected of his limbs and he was termed by the Senior Medical Officer as a 'cerebral palsied diplegic with added involvement of the right upper limb, and mild involvement of the left upper limb'. The doctor maintained that as long as the difficulties of the child were identified they could be treated — his emphasis was not on the diagnosis. He stressed that his treatment was based largely on his own observations of Robert and those of his mother and the staff at Hillside. The above section contains clinical descriptions of Robert aimed at illustrating those facts which were relevant to the profile. It is not to be viewed in isolation as it tells little about Robert himself and what he can and cannot do.

I interviewed Robert's mother in her home and at Hillside and was able to compile a detailed description of Robert's family situation. Whilst this information is extremely important to the overall picture of Robert, it is not possible here to include the detailed notes I made. Suffice to say that Robert was born into a caring and supportive family and the relationship between home and school was, and remains, favourable. Robert's mother maintained regular contact with me and was always willing to support our efforts by doing what she could to help at home with classwork, physiotherapy and by discussing any emotional upsets Robert may have experienced.

*Robert at school*

Robert appeared to enjoy school. He was always first to go and collect his work from his tray and always intense about practical activities. His number and reading skills were a little below the average level of his ordinary school peers, but his handwriting was clearly formed considering the slight weakness present in his left hand. Any manipulative skill required by Robert within a classroom situation was affected by his inability to co-ordinate hand and eye. Putting his work tray back into its space was a difficult task requiring more strength and co-ordination of both hands and arms than Robert had. Walking for Robert required considerable effort and he fell frequently.

Although his motor skills were limited Robert was able to do many exercises in PE sessions. His determination, and the strength of certain parts of his body appeared to account for this. Vital physiotherapy was received twice a week in order to strengthen the weak muscles in Robert's legs, trunk and back, to improve walking skills and to encourage the use of his right arm and hand. Robert also went swimming and riding weekly – again the aims were to strengthen weak muscles. He was examined at regular intervals by the Senior Clinical Medical Officer and monitored by the resident school nurse. Robert was able to undress and almost dress himself for PE sessions and could use the toilet facilities unaided. At lunchtime, although he fed himself, his tray was brought to him by a dinner lady as his balance could not be relied upon.

Although a number of Robert's characteristics could be directly related to his medical condition, I tried not to let this detract from his individuality. Robert was a hardworking, likeable boy with a wry sense of humour. He was enthusiastic about the more active structured aspects of the primary curriculum and enjoyed his swimming, riding and PE. Robert was also determined, stubborn and moody. If he was physically hurt or mentally frustrated it was almost impossible to console him – his wish was to be left alone. My examination of the medical, family and school situations resulted in possible explanations of social behaviour and physical development – explanations which helped me to understand the child and thereby avoid making mistakes in my judgement of his situation.

## Difficulties to be overcome

Although Robert's problems were more apparent in PE, it became clear that lessons in basic subjects could be just as hazardous for him. The motor programme produced for Robert had to be part of a total approach to his development. Towards the end of my data collection on Robert the same difficulties kept occurring with speech, poor balance, right arm weakness, attention lack and emotional and social problems. These were often inter-related, but for the purpose of my study I dealt with them as separate entities. When the motor programme was constructed I needed to have areas of specific difficulty defined so that I could deal with them.

### Speech

Until recently, an additional cause of Robert's frustration was his inability to make those around him understand what he said.

About half the children with cerebral palsy have speech and language difficulties of some kind. Robert's speech continued to improve, although to a stranger it may have seemed unclear at first. Unfortunately when Robert became excited, which was often the case during PE or soft play therapy, his speech was almost unintelligible. This affected interaction with his peers at a time when Robert had actually become involved with them in spite of himself. Linked to Robert's speech problem was his difficulty with swallowing which caused drooling, a common but anti-social problem.

Balance

Robert exhibited a mixture of spasticity and weak skeletal muscles. He was slightly ataxic, which meant he lacked a sense of position in space, walking like a sailor on a rolling ship. Robert was also known to have been born with a cerebellum cyst. All of these contributed towards Robert's lack of balance and rotation. When observed walking he seemed to fall from one foot to the other. He was unable to stand still without holding on to something, and all his lower limb joints were unstable, the right side being most affected. Robert's feet turned outwards, particularly his left foot. The problems caused by Robert's inability to balance were probably the most limiting in terms of physical activity. Jumping, running, climbing stairs, lifting and throwing, were just some of the tasks which were difficult for Robert because they were dependent on good balance.

Even the task of dressing and undressing depended upon Robert's ability to remain steady while moving the appropriate limbs. Although, seated on the floor, he was able to dress and undress himself by the time my research was nearing completion, both his mother and I were aware of the lengthy process of putting on socks, splints and boots, while attempting to keep his balance. Robert was unable to maintain a wide base which, coupled with his disinclination to use his weaker right hand as a prop on the floor, made the whole procedure arduous.

A PE lesson in the school hall, aimed at giving basic practice in foot and eye co-ordination, highlighted again the problems Robert experienced with balance. He was unable to stop a slow moving ball with either foot. Consequently, dribbling a ball between cones was almost impossible. Robert was fully aware of what was required but because of his balance problem he could not maintain position long enough to exert any control over the ball. Like many other young boys Robert had a love of football and being unable to participate in such an activity both at home and at school merely added to his frustration.

Where specific motor difficulties could be easily identified in a PE session, this was not the case within a classroom situation where over a short period of time Robert was faced with a range of challenges. There were a number of occasions during the course of one particular classroom lesson where poor balance caused difficulties for Robert. His posture in a seated position was poor — he sat on the edge of his chair with his legs fully extended underneath the table. This was a position which many of the ambulant children with cerebral palsy seemed to favour. As on a number of previous occasions, when Robert wished to show the class teacher his work (he had been cutting out shapes) he made no attempt to walk the short distance towards her seat in the middle of the room. On that particular occasion he sat for a few minutes with his left hand up, even though the teacher had her back to him. On reflection I tried to appreciate the effort required for Robert to rise from his awkward seated position and weave his splayed legs past chairs, between desks and cupboards carrying a sheet of paper. Robert called out — the teacher went to him. In the same lesson Robert was asked to collect the litter bin and take it to his seat and place his unwanted scraps of paper into it. He collected the bin using his weaker right hand to steady himself when he lifted the bin from the floor. He stumbled a little on his way back to his seat through a narrow space between the table and the wall heater. When asked if he needed help by the nursery nurse Robert declined her offer. Robert sat on the edge of his seat and successfully picked up all the pieces of paper that had fallen on to the floor. Sitting to do this was a wise choice on his part and illustrated to me one of the ways in which he had adapted to his disability. Robert returned the bin — this time asking another pupil to give him more space to manoeuvre. He held the bin in both hands and bent to slide it into position under the worktop — he fell on to his hands as he leaned forward. Robert fell again on his way back to his seat, this time on to his bottom with his left foot twisted. He became wedged between a chair and a wall heater and was rendered helpless until the class teacher came to his rescue.

My other observations illustrated that there was a point of balance which Robert could not maintain without falling forward — this was a factor observed by his mother when he tried to jump from the floor into the air like his younger brother. It was an issue I was to examine as I was convinced it was possible to 'teach' Robert how to use his own body to achieve maximum stability in an increased number of situations.

Right upper limb weakness
Robert had physiotherapy twice a week — these sessions were aimed at developing his walking skills and using his right arm and hand. Because of the limitation of that limb, fine motor control was affected and Robert was disadvantaged in any task measuring eye – hand co-ordination skills, that is, he found throwing a ball very difficult and he attempted to catch a ball with one hand only. However, the physiotherapist assured me that the movement of his hands could be improved upon.

I listed all the activities at home and at school when a two-handed approach would have been appropriate. I then divided that list into activities where two hands were used by Robert and activities where only one was used. A pattern emerged which led me to question the motives behind Robert's actions. What emerged from the observation was that Robert would use both hands in certain circumstances, that is when he needed to use them for an activity he enjoyed or when he was forced into using his right hand as a prop to maintain balance. He refrained from using his right hand for fine motor tasks when he could use his teeth instead — for example, separating cubes — or when he could adequately manage a task without using the hand.

Robert, aware of the considerable effort required to use his right hand, did not intend to waste any extra effort if he felt it was unnecessary. In PE periods Robert would use both hands only in a structured situation when it was unavoidable — for example, pulling himself along a bench, carrying an object, or steadying himself. In most situations his right hand was forgotten. From the perspective of the doctor, the physiotherapist and myself, it was important for Robert's future physical and social development to exercise, by usage, the weakest limb he had. The physiotherapist's view was that, in spite of some 'bad habits' which may have been established in the past, there was no reason to suppose that Robert's right hand and arm could not be improved with correct treatment. There was movement in the hand and the muscles could be strengthened. The problem was one of reluctance on the part of the child himself. Therefore, whatever our perspectives as professionals, my observation had shown that it was the attitude of the child that had to be positive if he was to improve and maximise his motor ability. It was my responsibility to find ways of motivating him.

Emotional and social difficulties

Robert was a child with limited movements who had to contend with frustrations that we may not be able to comprehend. Lack of success in some areas, or being unable to perform some of the simple tasks that other children complete without effort, can often result in a rigidity of behaviour of the kind Robert exhibited at home and at school. The more intelligent a child is, the more emotionally hurt he can become − such was the case with Robert. He was one of the more able of my pupils with cerebral palsy and wanted to be equal to other more active children. If he did not succeed he would withdraw himself. He would sit alone for the majority of playtimes because he could not play football in the hall. He would not go outside to play at home even though his mother informed me that the other children welcomed him. It may have been that Robert did not want his difficulties revealed to his peers, or reinforced through situations that constantly emphasised them.

Like many children with cerebral palsy, Robert experienced strong, easily aroused emotions such as frustration, stubbornness, anger and depression. One of Robert's most predominant characteristics was his refusal to work or co-operate in situations which he found difficult or which he believed were unnecessary. He remained unconvinced of the value of physiotherapy, not surprising in one so young, and put up a great deal of resistance for the majority of his weekly sessions. He would watch the faces of the teachers or physiotherapist, trying to judge reactions to see if they would relent before he did. It often became a battleground, but once resolved there was no ill feeling from either party − Robert bore no grudges.

Robert's emotional make-up affected his relationship with others around him. Donlon and Burton (1976) believed that most disabled children could make a choice between total withdrawal or self-stimulating activities or some other activity. For the majority of his playtime Robert chose to withdraw. Occasionally he watched the more active pupils play football in the hall, but usually he would sit in the same position for the majority of the 15 minute break. It was disturbing to observe this lack of motivation and interest in what his fellow pupils were doing. If given the opportunity he would chat to the member of staff on duty instead. He seemed to be more at ease with adults.

Attention span

Like other children with cerebral palsy there were times when Robert found it hard to focus his attention. Those periods were usually in a class lesson when he was writing. On those occasions he was not able to remain on task without constant encouragement and was easily distracted by any slight sound or movement.

During my analysis of Robert's difficulties I had attempted to explore those which I considered to be motor related. However it was difficult to ignore other problems which were apparent during observation periods. It is possible that, during the course of the implementations of my motor programme for him, issues not directly related to PE could still be considered and improved upon as part of the motor remediation process. Robert's difficulties interacted with one another and any programme of motor remediation had to reflect that interaction.

I had endeavoured to empathise with Robert, and understand the nature of his difficulties. In doing that I was able to construct a motor programme that considered these in a unified manner which hopefully would help him to discover more appropriate strategies for solving them. In previous years Robert had chosen the simplest way of doing things; he had used his strong muscles to the detriment of weaker ones. In his own way he had compensated for his difficulties, but in doing so had created more.

**The motor programme**

The motor programme I devised does not attempt to provide experience in all aspects of PE. It is not intended to be used in isolation but as part of the PE curriculum of the infant department in a school for physically disabled children. Although the programme itself is very specific in its attainment targets for one child, there are certain broad based aims which I believe should automatically be considered by a teacher engaged in the production of individual motor programmes. One of the most important of these is enjoyment. This applies to all children whether they are physically disabled or not. Physical activity must be pleasurable if it is to stimulate progress. The programme constructed for Robert included opportunities for experiencing a sense of achievement, physical development, fitness, motor skill, social development and current work in other curriculum areas.

One of the major considerations in the construction of a programme of motor education for a physically disabled child is that allowances must be made for the rate at which children develop. Unfortunately, many children with cerebral palsy like Robert, come to school with a low level of developmental motor functioning. It is vital therefore that learning about general body management and manipulation skills (related to game playing) should begin as early as possible so that a foundation is laid on which to build future recreational competence.

Robert's exposure to the experience and the practice provided in his motor programme will hopefully encourage him to develop an understanding of his ability so that he can work out for himself a method of performing movement tasks.

*Programme activities*

My first task was to list all of the activities which I felt would give Robert experience and practice in the areas in which he was having difficulty. A number of the activities would give Robert practice in more than one of these areas, others were more singular in their objectives. When this procedure was completed I grouped them under the following headings:

a. hand exercise
b. hand/ball control
c. throwing
d. transfer of objects
e. balance
f. foot control
g. muscle strengthening
h. balance games

As there is little space in this chapter for discussion of the content of the programme, I have given an example of activities within one area of the programme, that of balance. Improved balance was a factor for consideration in all the activities listed in the programme. No task was introduced without careful examination of the stability of Robert's position.

> Children's balancing skill can often be masked by lack of confidence. Assistance should be given at first, as well as much encouragement and praise, by the teacher or a partner.
>
> (Tansley 1980, p.30)

The examples given in Figure 5.2 are aimed at improving balance, co-ordination, manoeuvrability and confidence building, and can be done with the whole class.

*Social integration of children with cerebral palsy*

An essential aspect of PE is social interaction, but this level of functioning is often limited among disabled children. Such children often experience difficulty in sharing or co-operating and are unable to accept rules or defeat. The lack of clarity in Robert's speech affected his ability to engage in meaningful conversation with his peers – particularly in his own neighbourhood. Throughout the motor programme Robert would be encouraged to speak more slowly and clearly, particularly when excited. This difficulty could also be minimised by input from a speech therapist who could construct specific exercises which could be included in the programme of activities.

In addition to the motor programme I included a number of activities outside of the basic school curriculum which I felt would encourage practice of some skills which may be needed for future social interaction. A game of snooker, under the guidance of senior pupils, might exercise the use of Robert's right hand and also teach him to accept help and advice from others. Tricycle and scooter riding during the lunchtime break would give Robert a little extra practice in skills he wanted to improve upon.

Sherbourne (1989) suggests that younger children can progress when partnered by older children who in turn gain self-confidence and self-esteem. She believes that movement education helps to build these relationships, and her article includes a number of partner activities which contribute to 'the development of confidence and the experience of being successful and valued' (p.7). Brown (1987) points out that an additional advantage of

Figure 5.2 Example of activities to improve balance

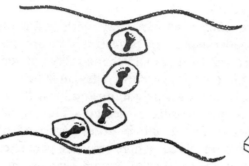

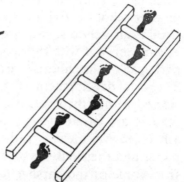

Stepping stone across the 'river'.

Walk between the ladder rungs.
Walk alongside the ladder with
feet apart.

In a soft play therapy room a
partner tries to shake Robert off
the half-moon. He has to keep his
balance.

such methods is the enthusiasm shown by older disabled children whom he claims 'are keen to offer their services to help in the teaching of skills to their younger colleagues, both in lessons and in after-school activities' (p.236).

Like all schools, we are concerned not only with academic attainment, but with the broader aspects of education. We are preparing all of the children we teach for life in a wider society outside. The social development of children with cerebral palsy must be considered within the context of their own neighbourhood. Ordinary schools are often viewed as microcosms of society. The special school environment is rather different and is often perceived by pupils and their parents as a 'safe island' where they are protected from some of the harsher realities of life. As teachers we are in a position to promote the building of valuable relationships between pupils, but there must be a degree of co-ordination with parents so that the child is encouraged to extend these friendships to include children from ordinary schools within the neighbourhood.

## Implementing the programme

A number of factors required careful consideration before Robert's programme could be implemented. Although my programme for him was an individual one I did not intend it to be carried out in isolation. It was to be introduced in the weekly PE sessions. It was envisaged that future programmes for other pupils would also be included in the existing timetable in this way. All available resources would be utilised and nursery nurses, auxiliaries and work experience students could be trained to oversee the performance of programme activities. The implementation of Robert's individual motor programme was to be a 'pilot' exercise, and until it was under way there would be many questions that would remain unanswered. How long would the programme run? How many times would the elements of the programme need practising? Were all of the activities contained in the programme appropriate? Would Robert improve? There was no way of knowing the answers until I had monitored and assessed Robert's progress.

## Conclusion

One of the benefits of this kind of investigation is the broadening of the researcher's experience and the enhancement of personal learning. I had become very close to the children I had been studying and my relationship with them, two years later, remains important to me. Also, since the research I still watch and learn. I believe my observational skills have improved and that this has enhanced my ability to assess the children in my care, and to anticipate and therefore alleviate some of the difficulties they may experience.

The research helped me to view my own teaching context from other people's perspectives, improved communications between various groups and enabled me to benefit from the expertise of others. I gained an increased understanding of parents' views of their children's disabilities and the effect of these on the homelife of both the children and their parents. This experience has led me to provide opportunities for parents to become more involved with the school and to improve communication channels between home and school. It has also encouraged me to go out into the community to meet parents in their own homes.

In an establishment where there is a multi-disciplinary approach to education, groups of employees see their roles in different ways. It seemed that, as a staff, we all suffered from the delusion that we knew what everyone else ought to be doing. The information gained on Robert initially often appeared to be conflicting, but this was due merely to differences of professional perspective and concerns. The research made very apparent the importance of our collective expertise if we are to give pupils the most appropriate care and education. The working relationships between members of a multi-disciplinary staff are vital factors in any plans for the development of the children's education. My existing knowledge and experience of specialist PE training was not adequate to allow me to work in isolation on the areas of a disabled child's motor education. I could not have designed an appropriate programme without the additional expertise of the school physiotherapist, the advice of the school nursing sister and speech therapist and the co-operation of willing parents. One of the major unintended outcomes of the research was the way in which it served as a catalyst for co-operation between the various professional staff involved with the children and generated interdisciplinary discussions which often extended into other aspects of our work and school life.

104

# References

Bell, J. (1987) *Doing Your Research Project*. Milton Keynes: Open University Press.

Bleck, E.E. (1975) 'Cerebral palsy', in Bleck, E.E. and Nagel D.A. (eds) *Physically Handicapped Children. A Medical Atlas for Teachers*. London; Grune and Stratton.

Bobath, B. (1985) *Motor Development in the Different Types of Cerebral Palsy*. London: Heinemann.

Brown, A. (1987) *Active Games for Children with Movement Problems*. London: Harper and Row.

Donlon, E.T. and Burton, L.F. (1976) *The Severely and Profoundly Handicapped. A Practical Approach to Teaching*. London: Grune and Stratton.

Hardy, J.C. (1983) *Cerebral Palsy*. Englewood Cliffs NJ: Prentice Hall.

Levitt, S. (1985) *Treatment of Cerebral Palsy and Motor Delay*. Oxford: Blackwell.

Sherbourne, V. (1989) 'Building relationships through movement'. *Special Children* 29, 7–8.

Tansley, A.E. (1980) *Motor Education*. Leeds: Arnold-Wheaton.

# CHAPTER 6

# *Parental Perceptions of the Professionals Involved with Children with Special Educational Needs*

Kathleen Murphy

Three colleagues and I wanted to address the issues of how the Educational Support Service (ESS), in which we worked, was seen by others. We also wanted to attempt some evaluation of how effective we were at supporting children with special educational needs in ordinary schools. It was hoped that such research would influence future decisions on LEA policy towards giving information and opening more channels of communication for parents within the Authority. The ESS is based in three regions, each with an Area Head, a Support Teacher and a number of Resource Teachers. In addition, there are specialist teachers, such as for the visually or the hearing impaired, who teach throughout the LEA.

It seemed to us that an ideal opportunity to gain the insights we needed was to embark on the University of York Outstation MA Course. It was ideal in that it required a team-based study in which each member was expected to pursue their individual pieces of research, linked to a common theme. One member looked at the perceptions of professionals from other agencies with whom we were involved, such as educational psychologists, medics and officers of the LEA. Another member sought the perspectives of the staff of some of the schools in which we worked. The third asked members of the Service for their own views of our functioning, and I sought the perceptions of parents. The Warnock Report (1978) and DES (1973) Circular 1/83 had emphasised 'parents as partners'. It recommended that parents should be seen as equal partners in the educational process of their children, alongside those professionals involved. I thought

105

it would be of value for one of us to try to discover how parents viewed this 'partnership' and therefore I chose to examine parental perceptions of the ESS.

The ESS was formed primarily to support the integration of children with special educational needs into ordinary schools. One of the main thrusts of the Service was to work closely with parents and other professionals. Part of the support work involved contacting parents of children who were about to begin the process of Formal Assessment, delivering the notice to assess and making regular follow-up visits to ensure that parents were kept up to date. Consequently, I sought to find out how much parents understood about the processes involved in Formal Assessment and the Annual Review of Statement. ESS members were also available to discuss problems and involve parents in the learning programmes for their children, if appropriate.

## Methodology

### The pilot study

I was asked by the university to conduct a pilot study mainly (so I thought) to practise techniques and check that questions were relevant. However, it became more than just an exercise imposed upon me. It proved vital in identifying the main concerns felt by parents and helped me to focus in on what they considered, rather than what I thought, were the relevant issues.

During the pilot study I attempted to focus the attention of parents on the role of the ESS, discover what they felt about the Service and discuss their understanding of 'special educational need'. I quickly found out that parents were unable to comment on all the aspects of the Service which I had identified. All parents expressed their concerns regarding lack of communication, but with a variety of professionals, rather than the ESS in particular. None had any knowledge of the role of the ESS in schools or of its connection with other professionals. Comments on special educational need were confined to their own children beyond whom they were unable to generalise.

I must admit that I initially panicked before I realised that refocusing was necessary. What I decided to look at in my main research was the parental perceptions of all professionals with whom parents came into contact, including the ESS, specifically related to the theme of 'communication'. The pilot study was therefore extremely useful as it demonstrated the direction the main research could take.

## Interviewing

It seemed that interviewing was the most appropriate way of collecting data. I realised I would not gain the feelings of closeness and rapport with parents if I was to request their expressions and concerns through the more impersonal approach of questionnaire. I was aware that this particular group, out of all the groups interviewed by our team, needed most encouragement and personal contact. The other groups were all professionals of various types, perhaps more used to arguing a case and being asked for their opinions. As communication, or lack of it, clearly emerged as an important issue I felt it would be beneficial for both the research and the ESS if information was collected through face to face contact. Later, I felt justified in the choice of interviewing as a method of gathering data, even though conducting and transcribing the data involved far more time and effort than I originally envisaged.

The constraint of insufficient time to handle large amounts of data and still meet the deadlines set limited the number of parents that I could include in the research. Three samples of parents were chosen to provide an overview of the three geographical areas into which the ESS was divided. Each sample contained the parents of three children with learning difficulties and one child with a visual impairment in ordinary schools, one child with a language disorder who was educated in a special unit attached to an ordinary school, and, in two of the areas, one child with learning difficulties in a unit and, in the third area, a child with hearing difficulties in an ordinary school. Seven of the 18 selected children were the subject of a Statement or close to the end of the process of Formal Assessment.

Of the 18 interviews conducted in the first round, there were 11 interviews where there were mothers only, three where there were fathers only and four where both parents were present. All except one father were interviewed in their own home, the one exception being conducted at the Education Office at the request of the parent. Six parents participated in follow-up interviews where I sought more in-depth information on communication issues.

Initially I introduced myself to some parents by telephone. However, I was informed by other Service members that this was causing unforeseen stress when parents became worried and concerned about being contacted by 'someone from the education department' whom they did not know. To reduce this stress, contact was then made through each ESS member who worked with, or who knew, particular parents. Parents were each given a brief letter, explaining who I was and what the research was for and that I would be in touch with them. I was indebted to the members for this help, but as they all had busy schedules some delay was caused in the timing of the interviews. Contact involved telephone calls, letters and home visits. In some cases the members kindly arranged initial interview dates. I was aware that there was little control as to how these requests were presented and that as a consequence, some parents may have had perceptions influenced by Service members. One parent telephoned one of my colleagues whom she knew to ask what she should say in the pending interview! It was emphasised to parents that they were under no obligation to either the researcher or the LEA to be interviewed, and that they could refuse if they wished to do so. In the event, none did.

The pilot study made me aware that the interviews would have to be handled as sensitively as possible, as there was a great deal of suppressed anger directed at certain professionals which had surfaced during these earlier sessions. I tried to keep a low profile, particularly in not over reacting or projecting any of my own feelings. Every parent had an initial interview in which the same open-ended questions were asked. I took care not to be too directive. The second group of interviews focused on issues which emerged from the first round and were, by necessity, more structured than the first. Sixteen of the 18 allowed me to tape record, and the interviews lasted between 30 and 40 minutes each. I attemped to take notes while the interviews took place, but in the end I found this to be obtrusive, reflecting my inexperience as an interviewer.

Tape recording the interviews had several advantages. I could play them back as often as I needed so that I did not have to rely on memory or being a fast writer. Keeping this in mind allowed me to relax and concentrate more on putting the parents at their ease. Taping also enabled me to spot some unforeseen themes during analysis. It proved useful in reminding me of issues which I later used to form questions for the second round of interviews.

Luckily, there were no major problems encountered in using this method of recording data.

I began each interview by asking parents to talk about their children and to explain any problems or difficulties they had with learning. This 'lead in' in most cases dictated the format and order in which the data were presented, in that parents gave an almost biographical history. These 'histories' usually began with their first contacts with professionals in the Health Service and later, their meetings with workers in Education.

## Data analysis

On reflection I found data analysis to be harder work than conducting the interviews. I needed a lot more space for storing data than I had envisaged. I spent a great deal of time preventing the rest of my family walking off with my treasured marker pens and unusually large pieces of paper! I decided that the first part of the analysis should involve a full transcript of each interview. These transcriptions were then transferred to larger sheets of paper which I then pinned up on the wall, enabling me to scan across all the interviews. This process was extremely time-consuming (and probably quite a clumsy method) but it gave me a much clearer picture.

I highlighted issues relating to the concerns that I had identified with coloured marker pens. Issues which were new or not previously identified were then simpler to spot. After this physical effort, further analysis appeared easy. The main issue which emerged interview after interview was that of 'communication'. This made me wary and perhaps contributed to my continual checking and rechecking for unforeseen issues. Common perceptions on communication were sought and placed under headings and those which were positive or negative were also highlighted.

Secondary issues began to emerge when I discovered a few comments which were inconsistent with other perceptions. These concerned parental views on 'integration' and further feelings relating to the difficulties involved in the Formal Assessment process. Again I grouped these 'secondary' issues to identify their common points. I then rechecked the transcripts by reading them through again to ensure that other themes had not been overlooked. It was useful to allow a time gap between each readthrough as it was easy to become saturated in the material.

The other team members were asked to listen to the tapes which were replayed and cross checked with the full transcripts and the comments which had been drawn out and placed under the colour coded headings. Any notes made during interviews were also used.

The second round of interviews was conducted with six parents only. They were questioned in more depth about 'communication'. I realised that I was much more relaxed during these second interviews and I remembered to probe by asking more 'why' and 'what' questions. These second interviews were also transcribed, colour coded and rechecked. I looked for new categories within the data until no new or further information was forthcoming. The findings will now be discussed under two broad headings: communication problems and the process of statementing.

## Communication problems

Parents complained of a lack of information from professionals generally and of little opportunity to express their points of view regarding the needs of their own children. Professionals such as paediatricians, medical consultants, teachers and headteachers were those who drew emotive parental comment. Most parents viewed these professionals as fulfilling the role of the 'expert' in the worst sense, that is, deskilling was intentional. Most parents felt forced into a passive role during encounters, where professionals held the power by witholding desired information. When they could obtain such information it was handed to them on a piecemeal basis, thus not enabling inclusion in decision making and therefore not allowing them to be true 'partners'.

### Professionals involved in the Health Service

All parents who made comments on paediatricians and consultants in my Area Health Authority expressed concern about the quality of contact they received. Written reports were not made available to them. They were given little or no chance to enter into discussion. Access to information relied solely on parental confidence in asking questions. Even parents who managed to do this, however, received little or no response. They resolved not to attempt this method of obtaining information from this group of professionals in the future.

Parents felt that: they were not listened to and their views were not taken into account; they were inadequately informed regarding the diagnosis or prognosis of their children's conditions; and, if they were given information, it was in a blunt and insensitive manner. One parent said: 'Even if I ask something he [paediatrician] never really answers me. We got nowhere really, he wasn't positive or helpful in any way and he hardly even addressed me'. Thomas (1982) described this situation as, 'an uneven balance of power' where the professionals, because they are seen as experts, have the authority. The management of the parent/professional encounter is more often organised around the 'experts'' view of the child and the encounter based entirely on that assumption:

> The expert sets up his technical authority against the global experience of the parent who is often uniquely qualified as the world's only 'expert' on his or her child. Most typically, that expert knowledge is discounted.
>
> (1982, p.122)

This group of professionals engendered strong feelings of emotion and anger from many parents months or even years after contact. These consultations were remembered quite clearly and one parent felt she 'could never forgive Dr ... for the way he treated me' and that she would 'never forget'.

## The Education Support Service

Parents were generally confused about the existence of the Service, its name, its role in schools and its connection with other agencies. Some parents saw us as being teachers. Others thought we were psychologists. Most were unsure of our connections with other professionals involved in education, realising we were not part of schools but that we visited them and sometimes saw their children there. Many thought we had power to dictate to the schools how their children should be educated.

As in the case of the other professionals, parents saw communication as being most important. They mentioned 'listening', 'help at home', 'giving information' and 'feedback' in describing what benefits they were receiving from the Service. Many parents reported that it was only when there had been Support Service intervention that they felt they knew what was happening to their children in school. Nearly all the parents had been pleased with this intervention, especially the home visits. These visits allowed them the opportunity to discuss their child's problems with someone whom they saw as having little or no connection with the schools, and who was therefore perceived as impartial. Parents were also more confident as they were on their own 'territory'.

Parents were positive about the way in which the Support Service provided a link between home and school by listening, and then responding by providing information or action. They perceived that they had the opportunity to be listened to and be involved with their child's programmes of work. It appeared that parents had very few negative comments to make on the ESS. Whether this was really so or whether they found it difficult to make any criticism when they were face to face with a Service member was not clear.

Most schools offer a booklet to parents containing information on staff, curriculum and approaches to special needs among other information. One of the suggestions I made at the end of my study was that ESS should do likewise and offer parents structured information on its function and relationship to other services.

*Schools and units*

In order to provide alternative situations in which to examine communication between parents and professionals, I deliberately selected the parents of children attending both schools and units. The schools were ordinary primary schools and the units consisted of one for children with learning difficulties and one for language disorders.

Most of the parents expressed difficulties regarding communication with staff in schools. Parents saw major barriers to good communication as:

1) lack of opportunity to talk to staff;
2) inability to discover the nature and details of their children's problems in school;
3) little information on strategies being used to help their children;
4) being labelled as 'fussy' and 'overprotective' when attempting to seek such information.

Most parents talked of difficulties regarding communication with their children's schools. A typical comment was:

> For me it would be interesting to know what they [the staff] were doing with him [the child] really. I'd like to know what they were doing but I can never talk to them.

I found that only four parents felt any encouragement to view themselves as 'partners' by staff in ordinary schools. These four parents perceived that schools were able to offer them good communication. All four agreed to the criteria for positive communication:

1) opportunities to build up relationships with school staff;
2) staff allowing time to listen to their views;
3) feeling involved in what was happening in school.

These four parents were content with the communication with their children's schools because they felt involved with what was happening and perceived that they were listened to and their views taken into account. One parent said that 'the school have been great all along ... the headteacher is good at listening'. Another commented 'I've a strong relationship with them. It's excellent − I can wander in and out at any time and [I'm] made welcome'.

Cyster *et al.* (1979) found that some parents in their study were grateful for the opportunity to see teachers when they collected their children from school, particularly when they had something to discuss. I found that few parents actually took advantage of formal contact. The reasons for this included difficulties experienced by the parents when they had to express what they wanted to say in a given time limit and 'feeling awkward' discussing their children when other parents were present. The information which parents so consistently required, but felt that they were not obtaining, was specific to their own children's progress and ways to assist them with their school work. They did not question the general curriculum, nor school management.

Implicit in the parental perceptions in this study was the belief that teachers and headteachers did not want increased parental contact, other than what was an administrative necessity. Where whole school policies of parental contact had been planned and developed, such as in the units, and parents made aware of strategies being attempted to help their children, positive relationships emerged.

It might be assumed that contact with the parents of the children in the units would present greater difficulty as the children were all bussed there. This constraint had been recognised by the staff in both units. However, they had adopted a specific policy to achieve effective liaison with parents. Comments from parents suggested that the units were more successful than schools in developing and maintaining communication. One parent said:

> I've got all the contact I want. I know for a fact that if I've any problems, I've only to ask [teacher] or speech therapy, and they'll come here. I can ring or send a message with the bus.

While opportunity for informal contact with the units may have been difficult for parents, the positive elements of a home/school diary and messages sent via bus escorts seemed to overcome most of the problems with physical inaccessibility.

All parents felt that they were included and informed of what was happening with their children and that they could easily initiate contact with staff. One parent was relieved to have her child bring work home so that she knew 'steps were being taken to help him' after his move into the unit. This mother had realised her child was having problems at his previous ordinary school but she had obtained little feedback and concluded he could not be receiving much help. She was aware that even when he was at the unit, his progress was still very slow. However, because she felt informed, both mother and child could cope.

It could be argued that involving parents was much easier for the units than the schools because of a number of factors: the units enjoyed a high staff/pupil ratio while teachers in the schools were dealing with much larger numbers single handedly; staff in the units were used to working in a multi-disciplinary setting; the units were staffed by experienced teachers of children with special needs; staff at the units had a background of working and co-operating with parents; and unit staff viewed parental involvement as vital in assisting their pupils' learning.

## The process of Statementing

Formal Assessment is conducted to establish if a child has special educational needs and to identify the nature of these needs. The assessment is carried out by professionals and is a statutory duty for each LEA under the 1981 Education Act. One of the main points in the 1981 Act was the involvement of parents in this process, as they are specifically requested to write comments and are allowed opportunity to read all other written comments submitted about their child. The result of Formal Assessment is usually a 'Statement' which outlines the needs of the child and the provision that the LEA will make to meet these needs. The Statement is then binding by law and reviewed on an annual basis.

In the second-round interviews I questioned parents further on their understanding and responses to the processes involved in Formal Assessment and Statementing. All six had children who were either in the process of being Statemented or who were already the subject of Statements.

The data showed that, because of lack of information, these parents were largely unfamiliar with the procedures and terminology, and were therefore unable to participate in any shared decision making. The DES Circular 1/83, in its outline on information for LEAs regarding information for parents, provided minimal guidance. It did, however, emphasise that it was the duty of LEAs to ensure that information on Statementing, and especially notices to assess, were in a language with which parents were familiar.

Parents were only informed on a piecemeal basis regarding the different stages of the process in letter form. Other information was passed on verbally, as the LEA relied solely on volunteer groups. Similar methods were used by other LEAs, as outlined by Rogers (1986) in a survey for the Centre of Studies on Integration in Education. At the time of this research my LEA had no published information about Formal Assessment available for parents of ethnic minorities.

### Statementing

The research revealed that:

1) Two parents did not understand the term 'Statement' and were confused regarding the written documentation they should have received from the LEA.
2) Four parents said they knew what a Statement was. Of these:
   - one parent was vague in his description and failed to expand any definition;
   - two parents mentioned either assessment of needs and provision, but not the two together;

- the other parent only mentioned Statementing in terms of the assessment of the needs of her child.

Four parents had received or were in the process of receiving the draft Statement and two parents were unsure as to whether they had received it or not. Two parents were in possession of a full (completed) Statement and their children placed accordingly in the school recommended by the LEA. None of the six parents could give a complete definition of a Statement and yet they had all agreed to the process of Formal Assessment which would take away their right to choice of school and become binding by law.

In another study, Sandow and Stafford also found that parents were uninformed:

> They [the parents] had remarkably little knowledge of the 1981 Act ... it was surprising that parents seemed to know so little, especially as all had recently had a child assessed under the Act.

> (1986, p.21)

### Named Person

The LEA did not have a 'Named Person' in the Warnock Report's sense of 'adviser and counsellor' for parents who would listen to their difficulties, provide information and seek to render their situations less stressful. However, parents had the opportunity to contact an administrative assistant, who dealt with queries relating to Formal Assessment, alongside her other heavy workload.

Not one of the six parents had any concept of the role of Named Person. Yet parents desired more information from 'a person who I can contact and speak to when I need help'. Their comments included:

- They've got to listen and understand your side of it; also they should be there to advise you on what's best and keep you informed.
- There should be people or a person who will listen to you, more than just once, to what you think and help you cope with all this jargon you meet.
- This person must be a good listener with lots of experience with working with families of this type of child. It should

be somebody who has your interests at heart not just the Authority's.

The lack of such information led to feelings of stress and concern. One parent commented on the fact that she had no one to refer to when the assessment process got underway. She said:

> We could do with somebody coming in the home and to talk to you about it ... We don't want to be sat in someone's office trying to take notes on what to do, or on the phone, when you don't know the in's and out's of it.

Sandow and Stafford found very few parents had received help in making sense of the procedures in their study:

> [Parents] were asked if anyone explained the procedures involved in deciding what the child's needs might be in the future. Thirty-six (69%) said no-one had explained this to them.
>
> (1986, p.21)

## Parental advice

The writing of their advice for Formal Assessment caused general confusion and, for one parent, particular difficulty. Where parents had submitted advice to the Authority it was evident that they had received help from individual ESS members, who were able to provide information about Statementing and also able to answer questions in parents' own homes.

I was aware that three of the six parents had not submitted any advice at all. One parent believed that advice could be written at any time and therefore she had not contributed until she felt she had something to say. She was not aware that it was vital that she should send in her advice if she had strong feelings about her child's future school placement. Advice to parents is crucial as it assists them to make mutually satisfactory decisions regarding future schooling. She said:

> I'm happy with where he is now [a special school] but as soon as he makes any progress I will write some advice to say that I want him moved into ordinary school.

The precise reasons why the other two parents did not submit their advice was not as clear. However, it was evident that these parents were unsure of the whole procedure and it was not through lack of interest or concern regarding how their children were supported with their learning difficulties or their future education.

*Annual Review*

Statements are reviewed annually by law when professionals who are involved with the child are asked to comment on the child's progress and both the appropriateness of placement and resources are checked. My LEA requests details of objectives for the child for the coming year, both short and longer term, and a detailed account of current functioning from the school and the ESS. This is seen as a process of continuous assessment and parents are usually invited to a Review meeting when the Annual Review form has been completed. These meetings are held in the child's school (although not all schools hold such meetings) and parents are requested to read the form, sign and comment if necessary.

Three parents said they knew about the Annual Review, but when asked to expand only one could give a definition. This was:

> I know that they [LEA] have to look at the statement on an annual basis to see if everything's OK. They'll check to see if she needs any more, em ... resources in the future.

The other two parents said that they had 'heard of' the term Annual Review; one said she 'had read up on it' but had forgotten, and the other said he had forgotten. Parents were similarly vague regarding Rights of Appeal.

Although parents did not make direct reference to having difficulties with jargon, which they encountered either in written information or in draft and full statements, it was clear from my interviews that they were obviously unsure of many of the terms used in the process of Formal Assessment. Cranwell and Miller (1987) in their study found parents frequently misunderstood such terms as 'self-image' and 'cognitive development'. The term 'auditory' was misunderstood 80 per cent of the time. Parents attempted to guess at their meaning rather than admit to not understanding and risk ridicule. Their findings led them to make suggestions and recommendations for written reports. These included: a glossary of terms; use of no more words than necessary; words with a high risk of misunderstanding to be omitted and if technical terminology was unavoidable, it should be directly related to the performance of the child and explanations given.

Hughes and Carpenter (1991) point out that Annual Review meetings are an ideal forum for parental contributions to be heard. However, most schools in my LEA seem to pay only lipservice to these recommendations in that parents are generally invited to meetings, but their views are often just added on at the end rather than being encompassed as an essential part of the review process. Hughes and Carpenter further note that such meetings are often dominated by professionals and any partnership is far from equal:

> Parents perceived the Annual Review meetings as dominated by professionals and, therefore, found them somewhat daunting ... The parents were relegated to a role of listening and responding while each professional submitted and summarised a report on their child. Consequently the parents' contribution to the meeting was not equivalent to that of the professionals.
>
> (1991, p.212)

In her study Wolfendale (1988) found that there were parents who saw little point in bothering to submit any views because they felt the professionals' reports would always be considered to be paramount. It is clear that unless parents genuinely feel involved in making decisions and observe outcomes of this participation, this response will continue.

Two aspects emerged from the data which I had not taken into account when framing my questions. These were, firstly, the length of time it was taking the LEA to complete a Statement and, secondly, parental feelings on integration. Parents made comments about the long duration of Formal Assessment and expressed particular concern that any advice submitted was becoming out of date by the time the Statement was written. Other comments were made about the LEA not contacting them to keep them abreast of the process. Five of the six mentioned integration. Four were strongly in favour of ordinary schools for their children and saw the role of the peer group as being important. Only one parent desired special education and saw this as giving her child more teacher contact time and extra resourcing.

## Conclusion

Several major points emerged about parental views of their contact with professionals. Parents:

1. felt strongly that they were not receiving enough information regarding their children's problems;
2. perceived that there were few channels of communication available for them to facilitate the exchange of opinion and to pass on feelings to professionals;
3. wanted easier access to professionals and more contact time;
4. wanted professionals to listen to them and take their views seriously;
5. required strategies from professionals on how best to aid their children at home;
6. wanted help to deal effectively with Formal Assessment and have more opportunities for discussion arising from this process with professionals.

I agree with Wright (1989) when he argues that the whole notion of 'partnership' between parents and professionals can be seen as 'unrealistic'. Parents cannot be said to be partners if information and the means to make sense of unfamiliar terminology are denied to them. Although the Warnock Report and Circular 1/83 (DES, 1973) had promoted equal partnership, they were vague regarding parental rights in practical terms.

There are more recent educational issues for which parents will need information. The National Curriculum, national testing and Local Management of Schools (LMS) may well affect LEA Assessment and Statementing procedures. LMS could prove to be a threat to the inclusion of children with special needs within delegated school budgets. Statements may include modifications and disapplication from the National Curriculum. Services such as the ESS still remain centrally funded but as LEA are looking to reduce spending wherever possible, the future of support services must be seen as unsure.

When I conducted my research, there were few opportunities available in my LEA to aid parents to acquire information about the issues discussed in this chapter. The mid-1970s saw the spread of the Portage scheme which involved Portage workers supporting parents of children with special needs in their homes and involving families in selecting their own goals for the child. Since my research such a scheme has been introduced into my Authority. One of the main aspects of the scheme is the 'key-worker' who is responsible, among other duties, for managing the transfer of relevant information between families and different networks of professionals. This person can be particularly valuable to parents as Silverman and Stacey point out:

> The advocacy role of the visitor was much appreciated. This was especially true where a family felt their child was not being assessed accurately in the clinical context or where they felt powerless and alienated from the system.
>
> (1989, p.19)

Also, at present there is a team of teachers who are connected to the ESS and who work in a similar way to Portage in that their primary focus is on pre-school children, except that they work with children who are developmentally delayed for various reasons and who may or may not require Formal Assessment. These professionals are potentially a great source of support to the family in general with their wide experience of teaching, working with parents and knowledge of Authority procedures.

For more general support, parents have had to look to a voluntary group called 'Network 81' which exists specifically to help them deal with Formal Assessment. This group was set up and is run by a parent of a child with a Statement within the LEA. Included in the support is help with writing advice and general queries. The group also offers home visits and a 'listening ear' outside office hours. Most importantly, perhaps, it holds up-to-date information on LEA procedures on Statementing and integration. It is more and more taking on the role of 'Named Person'.

Formal information channels may now be enforced through LEAs being directed by the 1989 Children Act and Circular 22/89 (DES, 1989) which among other changes strongly recommend parental and, 'wherever practicable', child attendance at meetings where children will be discussed. This includes Annual Review meetings where their 'attendance' should 'be encouraged' and the views of the parents 'should be included in formulating the outcome of the review'. An ESS Handbook was eventually produced specifically for parents, mainly in response to DES Circular 22/89 and not, I feel, much to do with the results of my study! (Although I know it has been read by officers of the Authority.)

Circular 22/89 directed LEAs to use:

> straightforward language ... and include names and telephone numbers of the various staff with whom discussions can be

122

held during the assessment process ... They should make leaflets
available in other languages for ethnic groups.

(DES, 1989, p.8)

These recommendations were included and the handbook also
attempted to outline the Formal Assessment process, describe the
structure and work of the ESS as well as other services parents might
encounter. It is a recognition that parents as well as professionals
needed written guidelines to help them with the composition of their
advice and other vital information. The handbook is currently in the
process of being updated and improved and I have been asked to be
involved in helping to rewrite it. I now know that one of the most
effective ways of finding out what type of information parents
require is to ask parents themselves. Carrying out the interviews
provided a chance for parents to put forward their views and
taught me both how to listen and how to ask relevant questions.
Perhaps this will be the start of more research on my part!

## References

Adams, F. (ed) (1986) *Special Education*. Harlow: Councils and Education Press.
Bond, G. (1973) *Parent-Teacher Partnership*. London: Evans Brothers.
Cranwell, D. and Miller, A. (1987) 'Do parents understand professionals? Termi-
nology in Statements of Special Educational Need'. *Educational Psychology in
Practice* 3, 27–32.
Cyster, R., Clift, P.S. and Battle, S. (1979) *Parental Involvement in Primary
Schools*. Slough: NFER.
Department of Education and Science (1973) *Assessment and Statementing of
Special Educational Need*, Circular 1/83. London: HMSO.
Department of Education and Science (1978) *Special Educational Needs: Report
of the Committee of Enquiry into the Education of Handicapped Children and
Young People*. London: HMSO.
Department of Education and Science (1989) *Assessments and Statements of Special
Educational Needs: Procedures Within the Education, Health and Social Services*,
Circular 22/89. London: HMSO.
Hughes, N. and Carpenter, B. (1991) 'Annual Reviews: an active partnership' in
Ashdown, R., Carpenter, B. and Bovair, K. (eds) *The Curriculum Challenge:
Access to the National Curriculum for Pupils with Learning Difficulties*. London:
Falmer Press.
Rogers, R. (1986) *Caught in the Act: What LEAs Tell Parents under the 1981
Education Act*. London: Spastics Society.
Russell, P. (1983) *The Education Act 1981 – The Role of the Named Person*.
London: Voluntary Council for Handicapped Children.
Sandow, S.A. and Stafford, P. (1986) 'Parental perceptions of the 1981 Education
Act'. *British Journal of Special Education: Research Supplement* 13, 19–21.
Silverman, D. and Stacey, M. (1989) 'Listen to the parents'. *Special Children*
27, 18–19.
Thomas, D. (1982) *The Experience of Handicap*. London: Methuen.
Wolfendale, S. (1988) *The Parental Contribution to Assessment*. Stratford-upon-
Avon: National Council for Special Education.
Woods, P. (1986) *Inside Schools*. London: Routledge.
Wright, J. (1989) 'New Circular – New Rights'. *Special Children* 33, 17–19.

# CHAPTER 7

# *Meeting Individual Needs in the Classroom in a Comprehensive School*

Thomas Farrell

> There may be every willingness on the part of teachers to go along with the aims of integration. Those same teachers, though, are the people who are in the best position to know that the high ideals underpinning the growth of integration will not easily be realised.
>
> (Thomas, 1986, p.19)

## Amalgamating schools: the research context

The view from the staffroom window of Livingstone Comprehensive School was dramatic. Beyond the playing fields the skyline was punctuated by cranes and chimneys and the unmistakable silhouettes of the blast furnaces. But closer inspection revealed an anomaly. The dust, the noise, and most of all, the smoke was missing. A walk over the school fields and across the main road took the observer into an area of old housing built up around 'the Works'. The streets of brick-built terraced houses had an air of dereliction, the boarded-up windows and the broken glass in the streets served to remind the observer that the skilled workforce that manned the steelyards and the docks had moved out as the heavy industries declined.

Redevelopment was taking place. Interiors were being ripped out and central heating and double glazing installed but the skilled and the enterprising had moved out to find work elsewhere, and those being re-housed in the converted terraces lacked both employment and hope. On the other side of the school there were some large, more modern, council housing estates and some small private housing developments. The whole of the area was served by three comprehensive schools which competed for the output of eleven primary schools.

Livingstone School (LCS) was a comprehensive school with a staff of 50 full-time staff and 650 pupils on roll. It had a reputation in the neighbourhood as a very caring school and, though its examination results were comparable with the other two comprehensive schools in the area, the local folklore painted an image of a non-academic institution.

Grenfell School was a school for pupils with moderate learning difficulties situated in the same neighbourhood as LCS. It was a small school with a good reputation of success. Each teacher had responsibility for a single class, as in a primary school, and this provided a secure and protected environment for the pupils who, in the main, had learning difficulties often combined with social/behavioural problems.

The proposed closure of Grenfell and the suggestion that the staff and pupils of Grenfell be transferred to Livingstone met with a mixed reception from the staff at Livingstone School. Some staff welcomed the suggestion as a possible solution to our falling roll problem; others were concerned that if Livingstone were to become known as a school for slow learners, it would worsen the parental choice situation and our numbers would fall away.

The merger took place in stages. In September 1986 two classes of statemented pupils from Grenfell joined the school, each with its own support teacher. In each of the subsequent years, the pupils who would previously have been sent to Grenfell School were redirected to Livingstone. The staff of Grenfell School were not amalgamated with the staff of Livingstone but came under the management of a Local Area Learning Difficulties Service which, whilst based in Livingstone School, had its own management structure and provided support teachers to two other local schools.

By the time the Grenfell building was closed in 1988 the problems of integration had become very apparent. The least of these problems was the mixing of the Livingstone and Grenfell pupils, most of whom played together in the streets daily. The main difficulties were being faced by the staff.

During the first year of the integration, only a few of the Livingstone teachers were involved in teaching the statemented pupils and these had been selected because they were thought to be sympathetic to the integration. By the time of the closure of Grenfell school, almost all the Livingstone teachers had some of these pupils on their timetables and the teaching problems were very apparent.

The statemented pupils within each year group were kept together as a group and were joined by a number of non-statemented pupils with learning difficulties to make a group of about twelve pupils. Most of the staff agreed that the non-statemented pupils had very similar learning difficulties to the Grenfell pupils, though with fewer behavioural problems. (It is interesting to speculate whether these pupils had avoided statementing by means of their superior social skills.) This group followed the same timetable as the rest of the year group.

Support teachers were attached to these groups and they accompanied the groups to all lessons. Each of these groups (two in year 9, one in each of years 8 and 7) had a permanent support teacher allocated. However, in order that the support teachers should have some non-contact time, some mainstream teachers were used in the support role.

Most teachers found these groups difficult to teach. The pupils appeared 'very fussy', they squabbled with each other, there were arguments, fights, temper tantrums and fits. The class teachers were, in the main, experienced teachers who found this kind of disruption to be quite threatening to their status. The teachers had all, at sometime in their careers, coped with this kind of classroom management situation, but this was an entirely new challenge. What was different was, firstly, the volume of the disruption and, secondly, the failure of the teachers' tried and tested strategies for coping with these difficulties.

The teachers were used to pupils reacting more or less immediately to instructions or reprimands. The pupils with special educational needs responded, however, with a sullen silence. When pressed further by the teacher they reacted, typically, with aggression, swearing or violence. Frequently they ended up running out of the classroom, either to home or to hide somewhere in school. The disruptive behaviour was rarely confined to just one child or to one area of the classroom. Once a teacher's attention was diverted to deal with one incident, others would manifest themselves in different parts of the room, making the situation completely unmanageable.

Sometimes these incidents would happen in the corridors or the dining areas and were observed by many other pupils. Teachers worried that some pupils were being seen to get away with the worst kinds of disobedience and insolence and felt that they were losing credibility in the eyes of the whole school.

At the point at which the research started the presence of the support teacher in the classroom went largely unacknowledged by class teachers. Indeed, some would have preferred not to have had another teacher in the room. Perhaps the initial attitudes towards, and reluctance to approach, the support teachers also had their roots in the way that the school and the support service were managed separately. However, teachers were beginning to realise that they were not going to solve the problems on their own; that under these circumstances it was necessary to employ the expertise and experience of the support teachers.

The broad aim of this research project was to try to find out why the pupils were so disruptive and to see if effective teamwork in the classroom might improve the situation for all concerned.

The National Curriculum Council circular number 5 (1989) draws attention to the effect of the school environment on pupils' individual needs:

> Special educational needs are not just a reflection of pupils' inherent difficulties or disabilities; they are often related to factors within schools which can prevent or exacerbate some problems ... It follows from this that pupils with SEN should not be seen as a fixed group; their needs will vary over time and in response to school policies and teaching.
>
> (1989, Paragraph 5)

More forcibly Sayer argues:

> If schools are not organised to meet real needs, they will cause them. The school is either part of the solution or part of the problem.
>
> (1987, p.17)

If teachers can identify the factors which contribute to the needs mismatch within their classroom then they can evolve strategies which alleviate rather than aggravate the problems.

When looking for assistance in the literature I was much impressed by an article by Thomas (1986) which puts the issues involved in integration and support into the context of classroom management. This focused my enquiry on the factors in relation to the management of pupils in the classroom which either help to meet or to aggravate their individual needs. Thomas also suggested some models of classroom management when there are two teachers in the room and these were useful as a basis for starting discussion between support and class teachers in our school. The message from Thomas's examples was about sharing the workload, and hence the responsibility, between the two teachers. Another major influence, from my reading, was Galloway (1985), who argues convincingly that there is a strong link between classroom management styles and the classroom behaviour of pupils.

## Collecting the data

My interest was not only in what happened in the classroom, but, more importantly, why it happened. My approach to data collection was to observe some lessons using a tape recorder for the dialogue and keeping longhand notes of what I saw happening – movement, interactions etc. As soon as possible afterwards I interviewed the class teacher involved in the lesson. During the data collection period I also interviewed each of the four support teachers who had participated in the observed lessons. In this way I had the possibility of gaining three perspectives on the lessons.

It would probably have been illuminating to have collected some pupils' perspectives on what happens in the classrooms, but, with some regret, I decided against interviewing pupils or discussing classroom behaviour with them, out of a concern that it might have an adverse effect on their behaviour, or at least be thought to do so by members of staff.

In all, I observed twelve lessons, seeing each of the classes and their support teachers in several situations. Apart from two sessions which had to be rearranged because the teachers were away on courses, the observations took place as planned. I had a feeling that staff tried hard to keep to the timetable because they knew I was giving up my non-teaching time to do the observations.

In planning the study I examined some interaction analysis recording systems, such as those derived from the work of Flanders and listed in Delamont (1976), but decided not to use this kind of approach. I believed I could gain more insight into why things happened if I could discern some patterns in the pupils' behaviour and concentrate on these, to the exclusion of whatever else was happening.

I used a tape recorder to capture the dialogue and wrote notes on what I saw happening. One useful trick that I learned was that the use of a stereo recorder allowed me, when listening to the tapes, to fade out one channel to concentrate on what was happening in one area of the room.

The interviews were carried out on a semi-structured basis. I used the same list of questions for each of the interviews. The questions asked were not specific to the events of the lesson observed, but the teacher was encouraged, in the introduction to the interview, to use such events to illustrate their answers. One question, for example, was 'Can you tell me about any strategies which you believe can contribute to the success of a lesson?' The question was deliberately phrased in a positive way. However, several interviewees used it as an opportunity to talk about occasions when things had not gone well.

The interviews were all tape recorded, but I took longhand notes too. I discovered that, because I was slow in writing, the interviewee would fill any silences by giving additional or anecdotal information which was often of a very high quality for my purposes.

## Finding a route through the data

As the observations and interviews progressed, I found I was collecting a great deal of data, but at that stage, could discern no unifying theme. However, an incident which I observed in a year 9 lesson set me thinking about the data in a different way:

> About mid-way through the lesson, whilst the pupils were working quietly at some duplicated worksheets, Josie announced in an unnaturally loud voice, 'What's the date today?'. This was instantly taken as a challenge by another member of the group (Kelly) who, before the teacher had a chance to respond, answered in an equally aggressive manner 'It's the 24th, you stupid cow!'. There followed a short exchange between the two girls but this came to nothing. The incident passed quickly and the teacher was able to attract their attention back to the work.

What I found interesting was that the incident was little more than a formality. Both girls knew the pecking order of the group and knew that it was unlikely to change as a result of this 'testing of the water' episode. In a less settled group this could have developed into a very disruptive incident, with those on the sidelines taking the opportunity to maximise the disruption. In this case it was little more than a ritual, which everyone in the group knew was not going to lead anywhere. So I wondered, why did Josie make the effort?

The nature of the exchange rang some bells and set me off searching the data for something I had seen in a year 9 geography lesson:

> Alan was struggling with a piece of work which he was finding frustrating. Eventually he put down his pencil and announced 'This work is stupid!'. Instantly Marie responded 'It's you that's stupid'.

Once again there seemed to be little conviction in either of the two protagonists and the teacher easily restored peace. Near the end of the data collection I was to observe almost exactly the same exchange between Alan and Marie in one of my own lessons.

It began to dawn on me that what I had seen was what I will refer to as a 'vestigial activity'. That is, they were repeating an activity that at some time had been of importance, but was now unnecessary and had become mere ritual.

At this point I digress momentarily. As a member of the British Deer Society I have spent many years observing deer in the wild. An interesting activity amongst roe deer is that of 'fraying'. The roe buck re-grows his antlers every year. Initially the antlers are covered in velvet, but when they are fully grown the velvet dries out and becomes irritating to the animal. He finds a suitable sapling and rubs his antlers up and down against it until he has removed the irritating velvet. This may take several days and often results in serious damage to the tree. What is interesting is, that at times of stress (dogs or people in his wood), he will return to his fraying stock and repeat the activity which previously had given him relief.

It occurred to me that the vestigial activities I had observed in the classrooms might be analogous to the roe deer's fraying. Were the pupils repeating an activity which at one time had provided them with an escape from a stressful situation? As the pupils had become more secure in the school had this activity degenerated to ritual?

## Coping strategies

With these questions in mind, I searched the data for entries connected with stress. I found some interesting evidence in an English lesson:

> The pupils were using cartoon drawings to make up stories. Maria was not showing any interest in the work and was trying to distract

John. When it came to the time when each individual had to tell the story to the rest of the group Maria still showed no interest. When asked to tell her story she was embarrassed. She tried to make something up. She struggled. No one helped. 'It's pathetic' she said. The teacher thanked the class for their stories. Maria was upset.

According to her teachers, Maria has a very restricted vocabulary, so I wondered where she had learned to call her effort 'pathetic'.

It would appear from the comments of the teachers interviewed that the pupils who are the subject of this study are particularly sensitive to criticism. The music teacher said 'By the time they reach secondary school age, they have already had a taste of failure and know that they are not very clever compared with other pupils'. This view is supported by Holt:

> How is it possible for children of only ten to have such strongly developed concepts of themselves, and these unfavourable almost to the point of self contempt and hatred?
>
> (1964, p.54)

One interpretation of Maria's behaviour in this lesson is that she was simply being lazy and was embarrassed when she was caught out. Holt raises another possible interpretation: that Maria did not believe that she was capable of producing a presentable piece of work, so she did not try. Holt called this 'a strategy of incompetence' and explained:

> For after all, if they (meaning we) know you can't do anything, they won't expect you to do anything and they won't blame you or punish you for not being able to do what you have been told to do.
>
> (1964, p.68)

and

> Incompetence has one other advantage. Not only does it reduce what others expect of you, it reduces what you expect or even hope for yourself. When you set out to fail, one thing is certain − you can't be disappointed.
>
> (1964, p.68)

In Maria's case, was she prepared to accept the embarrassment of being thought lazy, in order to cover up the indignity of being only semi-literate? Of course, a single incident like this tells us very little. However, if there were a pattern of cover-up strategies, then we might be able to draw some conclusions about Maria's self image.

Holt believes that we underestimate the amount of stress that schools place on pupils. He goes as far as to compare the child in the classroom with the soldier suffering from shellshock on the battlefield:

> Many will reject this comparison as being wildly exaggerated and inappropriate. They are mistaken. There are very few pupils who do not feel, during most of the time they are in school, an amount of fear, anxiety and tension that most adults would find intolerable.
>
> (1964, p.72)

Perhaps Holt exaggerates the number of pupils and the amount of time they spend in fear, but his words must be true for some pupils much of the time and for many pupils some of the time. Take for example, Donna: Donna is a year 8 pupil, rather round and plump but not really oversized for her age. She dresses in an old-fashioned way. She smiles a lot, in a vacant sort of way, which is very misleading because in no way is she lacking in mental capacity. She smiles even when she is being reprimanded, which tends to make her teachers even more angry.

Donna's statement of Special Educational Needs, with which she entered our school, describes her problem as an inability or unwillingness to communicate. This is not strictly true; she communicates quite well, she just will not speak or write. Some teachers believe she cannot speak at all, yet I have seen her shouting at other pupils who have pushed in front of her in the dinner queue.

Donna is quite demanding in the classroom. She constantly 'asks' for help with her work, either by pointing, or when she cannot make herself understood, by whispering the odd word. Her work is generally immaculately presented, though usually limited to a few words. She 'asks' about every detail of how she should set it out and requires confirmation of its correctness at every stage; thus most of the work is done by the teacher for her. When the teacher has had enough and tells her it is time she did some work for herself, she wastes time for a while, and then turns to the support teacher and continues in the same fashion.

Donna is terrified of failure or of being made to look foolish. She says little, and she says it quietly, in case it is wrong. She worries about every entry that she makes in her book in case it is wrong. What she does produce is neat and accurate. In spite of a degree of spasticity in her movement (which gets her out of PE!) she is perfectly mobile. Yet she is brought to school every day in a taxi, paid for by the LEA, because she is not deemed capable of looking after herself. In fact she is looking after herself very well!

Donna can speak and she can write, so why does she employ these devious strategies? Holt writes:

> Strategy is an outgrowth of character. Children use the strategies they do because of the way they feel, the expectations they have of the universe, and the way they evaluate themselves, the classroom and the demands made on them.
>
> (1964, p.56)

So what causes pupils to react to school in this way? The forces which motivate such pupils must be very powerful indeed if they can influence their lives in such an all-consuming way.

## Self esteem

Mrs Pillar, a support teacher, told me:

> They have no idea of self worth. They are accustomed to failure. They need constant reassurance that they have some worth. They need to find, establish and maintain their position in the peer group hierarchy which they see as permanently under threat.

But why should a lack of success in school exert such enormous pressures on pupils? Whilst it is true that parents and teachers place great importance on schooling, is this sufficient to cause the terror which apparently drives these pupils? Mrs Pillar provided some illumination:

> The big problem is that they seem to equate performance in school subjects to performance as a person. They think that if they are no good at school then they are no good as human beings.

If this statement is an accurate assessment of the way the pupils feel, then it becomes possible to see why the fear of failure is so great. Every critical comment becomes a character assassination, a comment on their worth as a human being.

At this stage I returned to the data to look for evidence of low esteem in pupils. What I found was several instances of pupils 'scoring points off each other'. For example, in a science lesson I noted the following:

The pupils were copying notes from the blackboard. Allan asks the support teacher for some help because the bit he is copying from the roller board has been scrolled out of sight. Now another pupil, Tracey, asks the classteacher to pull the board back down because her friend, Nahdir, has fallen behind.

The classteacher asks, 'who is not yet finished?' and Tracey tells us that Nahdir isn't finished.

Gray and Richer (1988, p.16) point out that pupils whose self esteem is under threat often resort to highlighting weaknesses in others as a means of bolstering their own self image. The data yielded several similar items varying from the one quoted above to the simple 'Sir, Craig is chewing!'

Hanko discusses the difficulty this defensive system can create for the teacher who is trying to improve the behaviour or work habits of an individual pupil:

> The child's group of co-learners, however, may not wish him to change − a frequent cause of frustration for teachers, when their sensitive handling of an individual child is brought to nothing by the reactions of the group, which may oppose his improvement.
>
> (1985, p.72)

Thus Hanko suggests that not only do some pupils enhance their self image by pointing out the weaknesses of others, but that they may actively resist, as a group, efforts made towards improvement by any individual, if this is seen as a threat to the self esteem of the others.

Another indication of low esteem was the high incidence of 'attention seeking' noted in the observations. It is interesting that this kind of activity, which was most prevalent in the year 7 group, and still very apparent in year 8, had virtually disappeared by mid-way through year 9. Within any particular group of pupils the attention seeking activity was always most noticeable at the start of the lesson and tailed off in the second half.

An example from the data might serve to illustrate the kind of behaviour covered by the expression 'attention seeking'. This one comes from a year 7 drama lesson:

> The pupils came in and hung their coats on hooks, supervised by the teacher, who asked them to find seats as

quickly as possible because they were going to make a
video film.

The group were fussy. They hung around the teacher's desk,
asking questions, but not listening to the answers. I counted six
pupils demanding attention in this way.

In interview, after the lesson, the support teacher commented that
the pupils had been more unsettled than usual at the start of the
lesson. She thought it was because they had not made a video
before.

Gray and Richer quibble over the term 'attention seeking':

The teacher's perception that the pupil is attention seeking is
half right. He is seeking attention. The point is that the
anxious pupil is unable to use the attention, his behaviour
is impulsive and incomplete, which is disruptive and extremely
frustrating for the teacher. It is also a classic form of anxiety
based behaviour.

(1988, p.21)

It appears that the pupils arrive at each new lesson in a
state of apprehension. They are concerned that they may
be put into a situation which may embarrass them in
front of the others or which may threaten their view of
themselves.

It would seem, then, that the pupils are not seeking attention
in general, but a particular kind of attention. They are seeking
reassurance and approval. They wish to be reassured that they are
not going to be placed in embarrassing or threatening situations
during the coming lesson and they need to be reassured that
they have some worth in the eyes of the teachers. Perhaps the
teaching teams can pre-empt attention seeking by giving the pupils
the support they need.

## Pupil reactions

The pupil activities I have described so far are probably best
described as unconscious strategies, in that I do not believe that
they are premeditated, but are reactions to situations in which the
pupils find themselves. I would like to look now at some activities
of a more conscious nature. It would not be fair, really, to call these
strategies premeditated because I do not believe they are planned in
advance. However, I do believe that pupils make conscious decisions

to do something, though those decisions may be forced on them by circumstances beyond their control.

Perhaps an example will help at this point. This episode took place in a science laboratory:

> The class were working quietly, writing up notes on an experiment they had done. John sat, pencil in hand, doing nothing. After a while, he got up and walked around the classroom, checking all the gas taps, to see that they were turned off. The teacher told him to sit down and get on with his work. John sat down and fidgeted for a while. Eventually he got up again and this time checked the water taps, until told to sit down again.

The support teacher referred to this incident in interview later:

> John has great difficulty with writing. Usually I help him with it, but on this occasion I needed to spend some time with Eric so John was left to his own devices. He couldn't do the work he was supposed to do, but he wanted to do something, he wanted to feel useful, to make a contribution, so he found something he could do.

Gray and Richer (1988) refer to this kind of activity as 'displacement activity' (p.22).

On this occasion, John's displacement activity did not cause any real disruption to the work of the rest of the class, but often these activities do. For example:

> Steven got up and opened the window. The other pupils complained about the cold draught and asked the teacher to close the window. Steven objected to this, maintaining he was too hot.

It is clear that this confrontation between Steven and the teacher was engineered by the pupils. However, the support teacher had seen Steven and his friends perform this routine before and was ready for it.

It is tempting to jump to the conclusion that Steven and friends jointly planned this activity before the lesson started, but I do not believe it happens that way. I think it happens as follows: One day, Steven is struggling with his work and he finds a displacement activity, he opens a window. He is surprised by the reactions of the rest of the class. He is aware that his action has released the class from the stress of the work and that this is appreciated by his friends. So he has gained in two ways; he has escaped from the stress of the work he cannot do, and he was responsible for easing the strain on his friends, which helps his self esteem. He remembers the relief gained from this activity and when he finds himself in a similar situation again, is likely to respond in the same way.

So far I have looked at what the pupils do, and have used evidence from the classroom and extracts from appropriate literature to try to explain why these things happen. The emerging themes are those of poor self image and insecurity, of apprehension and avoidance. If all this paints a rather depressing picture of school life, then that is not my intention. The evidence of the data was that by year 9 these strategies were seen to be becoming redundant. So how do the teaching teams go about building trust and confidence?

## Ways forward in meeting pupils' individual needs

### Building a good self image

Even when a pupil's avoidance strategies are discovered, it is not always obvious what to do about them. If the teaching staff take actions which negate the strategies then that will leave the pupil without any image protection system or any means of escape from difficult situations. This is bound to increase stress levels and may well result in even more disruption. If the pupils' strategies have to be dismantled, then it is clear that they must be replaced by something else. If the inappropriate strategies have to be replaced by more effective ones, then the teaching teams must provide the replacements.

Perhaps the way to start replacing the faulty learning styles is to help the pupils to improve their self images and so make their strategies redundant. The music teacher's approach to the problem was interesting:

> To go into life confidently, confidence needs building into them. Weak areas need confronting. I do not allow someone to fail. That only confirms a failure mentality and consequently a lower self esteem. If I find that I have pushed a pupil and he cannot do what I am asking, I give him a way out so that he does not lose face. This builds trust and security in me as a teacher. It encourages pupils to have a go because they learn that I will not allow them to fail or lose face in their own eyes or the eyes of others.

It is clear that this teacher has thought about the pupils' self-image problems and has developed strategies for working with such pupils.

*Minimising stress*

Whilst success in school work will help in the image building process, in itself it is not likely to solve the problem. The pupils have experienced many years of not being able to keep up with other pupils. They know they are slow learners. The solution suggested by the data is to try to break the link, which the pupils make, between academic performance and their worth as persons.

Both Holt (1964) and Gray and Richer (1988) describe how stress in pupils results in egocentricity, a self-protecting survivalist attitude. The worst aspect of this is the way in which the pupils are driven to score points off one another. The task for teachers is to convince the pupils of the value of being a member of a group. It must be within the remit of the support teacher to remind the pupils persistently that, whenever any individual makes a significant improvement, the value of the whole group rises too, and that when a group member is diminished in some way, the whole group is diminished. It is the class teacher's responsibility to use the whole group as a resource; to exploit the total sum of the members' experience rather than that of any individual. Perhaps if teachers worked at establishing a group ethos as soon as the pupils join the school, some of the damage to pupils' self image could be prevented.

The research suggested that pupils do not differentiate between what they do and what they are. When pupils are reprimanded for inappropriate behaviour, they will interpret it as criticism of their character, rather than a comment on their actions. The implications for teachers, then, are that class teachers in particular, should consider why the pupils act in the way that they do, before deciding how to deal with the problem. In this way they are less likely to raise stress levels in the pupils and in themselves.

The support teacher, who has a closer relationship with the pupils, is in a good position to explain that a criticism of inappropriate behaviour is not a condemnation of character. Mrs Pillar said, in interview:

> If you do have to confront a child, then you should choose your ground carefully. The pupils are far more willing to accept reprimands about work and effort, than they are about behaviour, because that is what they see school as being about. If it is necessary to talk about behaviour, it is best done in terms of the effect that it is having on their or someone else's work.

Several teachers pointed out the futility of trying to talk to pupils who have lost their temper, because the pupils retreat into a state of extreme egocentricity in which they are incapable of seeing any point of view other than their own. The talking must come later when the situation is normalised.

Several of the teachers mentioned that the beginning of the lesson was the most critical time in creating a good working atmosphere in the room, and this was supported by observations. Lessons which began with a lengthy introduction by the teacher, containing several instructions produced an insecure, unsettled atmosphere. Two teachers mentioned that continuity from the previous lesson was effective in keeping instruction giving at the start of the lesson to a minimum, thus keeping pupil's stress levels low, and maintaining a happy atmosphere.

*Groupings*

Mr Newton, the science teacher, commented on the importance of dividing the class into small predetermined groups for each lesson. He emphasised that breaks and lunchtimes were periods where bickering, bullying and fighting sometimes occurred. By choosing his groups carefully he could avoid these playground problems spilling over into the classroom. He used the judgement of the support teacher, who had been with the pupils all day, to determine the groups for the day. Mrs Pillar, the support teacher, added that often problems from the pupils' homes, particularly inter-family rows, can affect pupils' relationships in school. She said that generally she would be aware of what was going on and be able to keep the pupils apart.

Another advantage, from the point of view of classroom management, when working with the pupils in small groups, is that if a child is being difficult, the problem can be contained within the group so that it does not affect the whole class. This technique is particularly effective if it is possible to zone the room into different work areas and assign the groups to the different areas.

## Choosing appropriate teaching styles

Pupils take each new experience and internalise it by fitting it into the framework of what they already know and by so doing turn knowledge into understanding. This is illustrated by my observations of Jenny working with her support teacher at a computer. The program was an adventure game, but it involved quite a lot of reading and Jenny was struggling. The sentence on the screen read 'A troll inhabits a nearby bridge'. Jenny looked at the screen for some time, knowing that she had to read aloud to her teacher. Finally she read 'A troll lives under the bridge'. Her teacher then helped her with the new words.

Mrs Lintel told me later that Jenny has an active vocabulary of about 50 words. She said that whilst Jenny is perfectly happy to ask for help with her maths, she is unwilling to admit to having difficulty with English.

Jenny tries very hard to disguise her reading problems. When she is confronted by a sentence containing words that she does not recognise she looks for clues in the sentence and uses her patchy background to guess at the unfamiliar words. The thing she knew about trolls is that they live under bridges, so she used this to guess at the words on the monitor screen. In this case her guessing was fairly close to the mark. Often it is not and as a result she builds up some very strange concepts.

Teachers can capitalise on this patching strategy by matching it with an appropriate teaching style, as in the following illustration:

> Mrs Bishop revised their last lesson and then moved on to a discussion about jigsaw puzzles, and the pupils told her about the puzzles they had done. They discussed some strategies, such as finding corner pieces and edges.
>
> She had prepared six large jigsaw puzzles, each made up of eight pieces, and each one, when complete revealed two sentences from the story of Saul and David. The pupils worked in small groups and when all the groups had finished their puzzles, the pupils read out their sentences.
>
> Mrs Bishop then led the class in a discussion in which the

pupils patched together the sentences in the correct order to tell the story.

The pupils were good at patching the story together, because they do it all the time, in order to pretend that they can read as well as other pupils. It is a survival skill they have acquired to cope with ill-matched content or poor delivery, but in this example the teacher put it to good use.

The final part of the lesson involved the pupils making a 'wanted' poster based on the story. This was another well thought out teaching strategy as it does not penalise a limited vocabulary. The pupils wrote the words on self-adhesive labels and then had them checked by the teacher before sticking them on their card. Presentation of work seems to be important to these pupils and it is something that many of them find difficult because of poor motor control.

## Retrospective view

Looking back over a research project, even after a short time, lends a different perspective to the process. At the time I wondered if I would find some unifying themes emerging from the data I was collecting. In retrospect I realise that some of my difficulties were the result of not being rigorous enough in defining the research questions. On the one hand, I was interested in finding out why the pupils were behaving in a certain way and on the other hand I was looking for team teaching strategies that were effective. This two-handed approach meant that I was constantly changing viewpoints: from that of the pupil to that of the teacher and back again. Of course these two views are intimately linked. However, with the benefit of hindsight, I might have found it less confusing to have awarded one or the other the main priority.

It is interesting to note that for the teacher researcher, the process does not end with the writing of the report or thesis. The teacher continues working with pupils and teachers and cannot avoid observing and contrasting what is seen with the research findings which become more refined with time. One effect of this is that now, when I am confronted with disruptive behaviour, I find myself examining it as a piece of data. This lends distance to the activity which tends to take the heat out of the situation.

I have found that what I learned from research on 'special' pupils has permeated the whole of my teaching, since there is very little that is not applicable to 'ordinary' pupils.

## References

Delamont, S. (1976) *Interaction in the Classroom*. London: Methuen.

Galloway, D. (1985) *Schools, Pupils and Special Educational Needs*. London: Croom Helm.

Gray, J. and Richer, J. (1988) *Classroom Responses to Disruptive Behaviour*. Basingstoke: Macmillan.

Hanko, G. (1985) *Special Needs in Ordinary Classrooms*. Oxford: Basil Blackwell.

Holt, J. (1964) *How Children Fail*. New York: Pitman.

National Curriculum Council (May 1989) Circular Number 5. York: National Curriculum Council.

Sayer, J. (1987) *Secondary Schools For All?* London: Cassell.

Thomas, G. (1986) 'Integrating personnel in order to integrate children'. *Support for Learning* 1, 19–26.

# CHAPTER 8

# An Evaluation of Conductive Education in English Special Schools

Trefor Davies-Isaac

## Introduction: the Petö Institute

I was immediately impressed by my first sight of the Petö András Institute, high on a hillside overlooking Budapest. Within minutes of entering the building I realised that it would be incongruous to attempt a comparison with the average English special school for the disabled. There are only two points of similarity: both admit children with cerebral palsy and both are educational institutions.

The Institute's size is unique. The crowd of visitors, parents, adult patients and student Conductors within the main lobby was striking enough, but insignificant when I learned that there were also over 500 resident Hungarian children, about 100 foreign children and around 1,000 'out-patients', many of the latter attending 'mother and baby' groups. On any day, I was told, there could be around 1,000 children attending the Institute, all receiving Conductive Education.

The compelling impression was of a dynamic institution where something positive and successful was being done for many hundreds of disabled children. Little wonder that hopeful parents are so powerfully encouraged on first entering the Institute.

## What is Conductive Education?

Conductive Education, although claimed to be relevant to many types of motor disorder, is most commonly associated with the alleviation of the effects of cerebral palsy (c.p.) in children. The diagnosis of cerebral palsy and prognosis for a young child are still controversial and problematical areas; Bowley and Gardner offer one explanation:

> The one thing that all cerebrally palsied children have in common is a difficulty in controlling certain of their muscles ... Apart from this ... c.p. children have little else in common. Indeed it is difficult to find two c.p. children who are alike.
>
> (1972, p.1)

Although insufficient for a clear understanding of the condition, there is still wide acceptance of the definition offered by Bax (1964) who described c.p. as 'a disorder of movement and posture due to a defect or lesion of the immature brain' (p.295) and helpfully added (Bax, 1987) that c.p. is 'non-progressive but not unchanging' (p.689).

The underlying causes of the condition are, however, varied and incompletely understood. Causal factors continue to be researched and debated. Olow (1986), while recognising a lack of homogeneity in many aspects of c.p. points out that c.p. children have many similar disorders of development and learning, thus offering some support for those who argue that c.p. children require an educational provision directed towards their specific needs. The Spastics Society's schools have been developed on that premise, although the generic special school is still the usual provision in England and Wales for children with c.p.

As other disabling conditions have gradually reduced in incidence or have been virtually eradicated, c.p. has during recent years accounted for the largest proportion of physical disabilities in many English special schools. Dissatisfaction has been increasingly expressed with the conventional approach of physiotherapy, partly because of a view that physiotherapy was too infrequently available, partly because of a questioning of the value of physiotherapy for the treatment of c.p. Curricular innovations to meet a perceived new and pressing need have become increasingly common during the last decade and attention has particularly focused on innovations deriving from the practice in Budapest of 'Conductive Education'.

Increasingly pressed by parents to fund Conductive Education for their severely disabled children, my LEA sponsored my study of English practice in Conductive Education in order to decide whether some form of education based on Conductive Education principles should form part of the Authority's provision.

András Petö's Conductive Education began in 1945 with a group of thirteen severely motor-disordered children who could neither sit nor walk. His resources were meagre and he relied on voluntary helpers, usually medical students, among them Mariá Hári, the present director of the Institute which bears Petö's name. Therapeutic disciplines in Hungary existed at that time only in tentative emergent forms and Petö met the children's needs with a new profession – the Conductors – and a new discipline – Conductive Education – a holistic approach to management, care, treatment and education of the motor-disordered child.

Although it is not a school and its size is similar to that of a hospital, the Institute operates under the aegis of the Ministry of Education and must meet the requirements of the Hungarian National Curriculum. The Institute's basic aims are to enable motor-disordered children to meet the criteria for admission to school, whether it be special or mainstream. Hungarian children may not enter a school of any kind unless they can walk and follow a normal course of study without support and concessions. Other requirements include continence and freedom from debilitating conditions, such as chronic epilepsy.

Conductive Education (CE) has 'orthofunction' as its goal – a level of attainment at which children can respond appropriately to all the mental, social and biological demands made upon them at each developmental stage. An inability so to respond is 'dysfunction'.

Ester Cotton, the famous physiotherapist who first brought CE to the attention of English professionals has consistently sought to deny that CE is 'physiotherapy' (Cotton, 1974). Nevertheless the English perception of CE has tended to emphasise the motor aspects of the system, relying largely on the interpretation of other physio-therapists. This view has been perpetuated by the priority which parents usually place on the importance of achieving independent walking (Henderson, 1986). Yet walking (albeit imperfectly) is a motor skill achieved by the majority of c.p. children whatever the nature or degree of interventional help.

Tizard (1980) described himself as one of the 'sceptical pae-diatricians ... who have been able to witness over the years how well some children with cerebral palsy develop without physiotherapy, (p.74). He relates how he advised a mother that her non-ambulant child should attend a centre for spastic children. Although transport problems prevented the child from doing so, he was walking independently if unsteadily three months later: "'If we had sent him to the centre you would have given them the credit", I said ... "Yes, and so would you, Dr Tizard", she replied' (p.74). No such doubt about the value of its intervention is held by the English supporters of Conductive Education, although parents of some profoundly disabled children have been bitterly disappointed not to have been offered a place for their child in the Petö András Institute, which has contributed to the view that the Institute is selective. Although staff at the Petö Institute are evasive on this point, Bairstow (1991) suggests that Conductive Education is suitable for only 35 per cent of c.p. children.

Partly due to parental pressure, some English special school heads have felt compelled to offer a version of CE, incorporating at least some of its perceived principles. This is despite Dr Hári's denial that any analysis of CE can offer a set of principles from which one or more may be selected and applied to the management of motor-disordered children.

It is unfortunate that the unique nature of CE, the remarkable size of the Petö Institute, the wide variety of its services and some novel elements in the method have contributed to visitors' accounts which agree only in some details. Visitors' accounts offer confusingly different emphases, and even biased and distorted interpretations of the Institute's work, and there has been a disappointing dearth of published material from within the Institute. Nevertheless, one can identify those features of CE which have attracted the attention of most observers (Cottam and Sutton, 1986) and which are sometimes erroneously described as 'the principles' of CE.

## The Conductor

She (for most are female) trains initially for four years and works for several more years under the supervision of more experienced Conductors. The Conductor meets all the children's needs and 'combines in her function what medicine, education, physio- and logo-therapy [speech therapy], and psychology have to offer to the education of physically handicapped children' (Hari and Tillemans, 1984, p.19).

146

*The Group*

Much is made by the Budapest staff of 'the Group dynamic', which offers general as well as individual motivation. Foreign children at the Institute gain little from Group Dynamic because of their relatively short stay and the language barrier. The Group receives criticism, not the individual, and the Group profits and learns from the successes of individuals. Numbering between 20 and 25 except in 'mother and baby' and 'pre-kindergarten' Groups, the Group's homogeneous composition also allows of sub-grouping and a range of levels of attainment. Each Group has two or three Conductors.

*Task Series*

These are literally a series of closely related tasks which make physical, intellectual and aesthetic demands, each series leading to a clearly stated objective which is repeated to the children several times during each Task Series session. A Task Series may last as little as 20 minutes or as long as 90 minutes, and its construction is closely analagous to Programmed Learning. Conductors devise their own Task Series and may alter or adapt each series during its course.

*Rhythmic(al) intention*

This has been seen to be closely related to Russian theories of verbal regulation of behaviour involving language – spoken and internalised – to control actions, but is claimed to be an independently-developed pedagogic tool. It is less important in today's Institute, and the continued English emphasis on this part of CE is seen by Hungarians as proof of the lack of understanding of CE's principles.

*Early intervention*

A state decree requires all brain-damaged motor-impaired babies to be registered with the Institute. It is not thought to matter that many of the 'motor-impaired' babies may only be developmentally delayed, as those babies too will benefit from the early intervention – a view which contrasts with the views of some Western experts, such as Levitt (1982) and Robson (1983).

*Distinctive furniture*

This is specially manufactured for the Institute and its design is derived from the basic native furniture available to Petö in the early years, and used to advantage by him in the absence of more sophisticated 'aids'. Dr Hári denies that the furniture is essential to the practice of CE, but it remains a ubiquitous feature of CE and its variants.

*The totally structured day*

Days are far longer than in English special schools. There is little truly 'free' time, although children have play periods. Every activity, even during recreation, is structured and directed towards a required objective: all parts of the waking day contribute to the delivery of Conductive Education.

*Residential management*

About 500 Hungarian children are resident and up to 100 foreign children. Residential management offers opportunity for longer structured days, but the staff at the Institute also stress the importance of working with parents.

Dr Hári and her staff deny that an analysis of CE can offer educationalists an opportunity to select only those 'principles' which may seem attractive or adaptable to the English pattern of special education. Cotton (1974), too, emphasised the totality of CE: 'It should not be believed that CE consists merely of a few techniques' (p.641). It particularly annoys Dr Hári that many foreigners spend a short time at the Institute on familiarisation courses and, enthused by what they see, return to initiate programmes which they describe as CE or part-CE despite Hári's repeated firm statements that participation in such short courses bestows no qualification on the participants.

Nor does the growing practice of 'transplanting' one or two trained Conductors into English schools find favour with Dr Hári; when I suggested that this was considered useful she told me:

> If a Conductor with a Diploma is working with an inter-disciplinary group, she may do CE some of the time; but the rest of the time? It

is not possible. Experience in CE is like a Christmas Tree [and she sketched a pyramid with her hands] ... from the top to the lowest branches ... I go about as much as I can, and all the time I see mistakes, mistakes which must be put right. Even at this Institute there are mistakes; but with supervision they can be corrected ... Training takes a long time. It is very important for trainees to see the programme of many children from when they first come in, and are very dysfunctional, to the time when they have achieved an appropriate level of function. If they have not seen this many times they cannot truly believe that progress is possible. If they do not believe what is possible, how can they motivate children so that *they* will believe in their future achievement?

The child's own belief in success is said to be particularly important in CE: the child is encouraged to have 'intention' — not only the will but also the cognitive effort required to comprehend and therefore achieve each objective and the ultimate goals. CE is claimed to change the way in which the motor-disordered child learns: it is a cognitive process and its success is dependent on the level of the child's cognitive ability. Although the selection criteria for admission to the Institute are imperfectly understood by observers, the child's apparent level of intelligence must be an important criterion.

## Researching Conductive Education

CE is a global system and is, as such, difficult to evaluate. Quantitative measures alone seem inadequate and inclusion of qualitative data is called for in order to get a more complete and detailed picture of the developing child.

(Jernqvist, 1985, p.21)

In sponsoring my study, my authority had indicated an interest in examples of the use of CE principles in other English special schools. It was obviously necessary to establish a view of 'pure' CE by a combination of personal observation and a review of the substantive literature in order to provide me with a base-line against which I could evaluate derivative forms of CE and initiatives which claimed to be founded on one or more 'principles' of the original.

The study was not primarily intended to produce a comparative evaluation of orthodox CE but rather to describe English educational innovations, why those innovations had been introduced, and what advantages and disadvantages could be identified. It was, moreover, not within the compass of small-scale research to evaluate the comparative effectiveness of CE but rather to observe examples of its employment in some English schools, and to compare observations of practice with a personal view of CE gained not only from seminal sources but also from the commentaries of those seeking to interpret the Budapest practice to a wider audience. My study had to determine whether what I observed were genuine departures from the English conventions of practice and whether they were credible derivatives of 'pure' CE. I had also to determine, not on any quantitative measures but on the perception of a practising teacher, whether any of the innovations observed might be advantageously adopted.

As a teacher in the field of special education for the physically disabled I had constantly to ask myself whether I could identify with the reasons given in other schools for innovations and also whether in similar circumstances I would adopt a similar response to those circumstances; in simple terms my sponsors were saying, 'Tell us what we should ask you to do'. My study was bound to be conditioned by my subjective response, but I also expected interviewees to respond to my questioning with some considerable bias, since it would be most unusual for any school to deny the value of its innovation.

Ball (1984) warns researchers to beware of their subjective views. He concurs with earlier writers that researchers should seek from those observed some validation of their observations. I prefer Patton's (1980) suggestion that the observer might see things unnoticed by the observed. However, the two perceptions added together, though not necessarily concurring, should present a more comprehensive view of an educational 'programme'.

I knew that no school — except perhaps the Birmingham Institute, which admitted its first pupils in January 1988 — could be emulating the Hungarian holistic concept of the Conductor since no such profession exists in England. Also my reading suggested that some so-called CE innovations might consist of a re-statement of tried and tested teaching methods with only superficial CE characteristics added for the sake of being seen to be in fashion. Even were that to be the case, I needed to report sympathetically lest I ignore Burgess's (1984) warning against rendering harm to my informants. I was reminded of this warning several times when I was welcomed into those schools whose staff clearly believed that

I intended to follow their examples and introduce CE into my own school; only a few people doubted that I was a believer.

The substantive literature suggested that 50 or more English schools claimed to be offering some form of CE-style provision, although Sutton (1984) had noted the transitory enthusiasm of some schools. Their adoption of CE had been perfunctory and short-lived. I found, however, that the schools included in my study had all adopted CE only after careful consideration and deliberation, largely in response to the rising numbers of c.p. pupils. A few schools cited other reasons too, such as the more effective use by a group of scarce physiotherapy time, particularly those schools in my study which catered for children with severe or profound and multiple learning difficulties – children who, in the words of one headteacher, would have been rejected by the Budapest Institute. Two schools had long-established CE programmes, introduced before the more recent rise in the proportion of c.p. pupils and one other had lately committed considerable resources to its CE work. The more recently developed programmes had posed difficulties for the other schools – insufficient time in the conventionally short special school day, insufficient or unsuitable spaces in which to accommodate the children and the Petö furniture, difficulty in establishing homogeneous Groups and insufficient numbers of staff to extend CE programmes to older pupils.

Faced with such a number I considered using a questionnaire. However I rejected this method of gathering data since question-naires cannot readily be designed to collect illuminating personal views. Parlett and Hamilton (1977) warn that some participants in innovation who might be 'keen to express their views find the questionnaire a frustrating even trivialising medium' (p.17). I was also rather ashamedly aware of the low priority which I usually give to questionnaires – often very badly constructed – which so frequently land on my desk.

I chose to use a combination of observation and semi-structured interviews for my fieldwork, visiting fourteen schools. I took Bell's advice: 'A structured interview will produce structured responses. Is this what you want?' (1987, p.77). It wasn't, because I was work-ing towards, not from, a hypothesis. To borrow the analogy from 'illuminative evaluation' (Parlett and Hamilton, 1977), I was becoming well-acquainted with the script but I did not know how the actors would interpret the play in their separate performances. I had gained the impression during an earlier small-scale research study that a structured interview seemed to arouse anxiety in respondents who were nevertheless able to give me a wealth of comment and information over a cup of coffee when they thought the interview was over. I took notes as soon as possible after interviews or used a pocket dictaphone − sometimes in a staff cloakroom − in order to preserve as accurately as possible the authenticity of the verbatim comments. Interviews were refreshingly different in their development, occasionally resulting in my being interviewed too.

Towards the end of the 1960s I had participated in discussion and examination of CE, and seen some of my fellow heads adopt and adapt its principles in their schools. The renewed interest in the 1980s introduced a different element: that of implicit − and often explicit − criticism of the conventional English special educational provision for the physically disabled. For example, *Standing up for Joe*, (BBC, 1986) depicted the Petö Institute as the only place where a c.p. child might hope to overcome disability. Like many other professionals working in special education I felt personal hurt that my work should seem to be dismissed as worthless. The British Ambassador to Hungary, expressing strong sympathy for the parents of c.p. children who could no longer afford to remain in Budapest, declared in a 1987 BBC television programme *To Hungary with Love* that:

> they go back to minimal provision in England ... you see the real tragedy of parents taking their children back to work in conditions which they know are so inferior to what is happening in Budapest ... Their children are losing the one chance they had to achieve.

Such an undiplomatic statement had to be dismissed as an irrelevance born of ignorance and I had to determine that my readiness to observe and listen should not be coloured by a stubbornly defensive attitude.

I had also to guard against the vestiges of cynicism still lingering from the late 1960s and early 1970s when I had noted the 'bandwaggon' effect of CE on some schools in the London area who appeared for fashion's sake to be claiming the inclusion of 'Petö' in their timetables: one school incredibly claimed to 'do Petö' on Thursday afternoons only if it was raining! Common sense decreed that educational innovation, be it CE, programmed

152

learning, or any other, would attract its superficial supporters: the discovery of any such amongst the schools in my study should not detract from what might be perceived as the intrinsic value of CE.

## The practice of Conductive Education

Most schools agreed that the following were important:

1.  CE allowed early intervention and might therefore increase the chances of integration into mainstream;
2.  CE brought together the disciplines which conventionally worked separately;
3.  the use of the Group was economical of time, particularly of therapists' time;
4.  CE encouraged the children to see motor development as part of education;
5.  CE allowed parents to be more closely involved because it was not couched in difficult medical terms;
6.  Group work increased children's motivation and helped to reduce disabled children's dependency on adults;
7.  CE's avoidance of aids (wheelchairs, calipers, adapted type-writers etc) gave greater encouragement to children and their parents;
8.  CE was a programme specific to the needs of motor-disordered children and therefore best enabled schools to meet the challenge posed by increasing numbers of c.p. children.

Several points implied a criticism of physiotherapy, not only because therapists' time was said to be too limited, but also because it was claimed that the treatment of children within a physiotherapy department did not motivate the child to strive for motor progress in the wider context of daily living. This was interesting because the impetus towards CE had come, in most schools, from the physiotherapists and it was noticeable how much emphasis continued to be placed by all staff on the motor development of the children. In many schools the end of the CE (that is, motor activity) part of the day was clearly marked and I noted a sense of finality at the end of a task series which might allow children narrowly to identify motor objectives with a 'plinth programme' (the slatted bed-cum-table is also used as an exercise frame) or a 'hand function session', thus evoking the same criticism levelled against physiotherapy.

There were some surprising examples of adults' failure to carry task series' objectives through to other activities. In one school, having observed infants demonstrating their ability to stand steadily while holding on behind a ladder-back chair, and push it forwards as they took hesitant steps, I was surprised to see these children carried to the adjacent toilet area. While acknowledging a frequent need for haste to avert disaster, I wondered why the children were not then allowed to return from the toilet using the chair backs for support.

The most striking anomalies were in a school amply equipped with 'Petö' furniture, but adapted by the addition of footboards, winged head cushions and seat pommels. Some chairs had small castors fitted to the rear and many chairs had ski feet – a feature seen in other schools too and scathingly dismissed by Dr Hári, who emphasised to me the importance of retaining the slight instability of the ladderback chair in order to give the child kinaesthetic feedback. In this school I saw children taking slow unsteady steps with the aid of a chair back during their CE session and soon afterwards being wheeled about by teachers and classroom aides.

Only in one school did I see motor task series incorporated into a lengthy programme which included number work, language development, shape and colour discrimination, letter recognition and the 'daily news' – familiar to all teachers of infants. The smooth transition from one activity to another was impressive and although there were isolated moments of spontaneity arising from unexpected occurrences, these were fitted into a framework which must have required lengthy and thoughtful preparation. The headteacher explained that the school had adopted only those CE principles thought to have most relevance to the school's aims and made no claim to be a CE purist. Yet of all the schools visited, only this one demonstrated how task series could 'be brought into harmony with the whole of the daily schedule' (Hari and Akos, 1988, p.17).

In fairness to the schools included in my study, most of them did not claim to be replicating the authentic Hungarian model. One leading 'CE' school suggested in its Year Book that: 'it may be argued that it is inappropriate to call what we are doing Conductive Education' but added: 'We believe that Conductive Education offers a very appropriate educational response to our children, and we will continue to develop it within our situation'.

The Spastics Society's (1989) agreement with the Petö Institute to avoid the use of the term 'Conductive Education' in describing the programmes used within its own and affiliated schools suggests that the term has been too readily and inappropriately applied to the innovations observed in the schools I visited and one must recall Dr Hári's firm opinion that CE cannot be analysed and used in selective parts.

Even so, Sutton (1984) suggested that 'perhaps it is no bad thing that CE should not have been solely imported but also submitted to a vigorous grass-roots adaptation' (p. 129). Despite Hári protestations, is it possible that CE – English style is viable as a hybrid, preserving some of the basic strengths of the Hungarian model, but adapting the general form to accord with our educational culture? If CE is analogous to an excellent native wine which does not travel well, can we produce an indigenous wine of comparable quality by grafting the vines on to English rootstock?

The Director of the Birmingham CE Institute, Mike Lambert, thinks not and is quoted as saying 'there must be a limit to which you can adapt CE and still call it the same' (Nash, 1988, p.8). Levitt (1982) is a self-confessed eclectic and sees much common ground in what appear to be quite different methodologies and rationales and she rejects the totality of any method: 'In any system there are methods and ideas which are superfluous. It is not correct to say that "everything in a system depends on everything else"' (p.35). Scrutton and Gilbertson (1975) do not, however, subscribe to the view that one can 'pick the best bits', arguing that it takes too long to learn one method properly: to apply all methods equally well is probably to do them all badly. Whilst it might be argued that the eclectic demonstrates an open mind, my interviews and observations gave rise to some doubt about some of the practices I saw.

None of the schools offered 'proof' that CE achieved better results than conventional treatment: in those schools with longer-established CE programmes, children did not remain to school leaving age; and in the schools where CE had been introduced since 1980, older children did not participate in CE. Most staff interviewed were nevertheless optimistic about the effects of CE. Perhaps of greater significance was that there appeared to be a general belief in all but two schools that *staff* had gained in motivation and job satisfaction. Rooke and Opel (1983), describing a trial of CE-derived work in a school for SLD pupils noted that: 'teacher motivation greatly increased during the project, and "teacher attitude" may be a possible dependant variable in future studies' (p.397). Not all those I interviewed shared in that view, however, and doubts were privately expressed to me by a few teachers and therapists. One teacher took a weekly 'CE' session because he had inherited his predecessor's timetable. He felt that 'they' were 'pushing methods at children' and claimed that 'they' had recently introduced another sort of motor education programme, 'and that wasn't done properly, either'.

I was unable to spend long enough at any school to note how a Task Series might develop over a period of time. Explanations seemed vague: 'Well, when they can all do it', was one reason given for the introduction of new tasks into each Series. I frequently gained the impression that a Task Series had remained undeveloped for too long. Some children made only perfunctory attempts to execute a particular motor activity, often moving on to what they clearly expected to be the next activity and they were right. In two schools I observed a few children who loudly and enthusiastically joined in the Rhythmic Intentions and songs while carelessly performing the motor act which was next in the Series. In discussion afterwards I was told that a couple of children could do everything required of them and were probably bored, but could not be moved on to the next Group because there wasn't one. Only one school used the term 'Task Series', the other schools referring to 'plinth programmes', 'locomotor sessions', 'hand function training', etc. I could discern neither advantages nor disadvantages in the semantic variations.

All establishments claimed to have a system by which tasks were regularly analysed and linked together to form a series or programme; I was allowed to join meetings at two establishments where the morning's work was thoroughly discussed and the next three or four Task Series adjusted or augmented by consensus. In neither meeting was there a dominant professional perspective, although I was told that had a therapist advised against a suggested activity or movement, the advice would have been fully followed.

I was also fortunate to be invited to join a staff training session led by Ester Cotton in which she posed questions which the staff had to answer by a process of physical experiment, the application of some common sense and a great deal of knowledge about c.p. Even so, it was ably demonstrated to us that experience can blind us to the links between small movements — links which could be crucial to a disabled child's solution of a motor task, for example, 'Now turn on to your back'.

In one school, Task Series were determined by physiotherapists after consultation with teachers, whereas in two other schools the therapists advised on motor patterns and motor development while the teachers framed the therapeutic objectives into educational contexts. In the last two examples, I was interested to note how the therapists appeared to take no active part in programmes and busied themselves with other children whom they treated in their department.

Rhythmic Intention was used in every establishment, but there was considerable variation in the degree to which children participated in the vocal statement. In some groups this seemed acceptable and appropriate where the children appeared to be at Jernqvist's (1985) 'Preparatory Stage' of speech regulation, that is, being guided by aural and visual clues and being almost entirely 'other regulated'. Two schools claimed that my presence inhibited the children's speaking aloud, an explanation which I doubted since it was clear that visitors were commonly present in each school.

I was impressed by the children's evident enjoyment of so-called Rhythmic Intention in six establishments: in all of these there was a considerable use of singing, usually simple and well-known tunes — *Frére Jacques*, *Seven in a Bed*, *The Farmer's in the Den* — all clearly chosen because of their repetitive nature and the ease with which other words and actions could be fitted to the tunes. In five schools I observed songs and rhythmic chants used to promote group cohesion. Each child was greeted in turn by peers and adults, and there was frequent use of individuals' names during the Task Series, ensuring continued attention and also promoting peer awareness. These examples bore a striking similarity to some of the ways in which songs are used at the Petö Institute, but only in three schools was there a consistent use of Rhythmic Intention to retain attention and sustain motivation. In these, Rhythmic Intention seemed to fulfil Hari and Akos's (1988) function of helping the cohesion of the Group and aiding concentration. The 'Conductors' regularly called the attention of the Group to what was going on, gave regular reminders of the longer-term goal and in all three places left 'a task demanding a great deal of precision to turn to a less detailed one, like singing' (Hari and Akos, 1988, p.181). This use of light relief seemed to be deliberate, planned and causing no surprise amongst the 'Second Conductors' (staff assisting the leading adult). These well-planned sessions contrasted sharply with that in another school when the 'Conductors' literally ran out of lesson material and the session limped towards the end of morning school.

I was particularly interested to observe a programme led by a fully trained Hungarian Conductor whose command of English was excellent and whose pronunciation, although accented, posed no communication problems for the four-year-old children. Her 'Second Conductors' consisted of two of the school's staff and two seconded from another school for training. She frequently intervened, advising a 'Second Conductor' on 'facilitation' (handling) of a child or checked a child's accomplishment of a task in the series. She neither corrected every incorrect movement nor did she signal another adult to do so, but maintained the impetus of the programme at a pace which was stimulating and – not surprisingly – very similar to the styles I observed in Budapest. This was the most energetic and enthusiastic lead given by any 'Conductor' during my field studies, although whether a single trained Conductor could effectively train others to a standard which might result in the delivery of a recognisable form of CE is a matter for debate.

Hungarian trainee Conductors study theory and practice during an intensive four years' training and after that they are still not regarded as competent to work except under the supervision of Conductors with eight to ten years' experience who, in their turn, are monitored by even more senior Conductors. By comparison, English schools attempt to put CE principles into practice on the basis of very small amounts of training.

Whether CE can be adapted or cannibalised for its useful parts must be left to others to debate. Observation and interview in some of the schools in my study led me to cast doubt on their state of readiness for innovation. I had assumed that in order to introduce a CE programme into a school some detailed knowledge of the principles and practice would have been thoroughly acquired by at least the key members of staff. This was not generally true, with a very few notable exceptions.

Some initiatives had been introduced on the basis of little more than a short course on one example of English-style practice or attendance at a few study days. With the obvious exception of the Hungarian Conductor, no other 'Conductors' had undergone a validated course of training. In five schools at least one senior member of staff had visited Budapest one or more times, the more recent visitors usually attending a six weeks' 'introduction' course firmly described by the Petö Institute as *not* a qualification to practise. The majority of staff at most schools had acquired their understanding of CE from their colleagues and had in only a few cases also attended study days or visited a Spastics Society school well-known for its version of CE. All the staff in five schools had gained their 'knowledge' of CE by learning from others who had attended English courses. There appeared to be a general lack of knowledge even of key areas of the substantive literature and references to the practice in Budapest were usually based on no more than impressions gained from the popular media, particularly television programmes.

The importance of Rhythmic Intention was stressed to me, but rarely did I meet anybody who knew anything of the theories of verbal regulation of behaviour. Most thought it important to have a Group, but the reasons advanced were no different from those which would support the class teaching system. Although established schools of physiotherapy, most often the Bobath method, were criticised for their failure to meet the motor needs of c.p. children, the lay critics appeared to have made no efforts to understand what they were rejecting, and talked alarmingly about the redundancy of physiotherapy with the advent of CE, apparently assuming that a thorough knowledge of physiology and motor patterns was no longer necessary in the practice of CE.

## Conclusions

For the most part, I doubt if what I saw in the schools I visited was Conductive Education, nor could those adopted 'principles' be claimed to be derived only from Budapest, but rather from what might universally be described as good teaching practices. The various initiatives, despite the ubiquitous 'Petö' wooden furniture and CE jargon, appeared to have close similarities to other initiatives taken by special schools in England and other Western countries and as such deserve examination as ways of meeting a wider range of special educational needs than those arising only from c.p. The latter initiatives, rather than variants of CE, were recommended to my Authority.

These initiatives include:

1.  a longer school day, sometimes extending from and including breakfast time until a late afternoon or early evening meal;
2.  a high degree of structure throughout the school day, applied not only to formal lesson-time but also to play and other activities;
3.  task analysis and synthesis, with clearly stated objectives, known to and understood by all staff;
4.  an integrated, multi-disciplinary approach to the totality of each child's needs;
5.  early intervention in all cases of diagnosed or supposed motor disorder, sensory impairment or developmental delay;
6.  active involvement of children, to whom all objectives should be regularly explained in a way they can understand.

There is, however, a significant difference between the Hungarian approach and those English initiatives which owe no allegiance to CE. The latter take full advantage of sophisticated mechanical and micro-electronic aids to learning and physical independence, and it is interesting to speculate whether CE will eventually relinquish its stern rejection of such 'aids'. It seems to make little sense to persist in a philosophy which sets its face against technological progress and tries to make a virtue of the deprivation and austerity with which Petö first had to contend.

## References

Bairstow, P. (1991) *Evaluation of Conductive Education*. Working Paper no. 53(3). University of Birmingham School of Psychology (mimeo).

Ball, S.J. (1984) 'Beachside reconsidered: reflections on a methodological apprenticeship' in Burgess, R.G. (ed) *The Research Process in Educational Settings*. London: Falmer Press.

Bax, M. (1964) 'Terminology and classification of cerebral palsy'. *Developmental Medicine and Child Neurology* 6, 295–307.

Bax, M. (1987) 'Aims and outcomes for physiotherapy for cerebral palsy'. *Developmental Medicine and Child Neurology* 29, 689–92.

BBC TV (1986) *Standing up for Joe*. 1 April 1986 (repeated October 1987).

Bell, J. (1987) *Doing your Research Project*. Milton Keynes: Open University Press.

Bowley, A.H. and Gardner, L. (1972) *The Handicapped Child*. London: Churchill Livingstone.

160

Burgess, R.G. (1984) *In the Field: An Introduction to Field Research*. London: Allen and Unwin.

Cottam, P. and Sutton, A. (eds) (1986) *Conductive Education: A System to Overcome Motor Disorders*. London: Croom Helm.

Cotton, E. (1974) 'Improvement in motor function with the use of conductive education'. *Developmental Medicine and Child Neurology* 16, 637–43.

Hari, M. and Akos, K. (1988) *Conductive Education*. London: Routledge.

Hari, M. and Tillemans, T. (1984) 'Conductive Education' in Scrutton, D. (ed) *Management of the Motor Disorders of Children with Cerebral Palsy*. London: SIMP with Blackwell.

Henderson, S.E. (1986) 'Problems of motor development'. *Advances in Special Education* 5, 147–218.

Jernqvist, L. (1985) *The Use of Speech Regulation of Motor Acts in Conductive Education*. Göteborg Studies in Educational Sciences, no. 54. Göteborg: Acta Universitatis Gothoburgensis.

Levitt, S. (1982) *Treatment of Cerebral Palsy and Motor Delay*. Oxford: Blackwell Scientific.

Nash, I. (1988) 'A troubled road from Budapest to Birmingham'. *Times Educational Supplement* 28 October 1988, 8.

Olow, I. (1986) 'Children with cerebral palsy' in Gordon, N. and McKinlay, I.A. (eds) *Neurologically Handicapped Children, Treatment and Management*. Oxford: Blackwell.

Parlett, M. and Hamilton, D. (1977) 'Evaluation as illumination' in Hamilton, D. *et al.* (eds) *Beyond the Numbers Game*. London: MacMillan.

Patton, M.Q. (1980) *Qualitative Evaluation Methods*. London: Sage.

Robson, P. (1983) 'Motor screening'. Paper presented at Spastics Society meeting on screening procedures in health clinics (mimeo).

Rooke, P. and Opel, P. (1983) 'An approach to teaching profoundly multiply-handicapped children based on certain principles of Conductive Education'. *Mental Handicap* 11, 73–4.

Scrutton, D. and Gilbertson, M. (1975) *Physiotherapy in Paediatric Practice*. London: Butterworth.

Sutton, A. (1984) 'Conductive Education in the Midlands'. *Educational Studies* 10, 121–30.

Tizard, J.P.M. (1980) 'Cerebral palsies: treatment and prevention'. *Journal of the Royal College of Physicians* 14, 72–80.

# CHAPTER 9

## *Support Work in Primary Classrooms: Some Management Concerns*

Marion Tricker

Working in a team can be extremely rewarding and stimulating for all involved. Above all it can be fun. It demands commitment, patience and energy and especially in the early days of its development, it can be highly demanding of non-teaching time. This chapter hopefully will encourage others to try to find the rewards of shared teaching rather than to deter them from its practice. It highlights some pitfalls and some of the less obvious dangers that can prevent the development of a successful team situation before it gets off the ground.

I studied a school with a fairly well-established tradition of team teaching that had recently increased this commitment to include its special needs provision. The school was also just gearing itself up to the implementation of the first stages of the National Curriculum. It seemed important to find out why in some cases shared teaching was successful and in others it seemed to fail. Why was it that on some days teachers could be found in tears of laughter and on others in tears of frustration?

Ethnic Minority Support Service (EMSS) teachers had been involved in the school for over ten years but only for the previous six had there been any structured involvement in team planning and teaching. Often, pairs of teachers would work closely together over a period of time, getting to know each other really well, anticipating one another's needs, sensing moods and knowing when to support and when to duck if the atmosphere became fraught! The Special Needs Support (SNS) — for many years being identified as the 'remedial help' that was offered to children in withdrawal situations — had only recently begun a process of change. Support had moved into the classrooms and planning was cross-curricular. The extra support was seen as an integrated part of the total classroom provision, rather than isolated and 'add on'. It seemed that, since this new initiative to integrate Special Needs Support into the classroom, some problems had arisen and concerns were being quietly expressed.

The issue of support work formed the starting point for a case study which investigated the extent and nature of the involvement of the various groups of people who provided support and extra human resources in the first school in which I worked. The research aimed to investigate the roles, attitudes and perspectives of these groups of people and explore the effects their involvement had on the management of a first school classroom. The content of this chapter draws on research data which relate specifically to the provision and support for children with special educational needs, much of which are inextricably bound up in data relating to the wider organisational structure of the school.

The school that formed the subject of the case study was a five to nine first school with 300 pupils on roll plus a 40-place part-time nursery. The catchment area was mixed; some private housing, some council property, some rented accommodation. It included a 'women's refuge' and a travellers' site which was undergoing improvement but was still not designated 'permanent'. Hence some of the pupils were transient visitors. A third of the school intake was of Asian origin, the majority of whom were Punjabi speakers.

During the research period there were twenty staff members including the school clerk, two nursery nurses, two school assistants and a pre-five home/school liaison teacher. In addition there were 3.7 teachers from the Ethnic Minority Support Service and 1.5 teachers for special needs on fixed yearly contracts. There was also a temporary teacher for travellers' education to act as a link between the travellers' site, the first school and the rest of the school pyramid. The headteacher was non-teaching and the deputy headteacher was non-class teaching for two terms but had responsibility for the school's special needs programme and did some special needs support teaching in some classes.

As a policy for meeting all educational needs within the classroom evolved, changes in staff resources and the deployment of these had had a considerable impact on class teachers and support teachers. In many respects the class teacher had become a team manager rather than a team member, in terms of having to co-ordinate and plan the involvement of several other adults who now played an important daily role in the classroom. Support teachers were now seen to be part of the classroom management structure. This major departure from the traditional form of organisation − one adult to one class − had inevitably created new concerns. Initially, team teaching and integration worked well but, as the numbers of extra people grew, the management of their involvement became more complex and time-consuming and necessarily affected the way the class teacher worked and related to her class.

Classes were organised into year group teams under a team leader for the purpose of planning the termly curriculum for that year group. All members of staff associated with a year group were part of this planning team and met together essentially at the beginnings and ends of terms to review and forward plan for the term. Meetings during the term were on a more *ad hoc* basis. Each class teacher also related to a class team so that she and the relevant support staff could plan together weekly programmes of work. These class planning meetings always included the EMSS teacher and in some cases the SNS teacher but may also have included any one of the liaison staff and/or a teacher from an outside support service. An EMSS or SNS teacher may have related to at least two year group teams and in some cases up to three class teams. All planning meetings took place outside the normal daily teaching hours. Added to these demands on non-teaching time were the regular staff meetings, in-service training meetings and curriculum development meetings.

## Difficulties arising from support provision

Various difficulties seemed to be arising for which no obvious solutions could be found. Concerns were being expressed but not at a whole-school level. It seemed that many problems arose from, or were exacerbated by, the increase in workload and pressure staff were under to meet and plan with so many different people, who in their turn were having too many claims made on their time by members of several other teams. Not enough time was now available to do all the things which made a team run effectively. There appeared to be a lack of predictability as to whether or not a support helper or teacher would arrive when expected. Staff could not always rely on things remaining as planned. Sometimes changes were known about in advance, sometimes not. Absences sometimes increased the pressure on staff whose classroom planning might have relied upon the involvement of an extra person. There seemed at times to be a lack of flexibility and spontaneity in teaching because of the need to adhere to a rigid timetable. Some felt that too much time was spent in the 'organisation' of the children, staff and other support to the cost of the 'content' of the teaching.

Another cause for concern appeared to be that of the pressure of constantly working with other adults in the room with the result that teachers' classroom management and teaching were under the regular scrutiny of colleagues, parents and other professionals and helpers. The amount of work, preparation and provision of materials necessarily increased if three or more adults were working together in one classroom as a greater number of activities could be going on at one time. Teachers working with younger children in school talked of losing breaktimes and lunchtimes in the need to clear away and put out new materials for the next session – problems intensified by the necessity of sharing space and resources with another class.

Certain teachers had begun to rationalise their situation in different ways. Some had begun a system of withdrawal so that any extra professional help was responsible for a particular group of children and removed them from the class on a regular basis – a complete reversal of school policy. One teacher decided to plan for her class as if no one else was coming in, then whoever did arrive 'fitted in'. Others were finding it impossible to meet and plan in advance and therefore class teachers were planning for everyone the evening before and any extra adults involved the next day would either read the notes the following morning before school or before the session they were involved in began. This left the class teacher with a huge burden of planning and preparation and the ideas of one teacher were not always successfully carried out by another. Although some teams within this large staff were working successfully and co-operatively, most staff were aware of the difficulties of others and all felt that for a team to remain viable and dynamic more and more effort was being demanded. Gray suggests:

all organisations are in a complex state of internal (and external) conflict and that when conflicts can be resolved easily and quickly the organisation is in a healthy state; but when they are suppressed there is a build-up of frustration that leads to unmanageable crises. These conflicts have their origin in the wide variety of changing needs felt by members of the school, needs which require them constantly to renegotiate their terms of membership in an unspoken psychological contract.

(1975, p.253)

There appeared to be a strong need to renegotiate or reassess the organisation and management of support help in the school.

## Methodology

In my case study, survey, classroom observation and interview were used to provide information on the involvement and perspectives of supporting adults. This essentially eclectic design allowed for evidence from different sources to be examined, compared and cross checked. It may be argued that the greater the number of viewpoints on the same issue, the greater the chance of its validation. This cross referencing of data was advocated by Stenhouse: 'In order to establish what *really* went on we use "triangulation" taking bearings on the issue by using evidence from different sources to cross check' (1982, p.269). Differences in interpretation and disagreements about what actually happened are inevitable when many participants have a different role to play in the same action. Triangulation helps to highlight these different perspectives and broaden our understanding of the interrelationships between the methods used and the data collected. Understanding the roles and perspectives of others was found to be the key to many misinterpretations. From the data collected it became clear that each group − class teachers, EMSS teachers, SNS teachers and volunteers − felt that they had difficulties which the other groups did not have or appreciate and yet from the interview data many of these difficulties were common to all groups; pressure of work, undermining of status, lack of reliability, lack of uniformity in basic routines from one class to another or from one adult to another.

Triangulation can take many forms. I used within methods triangulation in confirming trends identified from the collection of data concerning the incidence and nature of support help within my own classroom, by asking other class teachers to replicate the survey I had used. I obtained representative data but not total participation in its collection. The problem was that I needed data to support my study but the use of a survey put extra pressure on people – something else to fit into an already heavy workload. Attitudes ranged from 'Yes, of course I'll help', to 'I've so much to do one more thing won't make any difference', to no response at all. Using survey, classroom observations and interviews involved between methods triangulation. It was intended that the different methods of data collection used would be compatible, mutually supportive and mutually illuminating.

Although teacher researchers in their own schools may have advantages over the outside researcher in that the teacher researcher is already accepted, tends not to be questioned or treated with suspicion and does not always need to negotiate entry to the research situation, there is in this position the disadvantage of bias. For example, being well known to prospective interviewees, as Woods (1986, p.64) points out, has the drawback that a person's values and interests are known to the interviewees. This may close up particular avenues of investigation about which the interviewee knows the interviewer holds strong views or attitudes. It was well known that I was very committed to team planning and involvement. Whether I therefore received some guarded or tempered responses had to be considered when analysing the data.

Interviewees may give an answer which is false or closer to what they consider to be the socially, or in this case, the more educationally accepted answer, than the response which would more truthfully reflect their views. An interviewer might consciously or subconsciously lead interviewees to answer a question or angle an answer in a certain direction which may add weight to a preconceived hypothesis. However carefully bias is eliminated from the interview questions it is very difficult to prevent bias from creeping in through facial expression, gesture, tone of voice. I found myself nodding agreement and colluding with statements at times: things a trained interviewer presumably learns to avoid.

In looking through the data I was of the opinion that people, in general, were very frank and tended not to cover up or gloss over problems or situations they felt strongly about or had a grievance about. All were assured of anonymity and were at liberty to decline to answer any of the questions they felt they did not wish to respond to, but in the event no one found this necessary. Most people reflected Measor's comment:

> Many teachers said that they had really enjoyed the opportunity to talk about their work and to air their grievances about their work situation. It may be that such research has a counselling function.
>
> (1985, p.67)

As I have suggested, as a class teacher in the school studied, it would have been impossible for me as a teacher researcher to have entirely eliminated subjective judgement and personal bias. In concentrating largely on data from support teachers and volunteers rather than from class teachers with whom I more readily identified, I hoped to avoid some of the more obvious problems of bias. However, in order to establish some trends and areas of investigation, my starting point, as a class teacher researcher, was my own classroom.

## The class teacher's perspective

I monitored my own classroom over a two-week period. The data, as can be seen in Figure 9.1, revealed that in this one class there was daily involvement of the EMSS, SNS and volunteer helpers, with intermittent visits from the home/school liaison teacher, the travellers' liaison teacher, the ethnic minorities liaison teacher, a school psychologist and the school nurse. Then there were irregular visitors such as students, advisers and parents. I found that on average, five times a week, what was expected to happen did not occur, which meant that I was often revising plans at the last minute. Sometimes someone arrived who I hadn't planned for; sometimes someone failed to arrive who I had planned for. For only three sessions a week was I scheduled to teach on my own in the classroom.

Having looked at the incidence and nature of the involvement of 'extra' people in my classroom I needed to investigate whether what happened in my classroom was a typical pattern of involvement for the whole school. I went on, therefore, to replicate my initial survey with as many staff as would agree to help. The information gained from the week's survey completed by the class teachers revealed an interesting pattern of involvement which could be traced throughout most of the school and which appeared to reflect

Figure 9.1    The involvement of extra people in one class: Week 1.

| Week Beg 16.11.87 | 9.00–10.35 a.m. | | | 10,50–12.00 noon | | |
|---|---|---|---|---|---|---|
| | Expected | Who came | Other interruptions | Expected | Who came | Other interruptions |
| MON | EMSS VH | EMSS VH | SA (5 mins) Parent (5 mins) Head (5 mins) | EMSS VH | EMSS VH | School Nurse (3 mins) |
| TUE | VH | | TLT (2 mins) | SNS | SNS | Parent (2 mins) |
| WED | VH | | School Psychologist and EMLT (5 mins) | EMSS SNS SNS | | EMLT (5 mins) |
| THU | VH Tutor and Student (Observing) | VH VH T and S | | VH | VH VH | CT called out to speak to T and S – EMMS covers |
| FRI | VH SNS | VH SNS | | VH | VH | CT called out to speak to adviser-Dep Head covers |
| MON | 1.15–2.20 p.m. | | | 2.30–3.15 p.m. | SNS | |
| TUE | EMSS 6 Par to discuss ch's work | 6 Par | HSL (2 mins) | 4 Par to discuss ch's work | 4 Par SNS | TLT (5 mins) Head (10 mins) |
| WED | EMSS | EMSS SNS | | | | Parent (3 mins) |
| THU | | | | SNS | | |
| FRI | EMSS SA VH | EMSS SA VH | | SNS VH | SNS VH | |

Key:   EMSS   Ethnic Minority Support Service     VH      Volunteer Helper
        SA      School Assistant                 CT      Class Teacher
        TLT    Travellers Liaison Teacher          SNS    Special Needs Support
        EMLT   Ethnic Minorities Liaison Teacher    Par     Parent
        HSL    Home/School Liaison Teacher        T and S   Tutor and Student

the pattern I found in the analysis of my own two weeks' data collection. EMSS, SNS, school assistant and volunteer help were involved in classrooms on a regular weekly basis. On an irregular basis the head, deputy head and the teacher for the partially sighted were also involved. Other people involved included a peripatetic music teacher, the school nurse, travellers' liaison teacher, pre-5 home/school liaison teacher, school psychological service and three unplanned, unexpected visitors (including a goat!).

The involvement of others seemed to be higher at the lower end of school. It appeared from interviews with two class teachers of the younger children that the involvement of others did have an influence on their planning and organisation which could be so finely tuned that it allowed little flexibility or spontaneity, or could be completely disrupted if someone who was expected failed to arrive. The reliability of support provision in the week studied was fairly high with people not coming when expected in only 17 sessions out of a total of 160. However, the absences were concentrated on the same classes. Eight sessions were affected in the class with the highest involvement of others (that is, 8 sessions out of 16). Three sessions were affected in the first-year class with the least involvement of others (that is 3 sessions out of 11). So where there was unreliability it must have had a considerable impact on those particular classes. In 12 of the sessions where extra help was expected but did not come it was volunteer helpers who failed to arrive. The other 5 sessions were due to support staff absences: the LEA did not supply cover for support staff absences. As a class teacher I found the unexpected non-arrival of help extremely frustrating, as a well-planned teaching session which was relying on another person being present could have to be abandoned.

An incidental factor to emerge from the surveys was that even when no extra help was in the classroom, classes were subject to interruptions (Table 9.1). These tended to be concentrated at the lower end of school and gradually became fewer higher up the school. The high interruption rate in the first-year classes may be accounted for to some extent by children coming for clothing (all spare clothing was stored here) or for books (a shared bookcase was situated in one of these rooms). Interest in the interruptions and surprise at their high incidence gave rise to much comment in the staffroom at the time of the data collection and there was an unexpected consequence. Data collection began on a Wednesday and the total number of interruptions for that day was 56. On the following Monday a note was sent round school from the headteacher asking teachers not to send children round school during lesson time with lost property, notes and non-urgent enquiries and requests. On Tuesday the interruptions totalled 17 – a dramatic drop. At least there had been one useful, if

Table 9.1 The number of interruptions for each class during one week

| Class | Wed | Thu | Fri | Mon | Tue | Total |
|-------|-----|-----|-----|-----|-----|-------|
| A1 | 9 | 2 | 7 | 6 | 3 | 27 |
| A2 | 5 | 8 | 2 | 5 | 1 | 21 |
| B1 | 7 | 4 | 3 | 2 | 0 | 16 |
| B2 | 8 | 4 | 4 | 4 | 5 | 25 |
| C1 | 6 | 2 | 2 | 5 | 0 | 15 |
| C2 | 9 | 2 | 5 | 4 | 4 | 24 |
| D1 | 9 | 1 | 1 | 1 | 0 | 12 |
| D3 | 3 | 3 | 5 | 7 | 4 | 22 |
| Daily Total | 56 | 26 | 29 | 34 | 17 | |

+9*      +8**

\* Unusual interruptions: 5 classes have visit from a parent, her child and a goat. 4 classes disturbed by visits from a member of SNS and an EMSS teacher to sort out a problem.

\*\* All classes have a school assistant in their room on Monday morning for collection of dinner money.

unintentional, effect of carrying out the survey. The collection of clothing was subsequently placed in a more central position.

## Classroom management and the SNS team

The SNS team began the school year as a team of four but gradually dwindled in size throughout the year as one team member became responsible for a new reception class in January and another in April. This immediately highlights a difficulty in the special needs provision: it was always changing. In the autumn term the school had 3.5 SNS teachers, including the 0.5 for travellers' children, between ten classes. The spring term had 2.5 teachers working with eleven classes and the summer term, 1.5 teachers working with twelve classes. In the final term the deputy head became a part-time class teacher of a third reception class, maintaining her role as co-ordinator of special needs and having limited time for her duties as deputy head. Therefore the SNS provision had very fundamental problems which some felt led to a lack of consistency and continuity in the provision for many children and teachers.

The early stages of the implementation of SNS integration gave rise to considerable discontent and in some cases opposition, much of which could have been due to the fact that the SNS programme was put into operation without the involvement of class teachers in the planning and discussion stages of the scheme. As Thomas and Jackson point out:

> It is important to identify *all* those who will be affected by the change ... and to canvass their opinions. People are far more

> likely to work for an innovation if they feel that they have been
> consulted and that they have contributed to the change.
>
> (1986, p.27)

Perhaps because of the early problems and because of the uncertainty as to the level of staffing and resourcing available for special needs support at any particular time the support at the time of the study lacked uniformity. It appeared to be provided quite differently by each individual and depended largely on the negotiations made between the support teachers and each of the class teachers they worked with. Not only did each support teacher work differently from the others but, as can be seen in Figure 9.2, each support teacher worked differently with each class teacher. No one was completely satisfied with the way she worked. The situation that received most approval was one in which the class teacher and the support teacher shared the planning and the SNS support teacher felt an integrated and valued member of a class team. Too often the support teacher felt that her work was 'added on' and as such was devalued. If a class teacher viewed support work as 'taking a group off their hands' that was giving no value to the learning experience being provided by that professional, relegating the SNS teacher's role to that described by a member of the EMSS team, of 'highly paid helper'.

The number of classes, children and class teachers supported by any one SNS teacher was also an issue. There was duplication of work and effort and little time for discussion with the class teacher or for joint record keeping. One teacher felt that the way in which she now worked was a compromise between what she felt she ought to be doing and what was practicable to hope for. She would have liked to have spent more time planning the provision for each child with the class teacher. However remarks such as 'I haven't time to spend talking about one child' were quoted as responses made by some class teachers to SNS staff seeking a time for discussion.

## Areas of conflict

SNS staff identified several areas which created the potential for conflict in the context of a shared teaching situation:

1.  Sometimes the work of a small group cut across the rest of the classroom working atmosphere. Especially in the older

Figure 9.2   The views of SNS teacher 2 regarding classroom management

| Organisation | Comments |
|---|---|
| a) 4 classes, 4 different year groups. | |
| b) To work only in classes with travellers. Then to work with the travellers and special needs children in those classes. SN children selected from the SN files. | Involved some juggling to gather all the travellers in certain classes. Lots of teachers changed the groups or the groups changed anyway as the children progressed through the year. |
| c) I work with 6 to 8 in a group normally. Sometimes withdraw if the class teacher requests. | There is a place for withdrawal. Having peace and quiet for children with poor concentration. Some activities require it − cannot say no withdrawal *per/se*. Withdrawal had seemed to have had results in settling in travellers. |
| d) In one class have planned with the class teacher and EMSS teacher and then planned within these guidelines for my groups. Not always the same group and sometimes the class teacher works with the SN group. | Support is cross curricular and not always with the same group, allowing chance for the same group, allowing chance for the class teacher to work with a group and me to supervise the class. I welcome the change of role and think it good to give the class teacher opportunity to give extra attention which as a class teacher myself, in the past, I have wished for. |
| In other classes I've had a group and I've done my own thing but always basic reading and writing skills. | Can be very monotonous. |
| e) Use shared notes but not always added to by the class teacher. | In some classes I feel added on, in some I feel part of the curriculum in a structured way. Rather disappointing in some cases − feel like a spare part. My success depends on the class teacher and the working relationship. |

classes, a group could be too noisy if they were playing a game and the children became excited. SNS staff found that their work often involved stimulating talk and therefore the learning situations they planned could be incompatible with the working atmosphere of the rest of the class.

2. Teachers allowed different working noise levels and the SNS teacher had to adapt to what each class teacher demanded. This could be difficult. One SNS teacher found it hard to work in a class where the teacher was 'loud': 'I find it very aggravating and it cuts across my concentration so it must cut across the children's'.

3. People had different methods and procedures and children did not always receive the same advice or instructions which could lead to confusion. The SNS teachers felt that organisation and routines should be more consistent throughout a school. For a support teacher there was a need for some continuity in basic routines when moving from room to room, as it was impossible to work efficiently and effectively when constantly required to readjust and adapt to different practices.

4. Sometimes control and general discipline created problems. One SNS teacher did not feel that this was her area of responsibility. SNS teachers, 'need to be aware of and keep within the confines of the task they are there to perform'. For two teachers discipline was felt to be a shared responsibility:

    I would discipline if the class teacher doesn't notice and vice versa.

    I feel guilty sometimes if I haven't noticed something the class teacher has but it works both ways.

    Neither is upset by the other if the relationship is right.

    One teacher said that she would not quieten the whole class as she did not view that as her responsibility. She would speak quietly to a child she saw misbehaving but who had not been noticed by the class teacher. However if she was responsible for a group she would not expect the class teacher to discipline her group: 'I would be offended'. There was nevertheless some consensus between SNS staff towards certain aspects of classroom discipline. All felt that they needed to support and confirm the class teacher's position of overall control and were sensitive to the undesirability of undermining the class teacher's discipline: '[we] need to be very sensitive to the class teacher's standards and expectations in terms of noise level and general discipline and control'.

5. 'It's not easy to please all of the people all of the time.' Personality was seen as a key issue and the teacher quoted above felt that it was much easier to give in and go along

with the majority. She had at times felt 'inferior' or that it was not her 'place' to object or question. She saw herself as the acquiescer: 'For the sake of relationships I am the one who makes all the overtures'.

It can be seen that the areas of conflict identified by the SNS teachers were largely concerned with the need to adapt learning tasks for children with special educational needs to a gamut of differing working environments. A lack of consistency in basic routines and expectations from classroom to classroom tended to make their role extremely demanding.

## Class-based special needs provision: advantages and concerns

In reviewing the advantages of their presence in school teachers identified many positive effects but countered these with several concerns.

A major advantage was that SNS provision enabled the special needs child to work in a small group or receive individual attention. Children were not left to struggle, as all teachers were more aware of their needs and had some means of meeting those needs. There was less chance of a withdrawn child in a large class being overlooked and there were more opportunities to help build up a child's self esteem.

When a support teacher was in a classroom the class teacher was often left with a smaller class group and therefore more time and attention was available for all children: every child benefited. As behavioural and social problems were supported, all the children in the class felt the effect because the class teacher was not having to give all her attention to one especially disruptive or demanding child. Awareness of special needs had helped to heighten teachers' sensitivity to the needs of all children. Sometimes an SNS teacher provided a figure for a child to confide in, to build a special relationship with that they might have been unable to form with another adult.

The mutual support gained from working with other adults was thought to be beneficial and reassuring. Problems could be discussed, ideas sounded out and staff felt that they learned from each other in a professionally stimulating environment.

An interesting point which emerged was that while withdrawal was discouraged because of the effect that identifying a 'special' group might have upon the esteem of the pupils in that group, it was possible to create a similar effect within the classroom – almost a case of a withdrawal group within the classroom. SNS teachers found that this could be a problem in some classes. Other children were envious of the special attention that some children received and SNS teachers worried that children connected the special attention with underachievement.

In considering the wider aspect of classroom support some SNS staff felt that at times there could be too many people moving in and out of the classroom. For very young children this could cause difficulties in identifying all the adults: 'All are helping but [they are] not sure who is their teacher'. In some classes it was made obvious to the children that one of the SNS teachers was there to support the travellers' children. How the children in a class viewed the support teacher was felt to depend on the attitude of the class teacher and the way in which she required the support teacher to work.

SNS teachers said that they tried to be sensitive to the class teachers' needs. They recognised that planning and organisation could be difficult. They felt that they needed to be constructive and tactful when making suggestions. Colleagues had to take care not to threaten one another's self and professional esteem. For some teachers collaborative methods of working were hard. Some teachers were not happy about or were too aware of another person in the room, a particular problem it was felt, if the support person happened to be a senior member of staff. The working atmosphere in these situations was not as relaxed as it should be.

## Planning and presentation

When and how SNS teachers planned and prepared their work, and how far their planning and preparation was carried out in collaboration with class teachers and other support teachers, was of central importance to the whole issue of the team approach to the management of extra personnel in the classroom. SNS teachers' accounts of their planning procedures gave little evidence of common practice. Only one teacher mentioned working, planning and recording as part of a full class team within which the SNS teacher, the EMSS teacher and the class teacher all appeared to take an equal share in all of these aspects of classroom management. The comment by one of the teachers would seem to have some substance: 'The use of the term team teaching suggests more of a shared philosophy/ethos than really exists'. SNS teachers varied in their level of commitment to planning, with one teacher leaving all the day-to-day planning and classroom preparation to the class teacher. This particular teacher, however, did mention planning outside school hours and so perhaps long-term planning and general guidelines were jointly decided. This SNS teacher also seemed to have had greater autonomy than other members of the SNS team in deciding the way in which she worked. Last minute changes in plans were said by all to be frustrating. Teachers disliked feeling ill-prepared and often found that the resulting teaching sessions were unsatisfactory.

A point of agreement between the EMSS staff and the SNS staff was that a major disadvantage of team organisation was the amount of planning that had to be done and the calls on time made by the many meetings and discussions with colleagues necessary for the smooth and efficient running of a shared teaching situation. However, data relating to planning and preparation by SNS teachers suggested some contradictions here. The class teacher in one particular case seemed to take the full weight of all the planning and preparation. For the fostering of good relations, though, it seems necessary to achieve some balance in the respective workloads of class teachers and support teachers.

It seemed that for SNS teachers, collaboration with other staff and especially with class teachers was difficult. The EMSS staff generally seemed to have a much closer working relationship with their class teachers, perhaps because they were more involved with larger numbers of pupils in fewer classes. EMSS involvement in school had a long tradition of working within the classrooms and as such many early problems had been resolved. Also the EMSS Service had a recognised professional structure at LEA level with an adviser having overall responsibility for the service. EMSS teachers met regularly as a group for INSET and the exchange of ideas. As a result, EMSS teachers felt that they had expertise to share and that their contributions were valued. The SNS teachers did not have this LEA training, backing or permanency. Provision was irregular and temporary.

## Conclusion

The provision and management of within-classroom support demands a shift away from the traditional roles of class teachers and support teachers. This could create problems for teachers who are unused to planning with or working alongside others. In the school studied class teachers and support teachers had had little or no training in team or shared teaching or working with parents or volunteers. Many interrelating factors such as personality, reliability, mutual respect, support and co-operation, shared philosophy, contribute to the success of within-classroom involvement of adults throughout a school. Commitment to and belief in an ethos may not, however, be enough to ensure its success. The data analysis suggested that, to some extent, for such a scheme to run smoothly the cardinal principle must be, as Gray (1985) states, to 'move towards the simplest structure' of management possible (p.26). The more complex the structure, the more demanding of people's time and energy it would appear to become.

Support staff clearly implied that a small team was more workable and remained more effective than a large team and the number of teams and classrooms that any one teacher had to relate to should be kept to the minimum. This study indicated that when the management of the support programme became too complex and time-consuming people tended to reduce their commitment to joint planning and teaching by adopting a level of interdependence, requiring less in the way of time, communication and co-ordination. There was some return to withdrawal methods; some class teachers planned without co-ordinating with their support teachers and helpers and some class teachers operated almost in spite of the support. Hence, if the management is out of sympathy with the practice, the resulting problems may detract from or possibly outweigh the clear advantages and rewards which can be gained from the successful utilisation of human resources within classrooms.

For the school studied, several factors mitigated against the design of a simple and effective management structure. The peripatetic nature of the EMSS, the lack of real commitment from the LEA to make SNS provision regular or permanent and the voluntary nature of the other support made organisation difficult both at class level and for the school as a whole.

If the philosophy and spirit of the 1981 Education Act are to be put into action then the nature of support for children with special educational needs in ordinary schools requires reappraisal. Extra human resources may mean extra teaching and support time for children with special educational needs, but may also mean increased pressure on staff, perhaps especially, the class teacher. The problem seems to stem from a lack of recognition of the management issues involved. Providing extra resources of any kind demands the added responsibility of providing training and guidelines if those resources are to be used effectively. Putting more adults in a classroom does not necessarily relieve the difficulties of meeting all needs within the classroom. Staffing for special needs in ordinary schools must also adequately represent the number of pupils requiring support.

Although the study identified many problems and disadvantages of support work, it must be noted that because they were high-lighted, many of the difficulties were talked through and began to be resolved. What was learned was that everyone has to be involved in any new initiative from the outset. Building sound working relationships and planning and implementing initiatives take time. As a teacher researcher I had my perceptions sharpened. I was able to focus on the way other people viewed the whole issue of classroom support. It led me to reassess my own practice and I feel that I am now more aware of the need to develop a classroom organisation which allows for flexibility and self-maintenance within a clear, whole-school management structure.

## References

Gray, H.L. (1975) 'Exchange and conflict in the school', in Houghton, V. McHugh, R. and Morgan, C. (eds) *Management in Education Reader 1: The Management of Organisations and Individuals*, London: Ward Lock.

Gray, H.L. (1985) *Change and Management in Schools*, Stoke-on-Trent: Deanhouse (2nd ed).

Measor, L. (1985) 'Interviewing: a strategy in qualitative research', in Burgess, R.G. (ed) *Strategies of Educational Research: Qualitative Methods*, Lewes: Falmer Press.

Stenhouse, L. (1982) 'The conduct, analysis and reporting of case study in educational research and evaluation', in McCormick, R. (ed) *Calling Education to Account*. London: Heinemann Educational.

Thomas, G. and Jackson, B. (1986) 'The whole-school approach to integration'. *British Journal of Special Education* 13, 27 – 9.

Woods, P. (1986) *Inside Schools: Ethnography in Educational Research* London: Routledge and Kegan Paul.

# CHAPTER 10

# Return to School from an Assessment Centre

Joan Normington

I am the headteacher of a school attached to a Social Services Assessment Centre which I shall call the Centre. Our primary function is to assess the social, physical, emotional and educational needs of the children referred to us. The Centre offers opportunities for various agencies to consider the children's needs and their home and educational circumstances before deciding on courses of action after the earliest and most simple interventions have failed. In many cases, however, such an assessment may have been left too late, and many options are no longer available. An example would be the referral of persistent non-school attenders when they are almost sixteen years old.

Shelagh was typical. Admitted from home following sexual abuse by her mother's second husband, she was a quiet withdrawn girl who had, nevertheless, a droll sense of humour. Her relationships with her family, never good, had deteriorated since her complaints against her step-father and she was finding it difficult to come to terms with the rejection and distress that resulted. Following an extended period at the Centre, where she had help from a specialist psychiatric social worker, it was decided to attempt a return to her original school at her request. Her home situation looked hopeful and there seemed a definite possibility that she could eventually go back to her family.

Various school problems were anticipated, contingency plans were made to cover these and Shelagh returned to school. All went well until family relationships again broke down and, in desperation, Shelagh took a drug over-dose. She was felt to be too vulnerable and so she returned to school at the Centre.

Other attempts at returning pupils to their ordinary schools broke down for reasons which were perhaps more within our control, hence this study. The study's main aims were:

- to investigate the feasibility of using existing documentary information about the children to predict, anticipate and avert difficulties which may be encountered by the children and their teachers when re-entry is attempted;
- to investigate specific difficulties which actually arise;
- to identify successful (and unsuccessful) strategies that can be used by those involved in helping children return to ordinary schools.

When a child is ready to go out to ordinary school our liaison teacher is usually, but not always, involved. I make the initial approach to the headteacher, particularly if it is a change of school, and arrange for a teacher to go to the school to make plans with their staff if they so wish.

If they agree to admit the child and to our involvement, the next step is often an introductory visit, with the child, to meet staff, discuss options, and agree on a time-table. It may be decided that a gradual introduction is necessary; it may be that parallel work is supplied so that we can ensure that the child is eased in with the minimum of academic difficulties; a contract may be drawn up, agreed to and signed; arrangements for each child are individual and are consequently varied.

The liaison teacher may take the child to school at first, then s/he will travel by public transport, and eventually the child will go alone. Visits to support the child and the school's staff will be arranged. Where possible, we liaise with the support services, house staff at the Centre or other community homes, parents and social workers.

## The assessment centre

Children at the Centre, boys and girls aged from eight to seventeen, may be referred by Social Services or by the Education Authority. Many of the residents attend the school at the Centre, as do a small number of day pupils. Their educational difficulties include poor attendance, underachievement and behaviour problems. Many are offenders and may be beyond parental control, whilst some are considered to be at risk or to be in moral danger. All have serious family and social difficulties and frequently find it hard to make and maintain relationships with peers and/or adults.

At the case conference following the six-week assessment period, social, emotional, physical and educational needs are identified and recommendations made as to an appropriate course of action. This may include a formal educational assessment under the 1981 Education (Special Needs) Act.

Many children, however, return to their original schools or change to another ordinary school depending upon individual circumstances. It is with these children that this research is concerned.

## Research methodology

I had ready access to pupil records going back over many years. However, there had been little systematic follow-up of the success or failure of subsequent placements. The recent emphasis on community-based treatment meant that an increasing number of children were returning to ordinary schools and the use of a specific liaison teacher had been an innovation intended to assist this process. I decided to concentrate on the experiences of children placed at the Centre during one calendar year, for whom resumed attendance at ordinary schools had been considered appropriate. In short, a series of pupil case studies.

This should have given studies of nine children. However, one did not want to take part. Another still involved the liaison teacher and looked like doing so for a considerable time. At his request I had agreed not to approach pupils or their schools during his involvement in case my intervention prejudiced the work he was doing. My sample, therefore, consisted of seven children whom I shall call Shelagh, Kevin, Jenny, Tina, Greg, Jeremy and Julie.

The research methods I used were:

1. Document study of each child's written reports prepared for the case conferences.
2. Interviews with the children and with teachers from the schools from which they came and to which they returned when different.

3.    Questionnaires administered to both the teaching and care staff at the Centre.
4.    A research diary in which I recorded observations made during the re-entry attempts.

'Case study is the examination of an instance in action.' (MacDonald and Walker, 1977, p.181).

I was examining seven 'instances in action'. My goal was to attempt some generalisation across the practices adopted to facilitate re-entry so that the research had a practical outcome.

Although I was looking at only a small number of children I felt this was perhaps out-weighed by the in-depth study and the fact that it enabled me to take into account the uniqueness of each individual. I chose to study particular cases rather than trying to consider the practice of re-integration into school as a general study as I believe the resulting data are real and enliven research. The evidence given is based on actual events rather than allowing people to describe what they like to think happens. The two are sometimes quite different — the difference between theory and practice.

The research was taking place within an institution over which I exert some control as the headteacher. Possibly my staff in school and the residential child care officers in the house would say the things they felt I wanted to hear rather than being frank. I am experienced at attending and chairing case conferences and reviews. It is possible to exert considerable influence on such occasions, particularly when the other participants are less experienced. There was, therefore, a possibility that I would be able to exert undue influence over the outcome. I hoped that the findings would help to identify necessary changes but made every effort to remain objective when analysing and evaluating the data. Awareness of the possibility of subjectivity was perhaps my best defence: 'The case study worker will recognize the need for a critical self awareness with regard to observation and interpretation as active, interventive processes, not passive or nonreactive' (Kemmis, 1980, p.113).

Nisbet and Watt suggest beginning case studies with 'an open phase, a general review without judgment' (1984, p.78). This occurred during a pilot study of one boy. I interviewed the boy, several social workers and teachers. Some completed Bristol Social Adjustment Guides. I studied the documentation. This process helped me to avoid duplication and focus on essentials in the main study.

## Document study

The documents available on each child are extensive; they are the reports typically collected for assessment at the Centre. They include a detailed social history prepared by the social worker based on existing records, interviews with the child's parents and with the child.

I chose not to involve the children's parents beyond asking their permission to study their children. Information regarding the home backgrounds came originally from them. Many are suspicious of any authority figures and would perhaps resent my questions, most of which they would have already discussed with a social worker with whom they have developed a relationship. I felt that the evidence in the social history, often obtained over many years of social work involvement with the family, to be more reliable than any I could obtain directly.

Other reports came from previous schools, educational psychologists, the school at the Centre, the Centre's house staff (this report is based on discussions with the child and observations made whilst the child is in residence), and medical information. Any other agency which may have been involved, such as the Adolescent Unit at the hospital or the Probation Service, will also have provided reports. The assessment report is completed by the summary of the case conference with its lists of needs and recommendations, and copies of any subsequent reviews.

I extracted information regarding the children's home circumstances from the documents in order to try to predict likely problems. Carroll (1977), Farrington (1980) and Galloway (1985) listed causes of adversity and stress in children's lives. By combining their lists I produced 26 factors which, whilst not necessarily causing disaffection or truancy from school, are often present in the histories of troubled and troublesome children.

As can be seen in Figure 10.1 all the children experienced multiple adversity. Despite some similarities it is evident that they have widely different problems at home which need to be appreciated when trying to re-establish a normal pattern of education. When the scale of the problems is considered it is not surprising that these children have experienced school difficulties.

Figure 10.1   List of Multiple Adversities

| | Tina | Julie | Shelagh | Jenny | Kevin | Greg | Jeremy |
|---|---|---|---|---|---|---|---|
| Live in a high-rise tenement flat, or older-type estate of semi-detached council houses. | • | | • | | | • | • |
| More than 3 children per bedroom. | | | | | | | |
| More than 4 children in family. | | | | | | | |
| Not living with both parents. | | | • | • | • | • | • |
| Child has history of chronic illness. | | | | | | | |
| Child has history of severe illness or accident. | | • | • | | | | • |
| One or more sibling has history of chronic illness. | | • | | • | | • | |
| One or more sibling has history of severe illness or accident. | • | | • | | | • | • |
| Mother has history of chronic illness. | | | • | • | | • | • |
| Mother has history of severe illness or accident. | • | | • | | | • | • |
| Father has history of chronic illness. | | | | ? | | ? | |
| Father has history of severe illness or accident. | | | | ? | | ? | |
| Bereavement of close relative. | • | • | | | | | |
| Child has been/is in care. | • | • | • | • | • | | • |
| One or more sibling has been/is in care. | | | | • | | • | |
| Parents are on social security/have been within last 12 months. | • | | • | | | • | |
| More than two weeks separation from mother. | • | • | • | • | • | • | • |
| More than two weeks separation from father. | | • | • | • | • | • | • |
| History of sociological problems. | • | | • | • | • | • | • |
| Parents unemployed or of low socio-economic status. | • | | • | • | | • | • |
| Low intellectual levels. | • | | • | • | | • | |
| Negative attitudes to school and clash of values with school. | | | • | • | | • | |
| Criminal parents. | | | • | | | | |
| Delinquent siblings. | | • | | • | | • | |
| Poor child-rearing practices. | • | • | • | • | • | • | • |
| Disinterested parents. | • | | • | • | • | • | |

GALLOWAY (1985)

CARROLL (1977)

FARRINGTON (1980)

What may be surprising is that they have not been more severe.

The various reports about the children proved to be a rich source of information. They offered valuable insights into the children's home circumstances and other problems, and also allowed predictions of possible school difficulty to be made.

*Interviews*

I interviewed all the children, except Shelagh, out of school hours. If the children had left the Centre I met them after school or on Saturday. We usually went for a meal first to renew our relationship. If the children were still living at the Centre we talked in a place of their choosing, usually their own bedrooms, although Kevin chose the office of the officer-in-charge as the venue. In Shelagh's case, as she was a girl who found it difficult to talk, she volunteered to write the answers to the questions in the interview schedule. This she did, very conscientiously, by herself during a time when I normally taught her group. She was not prepared to discuss the answers subsequently but I believe she gave her honest views. It is a system that she used extensively during her time at the Centre when she wished to communicate her inner feelings to the staff. She was only able to talk to adults that she really trusted and was fully at ease with − I was not one of them.

Although I have overtly amicable relationships with the children at the Centre I am still the headteacher and so some reserve was to be expected. However, there did not seem to be any alternative to individual interviews. I hoped that by the time we talked, my involvement in their lives would be peripheral but not too distant and so they would be less concerned with giving me the 'right' answer and more disposed to be honest. I also interviewed the teachers in the ordinary schools most closely involved with the children, asking questions concerning anticipated problems, the nature of the planning, co-operation with the Centre and the progress of the reintegration attempts.

## Pupils' perceptions of returning to school

It was important to establish how the children at the Centre feel about their ordinary schools and their eventual return to them. Given such information it should be possible to take their fears and expectations into account when developing re-entry plans.

*Missing schoolwork*

In group discussions, the major fears expressed were those about schoolwork. The more intelligent children commented that they were missing work in a wider range of subjects than we can offer at the Centre. After all at the high schools, as Greg remarked, 'You get more education 'cos there's a lot more teachers and everyfing'. There was some concern about missing examination courses.

Individual children were concerned with the problems of having to catch up missed work and Kevin in particular had been afraid that he would have to copy up nearly two months work. The two children who changed schools, Jeremy and Jenny, commented on the difficulties which arose from different teaching methods, curricula and experience. Jeremy said he found maths hard because, 'They're telling me to do it their way when I've already been taught how to do it my way'. Jenny thought that: 'It isn't fair 'cos they've had all the experience that I haven't. I get dead embarrassed and they all call me a divvy'. She also complained that one teacher acted: 'as though I'm like every other kid what's had all the experience and everything. But I'm not. I need more than anybody 'cos I've missed so much school'. She would not ask her class teacher to explain matters in case: 'He might say summat awful or do summat. He might shout at me'.

Interestingly the children thought this to be a more important issue than did their teachers. The teachers were obviously aware that this could be a stressful area for children but were not themselves worried. They emphasised the importance of timing. For example, Greg's school was anxious that he went back as soon as possible as he was at the beginning of the fourth year — a crucial time as GCSE courses are commencing and to leave re-entry until later in the year would mean that any attempt to fit in with existing courses would be well-nigh impossible. Pastoral care teachers were far more concerned to pre-empt difficulties by ensuring that individual subject teachers were aware of problems and, rather than expecting missed work to be completed, looked out for and helped with specific difficulties as and when they arose.

## Peer-group relationships

Six of the seven children expressed fears concerning peer group relationships. Tina, who had always tended to be solitary, expressed worries at meeting large numbers of people again. She found their attempts to care for her to be a source of annoyance: 'I know that if I do go to school I'm gonna get followed around by a lot of people. I just want to get away from them'. Kevin, Shelagh, Jenny and Jeremy were all aware that they might have to fend off a lot of questions about where they had been and why. Jeremy expected that 'everyone would be picking on me and seeing how hard I was'.

Most of the children at the Centre have peer-group relationship difficulties and all we can do is to try to provide positive help, whilst they are at the Centre, in the skills necessary to make and keep friends. Boys in a group discussion emphasised the troubles often caused when placing a child in a school in a different neighbourhood. 'Kids just didn't like me 'cos I came from —— and we used to have battles.' This should be born in mind when placing children in different schools. If there is evidence of local rivalry it should certainly be a consideration.

The teachers were well aware that peer-group relationships were a major source of potential problems and took what steps they could to prevent trouble arising and provide support if necessary. It is not an easy area in which to intervene. Teachers can only offer help in specific instances. For example, Jenny had problems with one girl: 'and nobody told me don't mess about wi' Michelle 'cos she won't like it at all'. Her form teacher helped solve that particular problem, caused when Michelle believed she was losing her best friend, by talking the problem through with all three girls. Kevin's form teacher explained his situation briefly to the whole class. Julie's deputy head asked the cookery teacher to speak to the group when they were being nasty to Julie. The interventions had varying success.

## Reception by teachers

The children had fears about the reception they might receive from the teaching staff. Their attitudes towards teachers were largely negative. They did not expect to receive help, particularly with personal problems, and were hesitant about asking for any. Many of them wanted help in school. One said: 'Teachers should try and help you more than they do. Half the time they're just sitting down marking books'. On the other hand Greg said that if he had any personal problems he'd talk them out at home, 'where they belonged'. In group discussions with girls the feeling that teachers should help was more pronounced: 'I've never been at a school where they asked you why you haven't been'. 'They don't listen to why you ran off'; 'One certain teacher at our school, she'll talk everything out with you.

188

She's all right'. Finally a damning comment, in my opinion, from one girl:

> They used to tell me when I was at normal school, 'Oh, you come to school to get away from your problems and work'. I was so upset I just couldn't. It was, 'This is school. We've got nothing to do with it. You leave your problems at home when you come to school'.

Given the reception the children had expected to receive from the teaching staff, they seemed somewhat surprised by what actually happened. They had expressed fears at their welcome all of which proved unfounded. The teachers I interviewed were prepared to go to great lengths to try to ensure the success of the re-entry attempts and genuinely understood the problems the children had to encounter in their home situations. They realised that most of the children were very much at the mercy of their home circumstances and needed understanding and concern rather than retribution. There was general regret at their inability to do more. As Tina's year head told me, she is responsible for the pastoral care of 290 children and has an hour extra each week in which to do it. Too many year heads have to act as disciplinarians only, as they have neither the time nor resources to devote to the well-being of individuals.

Individual arrangements were made for most of the case-study children to help ease their relationships with staff. For example, in Julie's case, she was given a different maths teacher, a major factor, and the deputy head organised her timetable so she had different teachers for all subjects except one. This was despite the fact that she had expected 'all hell to break loose [when Julie returned] and they'd all blame me'.

## The first day

In discussing the return to school generally, two of the children admitted they did not like school. All were apprehensive at the thoughts of returning, even Greg who desperately wanted to go back. Most admitted to being frightened on their first day. Tina said:

> I felt funny going to that school after I missed so long. I just didn't want to go. As soon as I saw it I wanted to go home. I was frightened of going back and didn't know what to expect.

It is obvious, therefore, that a great deal of re-assurance is necessary. Several preliminary visits are needed, first to meet staff (or even just one particular teacher at first), then to renew acquaintance with the class. Going to and from school could well be difficult and ensuring that the child is taken by a sympathetic but firm adult is a sensible precaution. Six of the children reported that returning had been easier than they had expected. Kevin's advice to other children is:

> Don't be worried to go back. 'Cos that's what people think, that if they go back the teachers will get at 'em because they've been missing school. They don't pick on you. They just try to help you.

Some of the evidence is perhaps unreliable. For example, Julie firmly stated that her classmates had welcomed her back and she had 'loads of mates', but her teacher reported the exact opposite. Greg and Jeremy would not admit to there being any problems at all, even minor ones, until I probed deeply. This may have meant that their determination to succeed meant that they were not admitting to any possibility of difficulty even to themselves and were hoping to fool me (and themselves) or that simply denying the existence of problems means they will go away. On the whole, however, I believed the data to be reliable − if only because the links between the problems anticipated and experienced by the children correspond closely with those reported by the teachers and that were predicted in the documents.

The fact that six of the re-entry attempts could be counted as being reasonably successful was due in great measure to the children themselves. Without their determination and effort nothing can be done. Perhaps their awareness of likely problems was an inhibiting factor. Certainly planning was vital. In all cases something had to change. In Greg's case, he changed although the school also made obvious efforts to accommodate him. Jeremy's mother had changed her life so that he no longer felt responsible for her and could concentrate on being himself. Similar changes, either in the children, their home circumstances or at school, happened in all the case studies, except Tina. In her case, nothing had changed, and re-entry proved impossible.

Problems encountered by children are individual and it is not possible to produce generalised solutions. Much depends on detailed knowledge of the children and their circumstances. Given this, it is possible to predict difficulties and plan to avoid them. Their wishes are of crucial importance. Unless they wish to return to school, and are determined to make every effort to do so, then the re-entry is unlikely to succeed. Adults can facilitate reintegration and do all they can to ensure its success. Only the children can make the plans work by their acceptance of the help offered.

## The process of reintegration

Planning for re-entry is crucial. Some were planned in great detail, occasionally in the face of criticism from other members of the school's staff. Greg's year tutor was asked, 'Why are you wasting your time on him?'. He believed that Greg had to see that the school cared about him and wanted to help. He felt that 'it had paid off'. The evidence pointed that way as Greg told me that he could tell the teachers wanted him back. Others were less detailed. Only in Tina's case was planning non-existent and this was a factor in the failure of re-integration.

Similar arrangements were made for all the children, with the exception of Tina, and their returns were effected successfully. In Tina's case previous reports indicated that she would be a poor attender, be solitary and be likely to gravitate to less desirable members of the community. She was taken to school by the Centre's deputy headteacher to choose her subject options before the end of the summer term. Her return coincided with the first day of the new academic year and followed her return home (at her parents' insistence) during the summer holidays. Her parents denied the existence of problems and refused all further offers of help. Her mother took her to school on the first day and, to quote the year head, she was 'dumped like a sack of peas'. She began to truant and the situation was soon out of control. This had been predicted and I believe we over-estimated Tina's ability to cope in unchanged circumstances. We had not anticipated her parents' unwillingness to co-operate with the agencies, although both her social worker and EWO reported that her mother had often promised change and support but never produced either.

Teachers in schools are often unaware of the very difficult home circumstances that some children have to contend with. By ensuring that at least the pastoral care teacher is fully informed we can enlist greater sympathy and understanding which secures a more tolerant approach, although some year heads questioned the amount of information that should be given to the teaching team. It all depends on individual circumstances and the precise nature of a child's difficulties: 'You can make awful blunders if you don't know'. Seeking to help rather than discipline can avert confrontation. Being well-informed enables teachers to prepare plans and strategies to handle difficulties and to attempt to pre-empt them.

A key issue in successful re-integration is the involvement of the school in the decision to take the child. Tina's year head pointed this out very strongly and vividly:

> I find that we are undeniably very important but we play 'Pig-in-the-Middle'. Our advice is not sought, we are a dumping ground when people have made their decisions in high places and ignored what we've suggested and recommended, and children are dumped back on our doorstep.

In my case studies no child was returned to a school without the staff's agreement. I feel strongly that if a school has to take a child it does not want, then there is less likelihood of that child succeeding. Persuasion and reassurance are more helpful than direction. It is essential, however, that the school receives truthful reports of the child's behaviour. Glossing over potential difficulties does more harm than good.

Planning and consultation are perhaps most important in that the schools feel more involved and become willing participants rather than seeing themselves as the only available option. Staff at one school pointed out that great care was taken when moving a child to some special provision, but the same care was not taken when the child returned. 'If all the people put enough effort into the return then it could be managed better.' The issue of advance planning seems to be closely bound up with that of monitoring a child's progress and a formal procedure might be of use. The most effective planning seems to take place when it involves all those who are going to be working with the child, that is teacher, parents and/or care staff, the support agency and the child. Several teachers remarked that they were confident that the Centre was 'on the end of a phone' and would be available if required.

Gradual re-introduction is sometimes a useful strategy although for it to be truly successful, the practical difficulties to be overcome are tremendous. If it can be arranged on a subject basis it is very valuable; otherwise, timetabling considerations usually mean that it makes courses of work almost impossible to follow. Jenny's headteacher remarked: 'Having a foot in each camp is an uneasy arrangement. They're always going to find something wrong with either place and want to escape to the other'. Most of the teachers I interviewed held the opinion that an 'all-in' approach was to be preferred as it caused less confusion, made re-establishing relationships easier, was a simpler option practically and ensured greater academic consistency. However, introductory visits, specific timetabling agreements and effecting changes where necessary were most important.

Opinions regarding a change of schools were also varied. Some felt that a fresh start might be useful as sometimes children are 'not allowed to forget their past mistakes very easily if they return to the same school'. On the other hand, returning to the same school meant returning to old friends, occasionally desirable as it is sometimes necessary to capitalise on existing friendships, particularly in secondary schools: 'They are so big and daunting. The more you can do to break that down and give them confidence to come and keep coming the better'. One of the girls underlined that point when she commented that, 'You'll get used to it pretty quick 'cos all your mates are there'.

The children thought of many small practical matters that perhaps the adults had not considered. They were all anxious to avoid needless embarrassment and asked for specific details to be attended to, such as not being given free bus vouchers in public. More sensitive attention to detail could avoid potentially difficult situations. Academic considerations were given less stress by teachers than by the children, although measures such as giving a child photocopies of work missed through absence was a helpful strategy. Trying to maintain children on parallel courses of work when they are out of school was extremely problematic and the benefits gained are sometimes not worth the effort.

Another issue is the pastoral care system in operation. The children who returned were placed as far as possible with teachers who were sympathetic and who were able to relate readily with their pupils. The role of the form teacher as primary point of contact, as emphasised by Reynolds *et al.* (1980) and Reid (1986), ensured that

Jenny was put in the class of an especially sympathetic, motherly teacher so that she had a readily available point of contact. The year head's ability to co-ordinate across subject and departmental boundaries was demonstrated by Greg's tutor who made changes across the subject groupings in order to ensure the right teachers and subjects. This is an important aim of successful pastoral care advocated by Kyriacou (1986). The extent to which they were prepared to be flexible was an important feature in demonstrating to the children that their schools wanted them back and valued their success.

HMI (1978) emphasised the importance of relating the aims of off-site units to the expectations of return to ordinary schools and also to the need for well-defined re-entry processes. This was born out in my study. Evidence from the questionnaire given to the staff at the Centre indicates that our ethos should be such that it is expected that a child returns to ordinary schooling in the normal course of events and succeeds there.

## Changes following the study

This study emphasises the need for individual approaches to 'difficult' adolescents and demonstrates the necessity for objective and sensitive management. There are no general solutions other than to consider children individually, learn as much as possible about them, then make decisions. One of the most practical implications of my research was the recognition that plans to facilitate pupils' re-entry into school can be developed on the basis of evidence, particularly that from the documents. The plans made in Shelagh's case can be used to illustrate this. She was expected to be the subject of gossip and so, to provide her with answers for curious classmates, she prepared a cover story with the help of her year tutor and the Centre's liaison teacher, which gave reasonable responses to all foreseeable questions without her having to lie. They arranged a system of written communication based on a lesson by lesson diary, as we knew that she found verbal communication difficult and also provided her with an in-school bolt-hole to prevent her from running off as she had done previously. The year head saw each of her subject teachers individually and explained Shelagh's circumstances in order that there was less chance of her being subjected to thoughtless, and perhaps insensitive, questioning. As the journey to school was long, she was given special dispensation for late arrival. An efficient communication link between the school and the Centre was established.

Effective planning for re-entry should be detailed, involve everyone and be based on knowledge. Any reports prepared for such plans should be accurate and very honest. It is useless to try to minimise a child's difficulties; it is also unwise to exaggerate them. Support offered should be realistic and within the competence of the agency offering it. It must be absolutely reliable for the sake of both child and school.

There were implications for the way in which we prepared our school reports. We lacked specific detail concerning academic matters although our comments regarding a child's social and emotional features were valued. We changed them in order to be more specific about basic subjects.

The general ethos at the Centre has changed radically. It is now expected that children go out to ordinary school if at all possible. We have also found that emphasising the likelihood of a return to school following the assessment period, both to children and their teachers, is a useful technique. The school then does not merely think they have 'got rid of a trouble-maker', but begins to think constructively of ways to manage the re-integration of children when, rather than if, they return. Children who may not be able to cope in ordinary schools on their admission to the Centre are returned to them as soon as they can. The exceptions are pupils who arrive during the latter half of their fourth year and who would not be able to be accommodated in their own schools because of examination courses. These pupils follow courses of study at the Centre, at the local technical colleges and at their own schools for particular subjects wherever possible. We strive for normality as far as we can.

We make more use of the peripatetic support agency for children with behaviour problems than we used to do. They are involved at the beginning of any attempt at reintegration. With their help, we are able to effect gradual returns when this is felt to be appropriate as they have a greater degree of flexibility. Their skill at working with families has proved to be valuable, particularly with non-resident children. Their greatest value, however, has been that they are better able to maintain continuity once the child has left the Centre altogether. In the first stages of re-entry, the Centre's staff play a prominent role, but as the child becomes more settled in the school and at home, then we progressively withdraw, leaving the peripatetic staff to assume the supporting role.

We have made changes in our own organisation. Instead of having a designated member of staff to liaise with schools, the member of staff who knows the pupil best is the one who undertakes the role of co-ordinator. They attend reviews, planning meetings and so on, as well as making all contacts with the school and support agencies. This way, the schools know who they are working with, child and parents have a specific contact person and the onerous task of liaison is spread evenly. The teachers at the Centre also feel they have a greater commitment to their groups and assume more responsibility for their care. It is a more satisfying approach. During the initial assessment period, my deputy or I act as primary contact for schools and other professionals. The changes have been brought about in part as a result of this research and partly because we now work with a greater number of day pupils who have been admitted on mainly educational grounds. This means that we are helping more children re-enter ordinary schools and so the work load is too great for just one teacher.

## Implications of recent legislation

The implementation of the 1988 Education Reform Act provides new barriers and new possibilities for the re-integration into ordinary schools of pupils such as those we have at the Centre. The Local Management of Schools threatens the very future of those services we provide. At present we are a resource funded by the LEA. If schools have to pay, then we must make sure that the service we offer is efficient and cost-effective. Until the system settles down, I do not envisage many governing bodies being prepared to sanction large amounts of money being spent to help pupils who are unlikely to contribute favourably to a school's performance in National Curriculum assessment. However, if help is not forthcoming, by developing whole-school approaches to prevent disaffection and to create environments where all children are catered for and valued for their uniqueness, as recommended in the Elton Report (DES, 1989), then this is likely to have serious adverse consequences for individual children, for the quality of life in schools and for the role of youth in the wider society.

To meet the requirements of the National Curriculum, we have

196

already changed maths teaching at the Centre and are similarly developing the English curriculum. There have been benefits. The increased demand that the core subjects should be practically based means greater relevance to the pupils. The reports we prepare are more precise. The information going into schools is, we believe, more relevant to the school staff, and the schemes of work and resources available (good computer software, for example) are stimulating for staff and pupils alike. However, both these subjects are easily organised on an individual basis. Science and technology have proved more of a problem for us and are stretching our personal and material resources. Science, together with history and geography, provides much content to be covered. There is a danger that pressures to cover this content might make our teaching less appropriate for pupils who have already rejected such a diet. For many years the Centre has concentrated on developing alternative learning programmes which ensure success and which are essentially practical, providing skills necessary for day-to-day survival.

However, the National Curriculum could assist the re-integration of our children through all schools working on the same curriculum and sharing a common language, highlighting the importance of matching tasks to individual need through differentiation and an increased demand upon fitness for purpose in relation to individual, group and whole-class teaching. Consequently a change of school might be easier to effect. In particular, it may mean that it is not too late for pupils in the fourth year to return to ordinary schools.

## References

Carroll, H.C.M. (ed) (1977) *Absenteeism in South Wales: Studies of Pupils, their Homes and their Secondary Schools*. Swansea: Faculty of Education, University College, Swansea.

Department of Education and Science (1989) *Discipline in Schools (The Elton Report)*. London: HMSO.

Farrington, D. (1980) 'Truancy, delinquency, the home and the school', in Hersov, L. and Berg, I. (eds) *Out of School, Modern Perspectives in Truancy and School Refusal*. Chichester: John Wiley.

Galloway, D. (1985) *School and Persistent Absentees*. London: Pergamon Press.

Her Majesty's Inspectorate of Schools (1978) *Behavioural Units: A Survey of Special Units for Pupils with Behavioural Problems*. London: Department of Education and Science.

Kemmis, S. (1980) 'The imagination of the case and the invention of the study', in Simons, H. (ed) *Towards a Science of the Singular*. Norwich: Centre for Applied Research in Education.

Kyriacou, C. (1986) *Effective Teaching in Schools*. Oxford: Blackwell.

MacDonald, B. and Walker, R. (1977) 'Case study and the social philosophy of educational research', in Hamilton, D., Jenkins, D., King, C., MacDonald, B. and Parlett, M. (eds) *Beyond the Numbers Game. A Reader in Educational Evaluation*. London: MacMillan.

Nisbet, J. and Watt, J. (1984) 'Case study', in Bell, J., Bush, T., Fox, A., Goodey, J. and Goulding, S. (eds) *Conducting Small-scale Investigations in Educational Management*. London: Harper and Row.

Reid, K. (1986) *Disaffection from School*. London: Methuen.

Reynolds, D., Jones, D., St Leger, S. and Murgatroyd, S. (1980) 'School factors and truancy', in Hersov, L. and Berg, I. (eds) *Out of School, Modern Perspectives in Truancy and School Refusal*. Chichester: John Wiley.

# CHAPTER 11

## *Unit Accreditation at a Special School*
James Powell


Rook Dale School opened in 1977 shortly after the reorganisation
of Local Authority boundaries and at the end of a period of rapid
growth in the number of special schools. The LEA's existing special
school headteachers had already expressed the view that the reduced
catchment area and the predicted falling roles in schools generally
would mean that there would be no demand for a new school for
pupils with moderate learning difficulties (MLD) – previously
known as schools for Educationally Sub Normal (Moderate)
Pupils (ESN(M)). They did, however, argue that the new school
should cater for pupils with emotional and behavioural difficulties
(EBD). Rook Dale staff would argue that this is the role which
the school now largely fulfils. At the opening of the school the
IQ range was higher than in the traditional ESN(M) school and
there was a noticeable number of pupils with marked behaviour
problems, including some who had previously attended residential
schools administered by other authorities. The number on role
eventually exceeded the established number but, as predicted, then
gradually reduced and at the time of the research was only 59. Few
were recommended on the grounds of learning difficulty alone and
the main criteria for recommendation by educational psychologists
was either a refusal to attend school or unacceptable behaviour.
During the year of the research only five pupils were enrolled, three
of whom were in their final two years of compulsory education
and all had that 'degree of disruptive or non-conformist classroom
behaviour' which Tomlinson (1981, p.202) suggests are significant
factors in the identification of ESN(M) pupils by headteachers of
ordinary schools.

   Pupils attending schools such as Rook Dale experience some
degree of intellectual impairment resulting from a combination
of factors – including heredity, pre- and post-natal environmental

factors, childhood ill-health, unstable and stressful family backgrounds, emotional and economic deprivation – and are likely
to have emotional and behavioural problems resulting from a
sense of failure. It is my view that, while special schools have
earned a reputation as caring, protective environments, in their
attempt to combat that sense of failure, some are insufficiently
intellectually challenging – an issue which is now being addressed
more widely owing to the entitlement of all pupils to the National
Curriculum following the Education Reform Act of 1988. The field
of education is increasingly having to become more accountable
to society, industry, parents and the pupils themselves and special
education is by no means excluded from this. The 1981 Education
Act requires that LEAs not only identify and provide for pupils
with special needs but, having made a statement of their needs,
the LEA must ensure that this is reviewed annually by a written
report and that a full reassessment of their needs takes place at
the age of 13 + years.

The present state of high unemployment is particularly relevant
to the problem of motivating pupils attending the special school.
Unfortunately for the pupil who already has a sense of failure adult
status is directly related to employment which provides not only a
source of income but 'allows social interaction and confers social
status and recognition, a personal identity, and a sense of purpose
or achievement' (Bookis, 1984, p.60). Unemployed young people,
it is argued, 'experience severe feelings of powerlessness and uncertainty . . . become increasingly critical . . . towards themselves and
their abilities' (Bradley et al., 1983, pp.1–4) and many fall 'into a
state of withdrawal and depression' resulting in them 'spending as
much time as possible in bed' (Widlake, 1983, p.79).

Schools such as Rook Dale are therefore faced with the challenge
of motivating young people who are disadvantaged intellectually
and socially and who cannot look forward to satisfying employment
with any degree of confidence.

## The introduction of a modular approach and accreditation

Many special schools have traditionally followed the primary
practice of having a thematic approach to class or whole school
areas of interest. While this had featured at Rook Dale it had
gradually disappeared. There was a need to reintroduce this with
more emphasis on the environment, science and problem-solving.

As headteacher I had made what were no doubt weak attempts to encourage this, but the insignificant resources which had been purchased were banished to the back of a cupboard.

A vacancy on the staff enabled a rethink of the use of the traditional 'boys craft room' and, with support from a number of LEA advisers, an environmental studies room was set up to encourage a thematic, cross-curricular approach involving primary science and problem-solving. An important management role of headteachers is to recognise potentials and skills in other staff and to help them release their energy. I was able to identify and persuade a relatively new member of staff to accept the role as co-ordinator of environmental studies. The development was enthusiastically supported by LEA advisers responsible for craft, science and environmental studies and they provided school-based inservice training and for the co-ordinator to undertake a part-time modular Diploma in Professional Studies which emphasised the primary science/problem-solving approach to the curriculum. The inservice training day confirmed the choice of co-ordinator who was soon given the support of other staff including those who had initially felt over-looked and disappointed. This development led to the school's participation in the Scheme of Unit Accreditation.

## NPRA Scheme of Unit Accreditation

The Northern Partnership for Records of Achievement (NPRA) was established in 1984 to assist those LEAs and schools who were developing new methods of assessment and recording achievement. It consisted of the five boards of the Northern Examining Association and 35 LEAs. Of the original 33 pilot schools, half chose to use the Scheme of Unit Accreditation. These Units are written by teachers based on the curriculum of the school and validated by the LEA who, after completed work has been assessed by the NPRA, issue a Statement of Achievement Certificate. At the end of their school courses pupils are issued with a letter of Credit listing all the Units achieved. Warwick (1987) suggested that the NPRA Scheme is: 'a more realistic approach to continuous assessment than the multifarious files, projects, audio cassettes and sundry course materials recently spawned by so many schemes' (p.6).

Before undertaking her new responsibilities for environmental studies the co-ordinator had been aware of a local comprehensive school acting as the LEA's pilot school for Unit Accreditation.

While the scheme may have been known to teachers in comprehensive schools the information had not been passed on to the special schools and both the head of the senior department and I failed to respond to her suggestion that we become involved. However, after accepting the role of co-ordinator she was as she later said, for the first time in her career 'promoted, responsible and able to influence her own work'. She was now able to introduce the idea of accrediting modules of work in her own area of influence. The science adviser involved in supporting her work was also responsible for supervising the Scheme of Unit Accreditation and he welcomed the opportunity to introduce it to one of the Authority's special schools. Again staff were able to take part in school-based inservice training and a firm decision was made to adopt the scheme.

## The research project

I adopted an illuminative evaluation research strategy (see Chapter 1, pp.12–14) to investigate the implementation of the Unit Accreditation scheme in the school. This approach to evaluation does not dictate which techniques of data collection should be used, but the main one in such studies tends to be the interview. Thus, in my study I interviewed a sample of six pupils, chosen to represent both the MLD and EBD groups and also the ratio of twice as many boys as girls in the school. It was my intention to interview the parents of each of these in order to assess the relationship if any between the views held by parents and child. This proved difficult for two of the EBD pupils. The girl, who was in the care of the Local Authority, was transferred, due to pregnancy, from a childrens' home to a foster-home placement. One of the boys had a poor relationship with his father and he asked me not to visit his home. In addition to pupils and parents, I also interviewed those teachers involved with Unit Accreditation and, since the school's governing body included a managing director, a personnel officer and the manager of a Youth Training Scheme, they or their representatives agreed to take part in the research.

Bell (1987) points to the adaptability of the interview as its major advantage and suggests that 'a skilful interviewer can follow up ideas, probe responses and investigate motives and feelings which the questionnaire can never do' (p.70). Questionnaires were also felt to be inappropriate for my research because users of questionnaires with less-able pupils have reported difficulties due to the phrasing of questions (Reid, 1984), having to read the questions in order to overcome reading difficulties (Taylor, 1981) and having to clarify what was required (Raby and Walford, 1981). Having decided to use interviews as the main source of my data, I then needed to consider what kind of interviewing strategy to adopt. Hopkins (1985) has suggested that when pupils are used to interview other pupils there are advantages, such as being more candid with each other. However, a recent exercise in the school involving video recording of pupil-led interviews showed that they were unable to probe when the respondee failed to respond to a particular question and I decided not to use this method. I also decided not to use an 'outsider' such as a school assistant who without considerable training could not have been expected to use anything other than a rigid interview schedule. In spite of the possible disadvantage of the headteacher – pupil relationship it appeared better for me to conduct interviews of a 'semi-structured' nature which would have the advantage of allowing respondents to express themselves at length but also giving sufficient shape to prevent aimless rambling (Wragg, 1984).

During the pilot stage of my own study I was interviewed as part of the TVEI Project in the Authority which I found difficult on two counts. Firstly, I was concerned about who would have access to the tape-recorded conversation, including very critical comments if I fully expressed my views, which in the hands of an experienced interviewer I did to a certain degree. Secondly, while the interviewer had had time to prepare his interview schedule I had no time to prepare my responses and when the interview was over I realised that I had not had the opportunity to say some things that I considered to be important. This experience influenced my approach to interviewing teachers and employers.

In spite of arguments that interviewers cannot take notes at the speed of conversation and therefore a tape recorder is essential (Corrie and Zaklukiewicz, 1985) and that interviewees quickly ignore a tape recorder (Stenhouse, 1984), I decided not to use one with any of the groups involved. I had attempted to do so during a pilot study but the results were poor due to inadequate equipment and loss of material in a group situation as a result of views being expressed out of range of the microphone. Delamont (1984) fearing that a recorder might fail also took notes which made me aware, for example, of the dangers of losing the information gained from an employer whose precious time would prevent a return visit. Although note taking has its limitations I decided to use it as my method of recording. I also decided with some adult groups, such as teachers and employers, to provide them with a prepared list of cue questions several days in advance along with a sample of Unit Accreditation Certificates and additional items in the school's developing Record of Achievement. This appears to have been appreciated and in some cases the information gained at the later interview was based on the views of several in the establishment. In another instance one employer who had to cancel my appointment and was finding it difficult to offer an alternative date used the prepared questions to provide written replies. While this approach appeared to be more of a fixed schedule not typical of qualitative case studies, they did act as cues at the actual interviews which took the form of conversations.

Cottle (1977) is an enthusiastic exponent of conversations as the main source of data gathering and like Ball (1984) many of my conversations took place in a variety of places such as the staffroom, pub and car, driving to and from school. These were recorded as soon as possible in a fieldbook and, in spite of some inevitable loss of information, formed a useful source of material when designing more formal interview questions as well as a check on the reliability of responses to those questions.

Interviews took place whenever possible on either neutral ground or the interviewee's own territory such as an employer's office or wherever the pupils felt comfortable. Wragg (1984, p.19) warns that even professionals used to meetings and telephones can 'feel on their guard when interviewed in an office with the questioner behind the desk'. Lang (1985) reported a significant change in the way pupils responded when the interview venue changed. My office is arranged to prevent the desk becoming a barrier but while many pupils feel free to visit my room to show me their work or just to say 'hello' it is also a threatening place on occasions for some who may associate it with a reprimand.

During a pilot study the school's clerical assistant had a long period of absence and I had to conduct pupil interviews in my office with resulting disturbances from telephone, visiting workmen and staff seeking keys which, at least for me if not the pupil, interrupted the flow of the interview. For the same reason I also had to give preference to the normal routine and interviews had to be at short notice when I could find the time and with whoever was available. Sometimes this was at the end of the day when pupils may not have been at their best and interviews had to be concluded in time for them to catch the school transport. On one occasion the only pupil available was a particularly disruptive girl who earlier in the day had been severely reprimanded. She had indicated that she was willing to be interviewed but once in my office it was quite clear that she had no intention of co-operating. As a result of these pilot experiences with pupils I avoided interviewing them other than in their own territory and only when they were available and prepared to speak willingly. I also avoided the term interview and asked if we could 'have a chat'. Similarly parent interviews took the form of conversations in their own homes with a minimum of note taking to reduce any anxiety they may have had. More detailed notes were then made in the car shortly after driving away from their homes.

Stronach (1988) suggests that in educational research there exists either visible or invisible authority 'and that if we do not know the who of the writer we cannot know the what and why of the written' (p.2). It is therefore important that readers are aware of my role as headteacher of Rook Dale School. I was responsible for opening the school and I brought with me a variety of experience, in both residential and day special schools, which had formulated my beliefs, opinions and biases but, as stressed in the current literature on whole-school management, headteachers should not expect to be the source of all the developments. Everard and Morris (1985) identify teachers as a major resource in the development of new ideas and, as I have already shown, Unit Accreditation was such a development.

There were times during the research when I needed to be aware of the conflict of the dual roles as headteacher and researcher. In any interview situation there are likely to be dangers such as respondents being eagar to please (Borg, 1981), friendly informants leading unwitting fieldworkers into a snare (Peshkin, 1982), 'researcher-wise' teachers who are able to 'fob-off' the researcher (Denscombe, 1983) and informants who may be dependant on the researcher for status and enhancement (Le Compte and Goetz, 1982). I was therefore aware of these dangers particularly when seeking the views of pupils and teachers who may well have been over zealous in justifying genuinely held views or alternatively covering up their lack of conviction on the innovation being evaluated. There is also a danger that headteacher-researchers will be anxious that innovations in their schools succeed which makes it difficult to maintain the neutrality and detachment required of a researcher. I was aware of this which, while it may not have totally eliminated bias, should have helped to control it.

## Perspectives on preparation for employment

Tomlinson suggests that:

> a major task of special education has always been to prepare pupils for routine manual work and some employers came to prefer special school leavers who were more docile, obedient and punctual than others. (1985, p.163)

While my experiences as a teacher responsible for careers in the late 1960s would not cause me to disagree with this statement, circumstances have changed and it appeared important that part of my study should consider what the participants thought about the employment issue. What were the expectations of parents, what were employers looking for and, if they wanted 'docile' young people, why were teachers attempting to motivate them through innovations such as Unit Accreditation?

The parents generally appeared to have an attitude of 'there's no chance for our children ... nobody in our family has a job'. One parent who regularly condoned her daughter's absence, such as extended holidays, indicated that it did not matter because she was not working for examinations and often parents appeared to relate job opportunities with examinations. One parent, however, expressed total despair saying: 'Basically nobody has any chance with or without exams ... my sister's got a load of O and A levels and it's just as bad for her'.

While parents were not hopeful about their children's employment prospects they were united in their rejection of Youth Training Schemes, a typical comment being:

> I don't agree with YTS ... it's cheap labour and there's no job at the end ... all the kids round here have been on a YTS and where did it get them?

Parents found it difficult both to accept that experiences and training were valuable to future employers and to see the value of much that school offered: 'You go to school to read, to write and do sums ... my son likes caving and canoeing but that doesn't get you a job'. Pupils' comments also reflected this view but clearly saw the 3-Rs as boring while activities which they saw as being relevant were welcomed. One boy expressed this quite clearly:

> I don't like some lessons ... what we are doing now ... world, maps ... What's happening and things like that. I don't know what's really happening ... if it's true or not ... it's boring.

but then he added:

> I like the motorbike unit, outdoor pursuits and gardening ... it's all outside ... it's more interesting ... the motorbike unit learns you stuff about the roads ... it'll be useful when I get a bike. I like gardening at home. I like going out on trips ... looking at the countryside where you haven't been before.

General comments by teachers throughout the study indicated that they did not necessarily see themselves as producing young workers. One teacher argued that it was difficult to assess just what employers wanted and concluded that teachers should not be aiming to use the Unit Accreditation Scheme to satisfy employers. Another teacher commented that: 'We may have to face quite different demands from parents and employers but there really shouldn't be any conflict because we should all be putting the children first'.

It was clear that 'putting the children first' was far from producing 'docile and obedient workers', but then the teachers generally challenged the idea that this was what employers really wanted. As one of them said:

> They did twenty years ago but the idea is now out of date ... although many special schools are probably still working to those aims, especially those with older headteachers. The attitudes employers are looking for nowadays are reliability, working with others, adaptability etc ... Yes, I'm sure obedience comes into it ... but docile ... I doubt that. Much of the work they do could be described as routine and manual but there will only be one sweeper and he'll probably have to turn his hand to other jobs.

Another teacher expressed the view:

> Some of our pupils would get on better if they were more docile ... there must be a happy medium between being docile and stroppy but we ought to be encouraging a questioning attitude.

This 'questioning attitude' was the whole basis for her work:

> I push science, not because there is an economic need for science, but because it makes pupils question and think about what and why they are doing things. I'm quite sure many employers want workers who show some initiative ... workers who think.

Employers were also asked to comment on the idea of docile, obedient and punctual workers. They clearly rejected the idea of 'docile' young people and were not too happy with the term 'obedient', although they agreed that there was 'a need for discipline at work'. This was described by one as a change in attitude from that of 'a teenager at school to that of a young adult at work'. Good time keeping and regular attendance were also aspects of discipline at work. Appearance and hygiene were considered to be important by two of the employers in the food manufacturing industry. A willingness to learn and the ability to work as a team were high priorities while, apart from some basic counting skills and the recognition of safety notices, the 3-R's were not listed as being of great importance.

## Unit Accreditation: teachers' views

During the pilot stage of the study four of the five teachers involved commented positively on the effect of Unit Accreditation on pupil motivation. However, one of them expressed the view that it would not motivate any more than any other 'satisfying non Unit Accreditation piece of work'. On a number of occasions she equated pupil motivation with the level of preparation and effort by the teacher and argued that teachers should not need innovations, such as Unit Accreditation, to encourage them to do this. Two of the staff referred to the fact that Unit Accreditation had resulted in more interesting lessons and that they felt motivated by the reaction of the pupils. One of them forecast that it would lead to a review of the senior school's programme:

> Unit Accreditation has helped me a lot. It has helped me to set out what to do and carry it out to a conclusion. It tells you what is important and what isn't. Unit Accreditation is a carrot for the kids and an incentive for the staff. Completed units and praise from the assessor gives staff a good feeling. It will encourage me to look at the whole senior programme. I used to have vague ideas about the outdoor education visits − now I have definite plans.

This expression of the level of commitment he had achieved in a relatively short period of time was in contrast with his initial views that 'Unit Accreditation has been a negative experience'. His change of opinion had come about as a result of writing units for himself:

> At first I was following other people's units and I got things wrong and the kids failed to get their certificates. Once we started writing our own I got a great deal of satisfaction ... I got a certain amount from putting down on paper the work I wanted to do ... there is also a great deal of satisfaction in following it through.

Unit Accreditation was often the subject of informal break-time conversations with comments being passed indicating that it has 'clearly defined the objectives', 'helped to structure the curriculum', 'helped me to focus and be specific' and so on. At times the rhetoric did not match my observations and I suspected some comments may have been made for my benefit as either headteacher or researcher by some staff. However, it was clear that a vast amount of effort was going into establishing Unit Accreditation. Towards the end of my study 55 units were available as part of the 14+ curriculum. Five of these had been written for other schools, four others had been modified to meet the school's needs while the remaining 46 had been written by Rook Dale staff. The vast majority of these were written by two teachers as individuals based on their own responsibilities and interests but they then exchanged units with each other for a second opinion. They also wrote a number of units together and appeared to appreciate the 'bouncing of ideas' between each other. Other staff and district college staff contributed to the writing of some units but one teacher in the senior school made no noticeable contribution and as a result felt left out of any decision making. He also found team teaching, which increasingly became a feature in the senior school, difficult and commented that he was beginning to feel like a student again. The structure which Unit Accreditation encouraged had taken away his 'professional freedom'. In contrast the two most committed stated that Unit Accreditation had motivated them and discouraged 'drifting along from one day to the next without any real aims or plan'. They also suggested that Unit Accreditation was particularly beneficial to supply teachers:

> In the past we haven't been able to point out just where we were up to in the senior programme and we would give supply staff some

time-filling ideas if they didn't have their own ... and the kids never helped because they didn't know what they were supposed to be doing. Now we know what each group and kid is doing ... they know where they are up to and can get on with it. Supply teachers can also be supported by team teaching.

This view was supported by some supply teachers who reported that they were happier with the increased guidance given to them and, based on their past experiences, the apparent improved behaviour of pupils.

## Unit Accreditation: a motivator of pupils?

It has been suggested that traditionally special school pupils have had nothing to show for their efforts in school (Burgess and Adams, 1985). Green (1987), however, now argues that the NPRA Scheme of Unit Accreditation is the closest approach yet to recognising the achievements of all pupils, including those with special educational needs, whose achievements and experiences can be recognised at the level they are able to achieve.

During the early stages it was assumed that pupils' work would be assessed, by an external assessor, twice each term followed by the arrival of the appropriate certificates within three weeks. It was thought that these would be the 'carrot' to keep the pupils motivated. As described in the previous section, staff were divided in their view on the effectiveness of Unit Accreditation. Some thought that only the brighter and more co-operative MLD pupils would respond while the EBD pupils would probably have little to do with it. On a more positive note the teacher responsible for introducing the scheme said:

If we are going to use Unit Accreditation it has to benefit all our pupils ... it is so adaptable it can meet the needs of each individual ... and that's what special schools are about.

During the pilot study a number of both internal and external hiccups reduced the regular flow of certificates. The school failed to request two possible visits by the assessor while external factors included a computer failure, which prevented the registration of pupils and printing problems which prevented the issue of certificates. The majority of the pupils appeared unconcerned that the certificates had not arrived regularly 'so long as I get them before I leave'. When certificates did arrive they were clearly valued. The level of interest was illustrated by the Easter school leavers who returned during the first two days of the summer term to see how successful they had been with the work assessed at the end of the previous term. One of them asked for a typed list of the units he had completed to use if he went to an interview before his certificates arrived. Conversations at the schools' Youth Club also reflected the interest being shown in the scheme. In spite of the predictions that the EBD group were less likely to respond to Unit Accreditation they were in fact quite positive, wanting to return their certificates to school for safe keeping after showing parents.

In addition to motivating pupils in their work it has been suggested that modular approaches can lead to improved attendance and better behaviour (SCDC, 1985). I made no attempt to compare attendance figures but relied on the views of teachers, pupils and parents. From the early stages there was a difference in teachers' opinions, from Unit Accreditation having little or no effect to claims that pupils were attending in order to complete the required number of outcomes even when their parents wanted them to stay away to do something for them. Conversations with pupils did not confirm that they had attended against the wishes of their parents or friends but one said:

> I haven't taken time off for ages ... probably got better as I'm getting old. Me mates say 'why do you go − you've only a few weeks left and you've no "O" levels to do' ... I just say 'I don't know'.

Although his mother was not able to confirm a link she was nevertheless aware that since the implementation of Unit Accreditation he had shown more interest in attending school. Other parents were also unable to confirm a link between Unit Accreditation and attendance but they were aware of the excitement when certificates had been gained and expressed the view that these had encouraged them to work. Both permanent and supply staff commented on improved behaviour from difficult pupils who now seemed to know what was expected of them, where they were up to and what to do next. One teacher's comments suggested that there was perhaps more than one reason for any improvements:

> I now have no behaviour problems in my lessons when I am working on a unit. I don't know if it's because they want

to work for a certificate or whether it's because I am better organised.

## Unit Accreditation and parents

Broadfoot (1986) has suggested that parents have traditionally seen alternative forms of assessment as being second class. When visiting the parents of those pupils involved in the research I took with me an example of the draft Record of Achievement being developed in the school including examples of NPRA certificates and the Letter of Credit. Rook Dale teachers had also designed illustrated sheets to record activities such as sport, outdoor pursuits, College Link Courses and work experience. Parents responded positively to these, with one mother commenting:

> My sister's girl has got one of these from the High School ... there's only a few pages and they are not very impressive ... it wouldn't do her any good taking it to an employer ... they might give a job when they see these ... I think they will like the Letter of Credit from the other people.

Other parents made specific reference to individual certificates which they thought 'shows what they can do rather than just saying it'. Although parents generally had a pessimistic view of their children's chances of employment there did appear to be some hope that Unit Accreditation and Records of Achievement might help. One parent complained that her son had attended for three interviews without being asked for anything, 'not even a school report or even which school he went to'. At this stage many employers had little experience of the Records of Achievement being produced by some schools, although those that had seen them valued both the academic and non-academic achievements illustrated. If such records were to succeed it appeared that pupils had a role to play by offering them to employers and employers had to request them if pupils were to value them. The National Record of Achievement should ensure that employers are aware of them and also introduce additional information, such as a pupils' school attendance record, which may be considered to be of importance. A recent National Evaluation of the Record of Achievement pilot schemes extension found that:

> despite some unresolved problems, the reactions of both students in special schools and their parents seem to be very positive, and

> the RoA process has helped to increase the involvement of many parents.
>
> (Broadfoot *et al.*, 1991, p.83)

## Conclusion

The introduction of Unit Accreditation at Rook Dale School appears to have been a very successful innovation, going beyond the initial intentions. A number of factors have contributed to this but the most important has been the determination and hard work of those staff committed to it. They worked long before the school opened each morning and long after other staff left for home and they would say that they have been rewarded by it. As one of them forecast, Unit Accreditation has led to a complete review of the programme being offered to 14+ pupils, giving structure to what already existed and revealing areas in need of attention. The senior curriculum now consists of compulsory core units and a wide choice of options. New developments and demands such as the National Curriculum can easily be accommodated by the introduction of new units, such as a recent unit on 'European Studies: Introduction to France'.

The response made by pupils during the period of the study was positive. Now that Unit Accreditation is established it is impossible to assess fully its influence on the behaviour and work patterns of the pupils currently involved, although there are some positive signs. Initially some teachers expressed the view that the EBD pupils would not respond, but the evidence suggested that they appreciated that their efforts were being recognised. During the past year one third of the school leavers, including some 'difficult' young people, requested an additional year in the school and working for more units was a reason given. A number of the Authority's educational psychologists appear to regard Unit Accreditation as a means of stimulating pupils who in their last few years have increasingly rejected schooling by truanting or displaying behaviour which led to long-term exclusions. During the past year seven such pupils have been transferred to the school from out of the normal catchment area and while behaviour may not always be perfect it is generally acceptable and they do attend school. One 'school refusal' from a 'travelling family' background, who came to the school with only eight months of compulsory education left, has now asked to stay on for an additional year. Parental choice has played a part in this and some of them have said that they chose Rook Dale from the options offered to them because of the Record of Achievement (see Figure 11.1) and Scheme of Unit Accreditation. Comments from several parents also suggest that they do not regard Rook Dale as a 'special school', but as a school that offers a programme which will encourage their children to attend school and improve their attitude towards learning.

Figure 11.1 The Rook Dale Record of Achievement

*Pupils' personal details.
*Summative Statement: the product of a joint discussion between teacher and pupil which belongs to the pupil and he/she should be able to understand it.
*Student Statement: completed after the pupil has taken part in activities to assist self-assessment and evaluation.
*Letter of Credit: issued by the NPRA listing the units completed.
*Statement of Achievement: individual certificates for the various units identifying the skills and knowledge demanded.
*Record of Work Related Experiences and College Link Courses.
*Work Experience Reports.
*Record of Residential Experiences, Outdoor Pursuit and Sporting Activities.
*Any other evidence which the pupil wishes to include, including photographs, reports from leaders of Youth Club or voluntary organisations.

# References

Ball, S.J. (1984) 'Beachside reconsidered: reflections on a methodological apprenticeship', in Burgess, R.G. (ed) *The Research Process in Educational Settings: Ten Case Studies*. Lewes: Falmer Press.

Bell, J. (1987) *Doing Your Research Project*. Milton Keynes: Open University Press.

Bookis, J. (1984) *Beyond the School Gate*. London: The Royal Association for Disability and Rehabilitation.

Borg, W.R. (1981) *Applying Educational Research*. Harlow: Longman.

Bradley, J., Crowe, M. and Scott, V. (1983) *The Transition from School to Adult Life*. Windsor: NFER.

Broadfoot, P. (ed) (1986) *Profiles and Records of Achievement*. London: Holt, Rinehart and Winston.

Broadfoot, P., Grant, M., James, M., Nuttall, D. and Stierer, B. (1991) *Records of Achievement: Report of the National Evaluation of Extension Work in Pilot Schemes*. London: HMSO.

Burgess, T. and Adams, E. (1985) *Records of Achievement at Sixteen*. Windsor: NFER-Nelson.

Corrie, M. and Zaklukiewicz, S. (1985) 'Qualitative research and case study approaches – an introduction', in Hegarty, S. and Evans, P. (eds) *Research and Evaluation Methods in Special Education*. Windsor: NFER-Nelson.

214

Cottle, T.J. (1977) *Private Lives and Public Accounts*. New York: New Viewpoints.

Delamont, S. (1984) 'The old girl network: recollections on the fieldwork of St. Luke's', in Burgess, R.G. (ed) *The Research Process in Educational Settings: Ten Case Studies*. Lewis: Falmer Press.

Denscombe, M. (1983) 'Interviews, accounts and ethnographic research on teachers', in Hammersley, M. (ed) *The Ethnography of Schooling*. Nafferton: Nafferton Books.

Everard, K.B. and Morris, G. (1985) *Effective School Management*. London: Harper and Row.

Green, P. (1987) 'Records of wider achievement'. *British Journal of Special Education* 14, 141–3.

Hopkins, D. (1985) *A Teacher's Guide to Classroom Research*. Milton Keynes: Open University Press.

Lang, P. (1985) 'Taking the consumer into account', in Lang, P. and Marland, M. (eds) *New Directions in Pastoral Care*. Oxford: Basil Blackwell.

LeCompte, M.D. and Goetz, J.P. (1982) 'Problems of reliability and validity in ethnographic research'. *Review of Educational Research* 52, 31–60.

Peshkin, A. (1982) 'The researcher and subjectivity: reflections on an ethnography of school and community', in Spindler, G. (ed) *Doing the Ethnography of Schooling: Educational Anthropology in Action*. London: Holt, Rinehart and Winston.

Raby, L. and Walford, G. (1981) 'Career related attitudes and their determinants for middle- and low-stream pupils in an urban, multi-racial comprehensive school'. *Research in Education* 25, 19–35.

Reid, K. (1984) 'Some social, psychological and educational aspects related to persistent school absenteeism'. *Research in Education* 31, 63–82.

SCDC (1985) *Curriculum Issues No.1: Modular Approaches to the Secondary Curriculum*. London: School Curriculum Development Committee.

Stenhouse, L. (1984) 'Library access, library use and user education in academic sixth forms: an autobiographical account', in Burgess, R.G. (ed) *The Research Process in Educational Settings: Ten Case Studies*. Lewes: Falmer Press.

Stronach, I. (1988) *TVEI in Caister High: a case-study in educational change*. Norwich: CARE, University of East Anglia.

Taylor, J. (1981) The integration of ESN(M) and ESN(S) Children within a New School: A Case Study. Unpublished MA Thesis, University of York.

Tomlinson, S. (1981) 'The social construction of the ESN(M) child', in Barton, L. and Tomlinson, S. (eds) *Special Education: Policy, Practices and Social Issues*. London: Harper and Row.

Tomlinson, S. (1985) 'The expansion of special education'. *Oxford Review of Education* 11, 157–65.

Warwick, D. (1987) *The Modular Curriculum*. Oxford: Basil Blackwell.

Widlack, P. (1983) *How to Reach the Hard to Teach*. Milton Keynes: Open University Press.

Wragg, E.C. (1984) 'Conducting and analysing interviews', in Bell, J., Bush, T., Fox, A., Goodey, J. and Goulding, S. (eds) (1984) *Conducting Small-scale Investigations in Educational Management*. London: Harper and Row.

# CHAPTER 12

# *Analysing and Validating Data in Teacher Research*

Graham Vulliamy and Rosemary Webb

As illustrated in the previous chapters of this book, teacher researchers are likely to produce a wide variety of data, including quantitative data where appropriate. The guidelines for analysing and validating quantitative data are well established in the methodology literature (see, for example, Ary *et al.*, 1972, for educational research in general and Bell, 1987, Ch.11 for small-scale educational research projects). These guidelines tend to follow logically from the expression of research questions or hypotheses in implicitly or explicitly quantitative form. Thus, for example, if one aim of a questionnaire survey is to ascertain whether male and female teachers have differing attitudes to the teaching of technology in special schools, then questions are asked to which the answers can be coded in numerical form (giving, for example, at the simplest level, percentages of 'yes' or 'no' responses or gradations of response from 1 to 5 on a Likert scale which can then be averaged to give a mean score). Analysis can then proceed by a comparison of the scores of female teachers with those of males and this analysis can be validated, or independently checked by others, by established statistical tests (for example, a chi square test for frequencies or a t-test for mean scores).

Qualitative data, however, pose much greater problems of analysis and validation since such data consist of a range of materials, most of which (fieldnotes, interview transcripts, documents and so on) consist of words rather than numbers. This is one reason why qualitative research is sometimes viewed as overly subjective and open to the bias of selection and interpretation reflecting a researcher's interests and prejudices. At one level, such a criticism is misplaced because it attributes a spurious degree of 'objectivity' to the procedures of conventional positivist research. As argued by Patton (1980), the manner in which measurements are derived from questionnaire responses or psychological tests are equally open to the intrusion of the researcher's bias as making observations to be recorded in fieldnotes or asking questions in interviews: 'numbers do not protect against bias; they merely disguise it' (p.336). At another level, however, such a criticism is well taken since, until quite recently, qualitative researchers devoted much more space, both in methodology textbooks and in discussions of their own research, to the procedures of collecting data than to the procedures of analysis and validation. It is for this reason that we are devoting the final chapter to this theme, introducing readers to the variety of procedures now used by qualitative researchers. We do this both by signposting some key literature and by giving actual examples of some of the techniques used with reference to our own research on the impact of the York Outstation Programme discussed in Chapter 1.

## Analysing data

Analysis refers to the process of bringing order to data by focusing on key issues, themes and categories rather than merely presenting a description of the raw data. Whereas in quantitative research data tend to be analysed in relation to pre-existing hypotheses, the aim in most qualitative research is to generate hypotheses and theory from the data. In this respect both the underlying philosophy and the procedures of qualitative research have been crucially influenced by Glaser and Strauss's (1967) pioneering book *The Discovery of Grounded Theory*. In this book, they discuss techniques for generating and saturating categories using what they call a 'constant comparison' method. To illustrate some of the underlying principles behind this, we can begin with a simple practical handout which is used on the Outstation MA Programme to help teacher researchers to get started on the analysis of their qualitative data:

1.  Categorize your data in relation to your research questions. Some data may be clearly relevant to one question. Other data may be relevant to more than one. The first stage provides a basis for deriving an overall picture of the data.
2.  Look in more detail at each category. Are there any issues,

themes, trends which form sub-categories/sub-patterns within it? Are some of these more widespread than others?

3. Look for similarities and differences in terms of who is saying or doing what — for example, differences between the attitudes of subject coordinators and the headteacher, the preferences of girls and boys.

4. Look for omissions in the data. Were there issues that you expected to come up but did not? How might you explain this? Could it be related to the way you conducted the research?

5. Make explicit the rules by which you have categorized/coded your data. If possible ask a team colleague to code an interview transcript or fieldnotes according to the rules that you are operating. Re-examine the rules if there is a substantial variation in analysis.

6. Have a 'rag-bag' category into which data which does not directly relate to your research questions can be placed for it may be needed as your research proceeds.

7. Suggest interpretations of the data and from these interpretations develop hypotheses or grounded theories.

8. Search for exceptions or negative cases which will help refine or disprove emerging hypotheses.

9. Compare findings with those of related research and seek to explain the similarities and differences between the theories forwarded and your grounded theories.

10. Consider how your findings/theories at the local, micro-level of the school relate to national, macro-level trends and events.

(Quoted in Webb, 1990, p.253)

The actual mechanics of generating and refining a set of categories from qualitative data varies in idiosyncratic ways from researcher to researcher. Thus, for example, Ball (1991) gives an interesting detailed account of how he first marks 'slices' of the data with a highlighter pen, also making short marginal notes to label parts of the data. He then photocopies all the pages of data and cuts them into pieces, putting all the examples of a single category into a separate envelope or file. The next stage is to 'map out pieces of analysis as diagrams which link together categories or concepts' (p.183). Other researchers use large sheets of paper, instead of envelopes, to build up and index an emerging category system. Such methods can be used for combinations of qualitative data, such as interviews, fieldnotes, documents or video transcripts. In addition to these 'low-tech' methods of qualitative data analysis, computer programmes have been devised to aid the process (see Fitz-Gibbon, 1989, for a brief account and Tesch, 1990, for a very full survey of software packages and their uses). Such computer software is increasingly being used for qualitative data analysis in large-scale funded projects with voluminous quantities of data derived from extended ethnographic fieldwork. However, it is less appropriate for small-scale teacher-research projects where, quite apart from the cost of the hardware and software, the sample size and characteristics of the data are unlikely to justify the time involved in setting up the data for analysis.

In our own work we combine short written analytic memos (Elliott, 1991) in the margins of the data with a word-processed index of categories. Figure 12.1 gives an extract from our first index following the analysis of the final stage of our research, which was based on the transcripts of interviews with twelve teachers (each lasting between 30 and 40 minutes).

Figure 12.1 Example of emerging category system

---

Changing other teachers' practices: AM1 pp.8,11; AS p.7; BR p.5.
External factors affecting possibility of change: BG pp.4,5; SL p.2; SS pp.2,4.
Gaining understanding of pupils' perspectives/abilities: AM1 pp.2,4,10; AS pp.4,6,11; JH p.2; GH pp.6,10.
Use of research to resist potentially harmful change: GN pp.6–7,8.
Changes to own teaching styles: SW pp.2,8; RS p.2; AS pp.3,4,5.
Support or lack of support from head: AM1 pp.3,4; BR p.3; GH pp.3,10; AS p.8; SL p.8.
Support from other staff: AM1 p.12; BR pp.3–4,8.
Resistance from other staff: AM2 p.7; JH p.8; BR p.8; GH p.7.
Research as 'private' enterprise (lack of climate for sharing): BG, p.5; AS p.8; JH p.8.
Raised own self-confidence: AM1 p.13; AM2 p.9; GN p.8; JH p.3.

Key: The letters refer to the initials of the interviewees (there were two AMs) and the page numbers to the interview transcripts.

---

As Jones (1985, p.58) argues, whilst it would be easy to decide upon your categories in advance and simply allocate appropriate sections to these pre-existing categories, this would undermine the principal strength of qualitative data which is the derivation of relevant, but unanticipated, categories from the concepts of the research participants themselves. Thus in producing our list we were interested in anything which pertained to our original research questions, which were: 'What impact, if any, does teacher research, conducted on the York Outstation MA Programme, have either on the professional development of individual teachers or on changes in their schools?' Some of the categories which emerged, such as 'support or lack of support from head' were very predictable given our prior knowledge of schools and the research literature. Others, however, were much less so. The analytic memo 'research as private enterprise' first appeared in the margin alongside a chance remark from one of the teachers that she didn't want to 'make a meal' of her research in front of the other teachers and consequently wrote up her notes during schooltime in the loo. This caused us to re-read the other transcripts to identify any similar feelings (or counter feelings). Later, through relating such data to analyses of teachers' and school cultures in the literature, this category was developed to form a central concept in one of our articles (Vulliamy and Webb, 1992, pp.46–9). Another unexpected category, 'Use of research to resist potentially harmful change', alerted us to the fact that the potential relationships between teacher research and change included not only the conventional one of the former leading to the latter. In this case, a secondary teacher who had conducted a case study of pupils' transition from feeder primary schools successfully used his findings to demonstrate the considerable benefits to pupils of detailed procedures which a new headteacher had planned to alter to save staff time and effort.

In our research a similar index of categories was developed for the responses to the large number of open-ended questions in a questionnaire mailed to all our ex-outstation MA students. When this index was merged with that of the interview data index, a process of further refinement of many of the categories took place. For example, 'support of the head' could be sub-divided into various forms. These included heads taking teachers' classes to release research time for them; heads reorganising the timetable to give extra free periods to teacher researchers; the expression of ongoing interest and commitment; and enabling a climate for sharing research findings through staff meetings. This process of the progressive refinement of categories can take place after all the data has been collected. However, in most qualitative research it also takes place during periods of data collection as well. As Woods puts it: 'As one observes, interviews, makes up field notes and the research diary, one does not simply "record". There is also reflection, which then in turn informs subsequent data collection' (1986, p.120). This ongoing process of data gathering and reflection contributes to what Glaser and Strauss call 'progressive focusing' — the continual funnelling process which limits and clarifies the scope and aims of a research project.

While we have concentrated on the manner in which we generated categories from our interview transcripts, there are other techniques for analysing qualitative interview data which some teacher researchers have found particularly helpful. We will mention two briefly here. The first is 'cognitive mapping', which is a way of charting people's beliefs and ideas in a diagrammatic fashion (Jones, 1985). In its simplest form, this involves summarising an interviewee's ideas in diagrammatic boxes on the page with relationships between them being indicated either with connecting arrows, where the interviewee has suggested that something has directly caused something else, or by a connecting line for a non-causal link. The second is Winter's (1982) use of 'dilemma analysis' which he later developed into a principle of 'dialectic critique' (Winter, 1989). Influenced by a strongly anti-positivist view of the social world, Winter argues that the latter is permeated by contradictions which are the impetus for social change. Since, as he puts it, 'motives are mixed, purposes are contradictory, relationships are ambiguous and ... practical action is unendingly beset by *dilemmas*' (1982, p.168), seeking out evidence of such dilemmas in interview transcripts can be a useful aid to identifying key themes.

The procedures for moving from initial category generation to the final written outcomes of a project vary according to the scope and emphasis of the research. Sociologists, used to handling large amounts of qualitative data derived from, perhaps, a year-long period of participant observation in a school, have devised strategies for analysis through sequential stages in the generation of grounded theory (see, for example, Turner, 1981). However, in smaller-scale projects, as is typical in teacher research, categories are likely to be directly grouped together in such a way that they might form sections of an article or chapters in a thesis. Thus, for example, in our Outstation Research we listed eight key themes, such as 'Factors facilitating change' and 'Factors hindering change', which, between them, could subsume all the 32 categories from the list of which Figure 12.1 is an extract. Sociologists also tend to put much emphasis on the generation of typologies and models from qualitative data (see, for example, Woods, 1986, Ch.6; Hammersley and Atkinson, 1983, Ch.8). These can also be useful for teacher researchers. Thus, for example, Best (1991) analyses the role of a support teacher in terms of a five-fold ideal type, following his keeping a research diary for two terms' experience of being a support teacher himself. His typology consisted of the support teacher: as the servant of the class teacher; as the servant of the child; as another pupil; as translator or interpreter; and as foreman. In each case, the ideal type directs attention to particular characteristics of the manner in which the support teacher role is adopted.

The final stage of analysis involves relating the categories, concepts and typologies which have been grounded in the data, to other published research and theorising. In quantitative research studies a review of the literature conventionally takes place before data collection and helps shape the research design in terms of specific hypotheses to be tested. In qualitative research, however, while reading around the subject may help formulate research questions, it is usually better to delay a more detailed review of the literature until after data collection and analysis. Glaser and Strauss argue this strongly, advising researchers 'literally to ignore the literature of theory and fact on the area under study' (1967, p.37) at the outset of a project. There are two reasons for this. Firstly, such prior reading is likely to create pre-existing categories and concepts which may then be inappropriately imposed on the data. As Riley puts it: 'the idea is to try really to hear what your own data have to say' (1990, p.47). Secondly, many of the categories emerging from qualitative data are likely to be unanticipated ones and therefore researchers will be unaware of which themes in the secondary literature to pursue until their data analysis has been completed. Thus, in the 'Research as private enterprise' example from our research discussed above, it was only after the emergence of this concept from our data that we were directed to particular reading. When writing up, such secondary literature is usually interweaved with extracts from the raw data to develop and refine the analysis, rather than appearing as a separate 'review of the literature' before a discussion of the collection and analysis of data, as is normally the case in positivist research. However, there may well be exceptions to this general advice where, for example, a teacher researcher explicitly wishes to build upon and refine the ideas developed in another teacher-research study conducted in a very similar context.

## Validating data

The validation of data concerns the processes whereby researchers can both have confidence in their own analyses and can present their analyses in ways which can be independently checked by others. In quantitative research, both of these can be achieved through the cross-checking of numerical data and the use of established statistical tests. However, in qualitative research, raw data cannot be summarised in convenient form and only very few extracts from such data tend to be used in written reports. Moreover, the process of qualitative analysis is itself partly dependent upon the creative insights and conceptualisation of the researcher. For these reasons, until relatively recently, the processes of qualitative data analysis tended to remain hidden from readers of the research. To remedy this, over the past decade an increasing emphasis has been placed by many writers upon the validation of qualitative data. Some, such as Miles and Huberman (1984), have argued for more rigorous techniques for data collection and analysis, each of which should be systematically recorded, seeing little difference between their uses in quantitative and qualitative research respectively. Others, such as Lincoln and Guba (1985), argue that the traditional concepts associated with positivist research are not applicable to qualitative studies. Consequently, at the theoretical level, they have suggested a detailed alternative language for qualitative research, where, for example, the concept of 'trustworthiness' replaces those of 'reliability' and 'validity' and where researchers should aspire to establish a study's 'credibility', 'transferability', 'dependability' and 'confirmability'. At a more practical level, they have suggested a variety of techniques, many of which can be found in the much earlier writings of sociologists and anthropologists, to help achieve these. Here we will concentrate on those techniques which are most appropriate and commonly used in teacher research.

Perhaps the most widely stressed validation technique in the teacher-research literature is triangulation. While this term has been used in a variety of different ways, including the use of 'unobtrusive measures' in conventional positivist research (Webb et al., 1966), it is most commonly used in two ways in teacher research. Firstly, there are the kinds of mixing of methods and data sources discussed by Denzin (1978). Thus, for example, in order to check and enhance the validity of one's data, the same method can be used on different samples and on different occasions (for example, interviewing both teachers and pupils on the same theme) and also different methods can be used in relation to the same sample (for example, interviewing and observing the same teachers). Secondly, a more specific variety of triangulation has been advocated by Elliott and Adelman (1976) in an action research context. This involves providing and comparing accounts of classroom interaction from a triangle of three perspectives: those of the teacher, the pupils and another participant observer. This technique has been further adapted and extended by McKernan (1991) with the use of videos and collaboration between a teacher researcher and an external researcher, although whether his new term for this 'quadrangulation' catches on remains to be seen!

The basic principles of triangulation are common sense, in that if a variety of different methods and sources of data point to the same conclusion then this lends credibility to that conclusion (in much the same way that detectives might use a variety of cross-checks on their evidence). However, what is perhaps not stressed enough in the teacher-research methodology literature is the fact that we might often *expect* different methods to produce different results. For example, Keddie (1971) shows how teachers, knowingly or unknowingly, present accounts of their teaching in interviews which are strongly at variance with direct observations of their teaching. Similarly, as suggested in Chapter 1, in evaluating educational innovations the use of questionnaires and one-off interviews are likely to reproduce the rhetoric rather than the reality of the innovation. In such circumstances researchers must use their judgement as to why different research techniques may have produced conflicting evidence.

Another validation technique, that of saturating categories and the search for negative instances, is associated with the Glaser and Strauss process of category generation discussed in the previous section of this chapter. Once concepts and hypotheses have been generated from the raw data, the researcher deliberately seeks out examples which might modify or disprove them, either by collecting new data or by searching the existing data for alternative explanations. Seeking examples which disprove emerging hypotheses leads to a progressive refinement and modification of them until a point is reached when a succession of new data merely reinforces the existing categories − at which point they are said to be 'saturated'. Hopkins (1985) provides examples of how such procedures operate in the context of teacher researchers studying their own classroom practice.

The validation techniques discussed so far − triangulation, saturation of categories and the search for negative instances − can each operate simultaneously with both the processes of data collection and analysis. Other validation techniques are designed to be undertaken after the completion of a research project. One example, derived from the work of Schwandt and Halpern (1988) and discussed in the context of school evaluation research by Hopkins (1989), is the setting of audit trails. Using the analogy of a financial audit, whereby an accountant requires access to certain documentation to assess the financial state of a company, an audit trail refers to the documentation required for an independant assessment of the procedures and validity of a qualitative research project. Schwandt and Halpern (1988) argue that setting an audit trail serves two important purposes. Firstly, by forcing researchers to keep careful records of the details of their research, including the actual procedures used in data collection and analysis, this tends to result in researchers approaching their task in a more self-critical and systematic way. Secondly, it can provide readers with the kinds of information they require to assess the trustworthiness of a piece of research. Figure 12.2 illustrates what an audit trail would consist of for our own Outstation Research discussed earlier, using a simplified version of the desirable components suggested by Schwandt and Halpern (1988, Table 4.1, pp.83−5).

Audit trails have proved particularly helpful in the context of teacher research for an award-bearing programme, such as the York Outstation MA. When the course began in 1983, expectations were such that very little of the content of Figure 12.2 would be required in a thesis and the emphasis was upon data collection techniques (where, for example, items 2a and 2b might be included as appendices). Following the upsurge of interest in qualitative data analysis, we now find that some external examiners require that most of section 5 in Figure 12.2 should appear in the thesis, either in a methodology chapter or in an appendix.

Figure 12.2 A simplified audit trail

---

1. Aims and History of Project
a. Documents relating to the background context and aims of the project. Identification of the key research questions: What impact, if any, does teacher research, conducted on the York Outstation MA programme, have either on the professional development of individual teachers or on changes in their schools?
b. Document showing the timing and sequence of stages of data collection, analysis and writing-up throughout the project
2. Data Collection Techniques
a. Copies of the pilot and the final questionnaires
b. Copies of the interview schedules used for each of the three groups of in-depth interviews (teachers in 1986 and teachers and advisers in 1989)
c. Methodological notes (e.g. rationale for conducting interviews with 4 LEA advisers, which had not been part of the original research design)
3. Raw Data
a. 127 questionnaire returns
b. Transcripts of interviews in 1986 with 19 teachers and 5 headteachers and in 1989 with 12 teachers and 4 LEA advisers
4. Data Reduction Sources
a. Summaries of questionnaire responses for each of the 7 out-stations
5. Data Analysis Procedures
a. Tables of quantifiable responses to closed questions in questionnaires
b. Coding procedures and ensuing tables of data from some open-ended questions in questionnaires
c. Several versions of indexes of categories from interview transcripts and from questionnaire responses to open-ended questions (initially conducted independently by each researcher and then combined)
d. Document on 'Key Issues' designed to group together categories from 5c into larger inter-related sections to assist the process of writing a research report
e. Lists of relevant quotations from other related published research and analysis
f. Analytical memos concerning the development of concepts from the research (e.g. 'Teacher research as private enterprise')
6. Final Written Products
a. An in-house research report
b. Two academic journal articles

---

The validation techniques discussed so far have been principally concerned with making the research process itself more rigorous and more explicit and they have been derived from a combination of the work of sociologists and qualitative evaluators, especially in the United States. A rather different approach to validation in teacher research has been developed in Britain, associated with the action research styles developed by Jack Whitehead at the University of Bath and Pamela Lomax at Kingston Polytechnic. They argue that the principal purpose of action research is to enhance professional development and to change practice by exposing contradictions between teachers' values and their current practices. Lomax considers the implications of this for validity:

> As action researchers we do not claim to find the final answer to a question, but we do claim to improve (and change) educational practice through the educational development of practitioners ... The validity of what we claim would seem to be the degree to which it was useful (relevant) in guiding practice for particular teachers and its power to inform and precipitate debate about improving practice in the wider professional community.
>
> (1986, p.48)

Consequently the validation process is not so much about method, but more about people and their claims to know the nature and substance of their own professional development.

At a theoretical level, Whitehead and Foster (1984) suggest that there are four standards by which to assess these claims — methodological, logical, ethical and aesthetic — and argue for a form of social validation influenced by the German philosopher Jurgen Habermas. At a more practical level, McNiff (1988, Ch.11) discusses the various processes which this might entail. Central to these, and used extensively on both the Bath and Kingston Polytechnic courses, is that of peer validation (Lomax, 1991). Validation groups might consist of between about three and ten people, usually predominantly other teachers (from both within and outside the institution in which the research project is located), together with course tutors and supervisors in the case of an award-bearing course. Their role is to listen to teachers' claims about their values and actions and to assess, in a critical but supportive manner, the accompanying evidence for such claims, which might be in the form of videotapes or documentation. As a process this has some parallels with the more traditional emphasis in ethnographic research on the importance of 'respondent validation', whereby researchers feed back their emerging analysis for comment to those who are being researched (Hammersley and Atkinson, 1983, pp.195–118; Delamont, 1992, pp.158–119). This can have the benefits of participants providing alternative perspectives and knowledge of the research context which may help refine the researcher's interpretations of events; it can also pose difficult ethical and political problems, as illustrated in Ball's (1984, pp.83–90) detailed account of teachers' responses to feedback seminars he gave towards the end of his long period of fieldwork for the book *Beachside Comprehensive* (1981).

The ethnographic principle of 'respondent validation' is also strongly stressed in other qualitative research traditions, albeit with different terminology being given to it. Guba and Lincoln (1989), for example, refer to 'member checks' which they describe as 'the single most crucial technique for establishing credibility' in a qualitative evaluation study (p.239). They argue that this should be a continuous process throughout the research and should involve allowing interviewees to check interview transcripts for accuracy and feeding drafts of an unfolding case-study report to interested parties for comment. In teacher research, this process has been viewed as a vital component of triangulation and also as a desirable attribute of a more democratic approach to the research process. In this respect, it is worth stressing that there is an added dimension to its rationale in the case of a teacher researcher, who is an insider in the research context, from the more conventional ethnographer or evaluator who is an outsider to the institution being studied. For both ethical and political reasons there are stronger obligations on researchers to share their findings with their colleagues working in the same institution. Moreover, if as is usually the case, one of the underlying purposes for a teacher-research project is to promote improvement and change, then the change process is itself facilitated if findings and understandings are shared with colleagues en route throughout a study, rather than coming as a surprise at the end of it.

## Conclusion

Teacher research, together with qualitative research more generally, has sometimes been criticised for being overly impressionistic, anecdotal and lacking in rigour. Whilst we believe that some of these criticisms are symptomatic of spurious assumptions of 'objectivity' in more conventional quantitative research, we nevertheless feel that the processes of teacher research would benefit from being made more systematic and explicit and that this would assist in the growing recognition by the wider research community of the

228

valuable contribution it can make to the understanding of education as experienced by pupils and teachers. To date, rigour in the analysis and validation of data in teacher research has lagged way behind that in the collection of data. This is why we have chosen to end this book on teacher research and special educational needs with a chapter specifically on this theme. We hope that, by doing so, the book will not only stimulate further teacher research in the area of special educational needs, but will also increase the power of such research to make the maximum impact on policy, practice and teachers' professional development.

# References

Ary, D., Jacobs, L.C. and Razavieh, A. (1972) *Introduction to Research in Education*. New York: Holt, Rinehart and Winston.
Ball, S.J. (1981) *Beachside Comprehensive*. London: Cambridge University Press.
Ball, S.J. (1984) 'Beachside reconsidered: reflections on a methodological apprenticeship', in Burgess, R.G. (ed) *The Research Process in Educational Settings*. Lewes: Falmer Press.
Ball, S.J. (1991) 'Power, conflict, micropolitics and all that!', in Walford, G. (ed) *Doing Educational Research*. London: Routledge.
Bell, J. (1987) *Doing Your Research Project*. Milton Keynes: Open University Press.
Best, R. (1991) 'Support teaching in a comprehensive school: some reflections on recent experience'. *Support for Learning* 6, 27–31.
Delamont, S. (1992) *Fieldwork in Educational Settings: Methods, Pitfalls and Perspectives*. London: Falmer Press.
Denzin, N. (1978) *The Research Act: A Theoretical Introduction to Sociological Methods*. New York: McGraw Hill.
Elliott, J. (1991) *Action Research for Educational Change*. Milton Keynes: Open University Press.
Elliott, J. and Adelman, C. (1976) *Innovation at Classroom Level: A Case Study of the Ford Teaching Project*, Unit 28, Open University Course E203: Curriculum Design and Development. Milton Keynes: Open University Press.
Fitz-Gibbon, C. (1989) 'Computer analysis of qualitative data'. *Research Intelligence*, Summer, pp.12–14.
Glaser, B. and Strauss, A. (1967) *The Discovery of Grounded Theory*. Chicago: Aldine.
Guba, E.G. and Lincoln, Y.S. (1989) *Fourth Generation Evaluation*. Beverley Hills: Sage.
Hammersley, M. and Atkinson, P. (1983) *Ethnography: Principles in Practice*. London: Tavistock.
Hopkins, D. (1985) *A Teacher's Guide to Classroom Research*. Milton Keynes: Open University Press.
Hopkins, D. (1989) *Evaluation for School Development*. Milton Keynes: Open University Press.
Jones, S. (1985) 'Depth interviewing', in Walker, R. (ed) *Applied Qualitative Research*. Aldershot: Gower.
Keddie, N. (1971) 'Classroom knowledge', in Young, M.F.D. (ed) *Knowledge and Control*. London: Collier MacMillan.
Lincoln, Y.S. and Guba, E.G. (1985) *Naturalistic Inquiry*. Beverley Hills: Sage.
Lomax, P. (1986) 'Action researchers' action research: a symposium'. *British Journal of In-service Education* 13, 42–50.

Lomax, P. (1991) 'Peer review and action research', in Lomax, P. (ed) *Managing Better Schools and Colleges: An Action Research Way*. Clevedon: Multilingual Matters.

McKernan, J. (1991) *Curriculum Action Research: A Handbook of Methods and Resources for the Reflective Practitioner*. London: Kogan Page.

McNiff, J. (1988) *Action Research: Principles and Practice*. London: MacMillan.

Miles, M.B. and Huberman, A.M. (1984) *Qualitative Data Analysis: A Sourcebook of New Methods*. Beverley Hills: Sage.

Patton, M.Q. (1980) *Qualitative Evaluation Methods*. Beverley Hills: Sage.

Riley, J. (1990) *Getting the Most from your Data: A Handbook of Practical Ideas on how to Analyse Qualitative Data*. Bristol: Technical and Educational Services Ltd.

Schwandt, T.A. and Halpern, E.S. (1988) *Linking Auditing and Metaevaluation: Enhancing Quality in Applied Research*. Beverley Hills: Sage.

Tesch, A.R. (1990) *Qualitative Research: Analysis Types and Software Tools*. London: Falmer Press.

Turner, B.A. (1981) 'Some practical aspects of qualitative data analysis: one way of organising the cognitive processes associated with the generation of grounded theory'. *Quality and Quantity* 15, 225–47.

Vulliamy, G. and Webb, R. (1992) 'The influence of teacher research: process or product?'. *Educational Review* 44, 41–58.

Webb, E.J., Campbell, D.T., Schwartz, R.D. and Sechrest, L. (1966) *Unobtrusive Measures: Nonreactive Research in the Social Sciences*. Chicago: Rand McNally.

Webb, R. (1990) 'The processes and purposes of practitioner research', in Webb, R. (ed) *Practitioner Research in the Primary School*. London: Falmer Press.

Whitehead, J. and Foster, D. (1984) 'Action research and professional educational development'. *Classroom Action Research Network Bulletin* 6, 41–5.

Winter, R. (1982) 'Dilemma analysis: a contribution to methodology for action-research'. *Cambridge Journal of Education* 12, 161–74.

Winter, R. (1989) *Learning from Experience: Principles and Practice in Action-Research*. London: Falmer Press.

Woods, P. (1986) *Inside Schools: Ethnography in Educational Research*. London: Routledge and Kegan Paul.

# Index